Unreal™ Engine 4 for Design Visualization

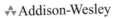

Unreal™ Engine 4 for Design Visualization

Developing Stunning Interactive Visualizations, Animations, and Renderings

Tom Shannon

✦✦Addison-Wesley

Boston • Columbus • Indianapolis • New York • San Francisco
Amsterdam • Cape Town • Dubai • London • Madrid • Milan
Munich • Paris • Montreal • Toronto • Delhi • Mexico City
São Paulo • Sidney • Hong Kong • Seoul • Singapore • Taipei • Tokyo

For information about buying this title in bulk quantities, or for special sales opportunities (which may include electronic versions; custom cover designs; and content particular to your business, training goals, marketing focus, or branding interests), please contact our corporate sales department at corpsales@pearsoned.com or (800) 382-3419.

For government sales inquiries, contact governmentsales@pearsoned.com.

For questions about sales outside the U.S., contact intlcs@pearson.com.

Visit us on the Web: informit.com/aw

Library of Congress Control Number: 2017942002

Publisher
Mark Taub

Acquisitions Editor
Laura Lewin

Development Editor
Sheri Replin

Managing Editor
Sandra Schroeder

Senior Project Editor
Lori Lyons

Production Manager
Dhayanidhi

Copy Editor
Paula Lowell

Indexer
Tim Wright

Proofreader
H S Rupa

Technical Reviewers
David Sparks
Luis Cataldi
Tim Hobson
Sam Deiter

Editorial Assistant
Courtney Martin

Cover Designer
Chuti Prasertsith

Compositor
codeMantra

To my Mom. I love you.

Contents at a Glance

Contents

PREFACE

Unreal Engine 4 (UE4) is quickly becoming the next big thing in games, visualization, and even feature films. Visualization firms, hobbyists, and professionals are eager to explore its possibilities. Unreal Engine 4 is a massive application with thousands of features, hundreds of hours of training videos, and countless tutorials, wikis, and community guides available. These resources can answer many questions about UE4, but finding what's important for visualization can be overwhelming. Almost all the learning resources available are geared toward creating games, not visualizations.

UE4 can seem both very familiar and very alien to people who know how to create traditionally rendered content. There are many similarities that can make learning UE4 easy; other times, things are only similar in name, but in practice are very different. The wrong assumptions can cause frustration and seem insurmountable.

This book aims to act as a guide to visualization studios and individuals, filtering out the noise and presenting the most relevant information using real-world examples, solid workflows, and some tools and tricks as well. Unreal Engine 4 (UE4) is quickly becoming the next big thing in games, visualization, and even feature films. Visualization firms, hobbyists, and professionals are all eager to explore its possibilities. However, Unreal Engine 4 is a massive application with thousands of features, hundreds of hours of training videos, countless tutorials, wikis, and community guides available. These resources are overwhelming and lacking focus. Almost all are geared toward creating games, not visualizations.

Who Should Read This Book

This book is aimed at visualization professionals looking to create the most visually impressive, interactive, and innovative real-time applications, renderings, and animations in Unreal Engine 4. It is also aimed at the technical lead who needs to bring a team of visualization artists, and maybe even a programmer, up to speed and needs to know exactly what to do to get there.

You should already understand how 3D rendering works at a professional level before tackling this book. Concepts like Materials, Global Illumination (GI), polygon modeling, and UV mapping should be familiar to you. I will not be covering specific visualization data workflows outside of UE4. It's expected that you are already adept at taking the raw data provided to you and manipulating it into an organized, optimized 3D format ready for rendering. It is also assumed that you are adept at raytraced rendering techniques and terminology, such as refraction, and Fresnel falloffs should be familiar to you.

If you are interested in Blueprints, I highly recommend you have some background in scripting or programming or computer logic. Concepts like For Loops, If Statements, Variables, and variable types like Booleans, Floats, and Strings are used throughout Blueprints and UE4 in general. This book provides an overview of programming techniques in Blueprints, but it is not a programming tutorial. However, Blueprints are exceptionally user-friendly, and anyone who has experience with scripting, especially in a 3D application, will be able to jump in easily.

If you are a more advanced scripter or programmer or UI developer, you should feel right at home in Blueprints. Functions, typed variables, and object inheritance act much like any object-oriented programming language. Like any programming language and development platform, Unreal is very specific about how it does things, so you should probably take a look at the early chapters to get a better idea of what's going on under the hood. Creating visualizations takes a combination of strong technical skills to understand the data provided, harness the available tools, and a keen artistic and design sense to master the presentation and polish that's expected by today's sophisticated visualization clients.

How This Book Is Organized

This book is divided into three parts. Part I is a technical overview of UE4—its major features, systems, and workflows. Part II demonstrates a simple UE4 interactive application built with included sample content where you learn the basics of the UE4 Editor and begin creating your first Blueprints. In Part III, you look at a real-world architectural visualization project from start to finish—starting with client data in 3ds Max, adding lighting with Unreal Lightmass, creating and applying Materials, creating a Sequencer camera animation and rendering it to disk, and finally following through to create an interactive visualization application with a full UI, interactive elements, and photorealistic rendering quality.

In Part I, you begin exploring UE4 from a conceptual and technical perspective—basics like installing the Launcher and the Engine, creating Projects, and understanding Level, Maps, and Assets. You'll learn important terminology and technologies, ensuring that as you read the book and seek help elsewhere, you have a good grasp of what's being talked about. I'll attempt to explain how things work from a technical perspective so you can take these lessons and apply them more easily to your own brand of visualization. You will look at this material from the perspective of a V-Ray or mental ray user who is opening Unreal engine 4 for the first time and is having to face the differences between offline and real-time rendering head-on.

After you have covered the basics and have a firm understanding of what's going on under the hood, you begin to dive into real-world examples. These are written in a more tutorial style with detailed walkthroughs. All project source files (both .MAX and UE4 project files) are available for download at **www.TomShannon3D.com/UnrealForViz** so you can follow along each step of the way.

Part I: Unreal Engine 4 Overview

Chapter 1, Getting Started with Unreal Engine 4. With a detailed overview of UE4, you learn what UE4 brings to visualizations, what challenges you'll face and how to overcome them, where to get help, and how to start planning your first UE4 projects.

Chapter 2, Working with UE4. UE4's workflow is likely quite different than anything you as a visualization professional have used before. Learn how the major elements of UE4 function together as a whole to create, edit, and distribute interactive applications.

Chapter 3, Content Pipeline. Getting your content into UE4 can be one of the most initially confusing and challenging aspects of learning to use UE4. Learn how UE4 imports and processes 2D and 3D content from other applications and get some ideas how to integrate that into your existing pipelines.

Chapter 4, Lighting and Rendering. UE4 introduces a revolutionary physically based renderer that produces amazing results in a fraction of a second per frame. You learn to take your years of rendering know-how and apply it to UE4's Physically Based Rendering (PBR) Lighting system.

Chapter 5, Materials. Creating rich, lifelike Materials is essential for achieving photo realism. Materials in UE4 are an integral part of the PBR workflow and are different from any material system you have previously used. Learn how Materials are constructed, how the various components of PBR work, and begin to see how Material Instances make creating Materials in UE4 interactive and fun.

Chapter 6, Blueprints. Blueprints are a revolution in scripting and game programming. You can now develop rich, cutting-edge applications without ever writing a single line of code. However, Blueprints are still a programming language, and learning the basics will enable you to jumpstart your development.

Part II: Your First UE4 Project

Chapter 7, Setting Up the Project. Learn to define the project goals, and then discover how to create a new project and setup the basic Project settings to start with a selection of pre-made Starter Content to build your level from.

Chapter 8, Populating the World. Using the Starter Content, you explore using the Editor for the first time, placing assets into the world to become Actors, moving them, modifying them, and then placing lights to illuminate the scene.

Chapter 9, Making It Interactive with Blueprints. Build your first Blueprint classes, the Player Controller, Pawn, and Game Mode. You assign Input Mappings and program the Player Input, allowing the Player to move around the level in first-person view.

Chapter 10, Packaging and Distribution. After your project is working, it's time to get it ready to be distributed as a standalone application. In UE4 this is called Packaging, and it creates an optimized, easy-to install and run application you can easily zip up and send off.

Part III: Architectural Visualization Project

Chapter 11, Project Setup. You once again define your project goals—this time for creating a high-end architectural visualization with several key deliverables: an interactive application and a pre-rendered walkthrough animation rendered with Sequencer.

Chapter 12, Data Pipeline. Learn how to prepare and organize your 3D data before exporting it to FBX. You learn the differences between Architecture and Props. Then, you explore several methods for getting your data into UE4, focusing on the FBX import and export workflow.

Chapter 13, Populating the Scene. After your data is imported to UE4, it's time to get it into your UE4 level. There's several strategies to learn, and you'll see several used here to get both your Architecture and props into the scene where you want them.

Chapter 14, Architectural Lighting. UE4's Lightmass Global Illumination solution is beautiful but also a huge departure from how you've ever rendered a scene's lighting before. Learn to get stunning high-dynamic range lighting for your scenes that render in a fraction of a second.

Chapter 15, Architectural Materials. Building upon the basics you learned about Materials in the first part of the book, you start to build a Master Material, programming parameters, and other shader logic to achieve a flexible, fast and beautiful set of Material instances to apply to the scene.

Chapter 16, Creating Cinematics with Sequencer. Being able to render photo-realistic animations in a fraction of a second opens a world of creative possibilities. Learn to create Sequencer animations, using Cine Cameras to achieve physically correct, filmic looks including effects like depth of field, motion blue, and vignette. Once complete, you'll see how you can record the 90-second walkthrough to disk at a resolution of 4k and 60 frames per second in a matter of minutes.

Chapter 17, Preparing the Level for Interactivity. Collision is absolutely essential for a great interactive experience, and it's also one of the most complex and misunderstood areas of UE4 development. Because video games require so many interactive elements, collision has been developed to be fast, but sometimes hard to setup. Learn how to easily get your level ready to walk around without falling through the floor or a wall.

Chapter 18, Intermediate Blueprints: UMG Interaction. One of the greatest powers of Interactive Visualization is the power to compare options in-context and in real-time. You learn how to setup streaming levels and then swap them at runtime using Blueprints. You expose this functionality to the Player by creating a simple User Interface authored in UMG.

Chapter 19, Advanced Blueprints: Material Switcher. If you're really looking for a challenge, this is the chapter for you. Here you see how a production-ready material switcher Blueprint is developed. Not only does it expose advanced functionality to the Player, but also to the Level Designer (LD), allowing them to visualize the setup in-editor, creating a complete toolset that could be reused on any project.

Chapter 20, Final Thoughts. This book only scrapes the surface of the iceberg that is UE4. I hope to leave you with a good foundation to build upon and some inspiration for where to go next. In the conclusion, I will discuss where UE4 and the industries that use it are heading, and how that will affect Visualization's future.

Source Files

All the UE4 project files and 3ds Max source files are available on the book's companion website at **www.TomShannon3D.com/UnrealForViz.**

You will also find additional resources and links for each chapter. As UE4 is a quickly developing piece of software and I will keep information as up to date as possible.

Conventions Used in This Book

The following typographical conventions are used in this book:

- **Bold** indicates new terms, and variable and parameter names
- *Italic* indicates values that properties and parameters may be set to.

Register your copy of **Unreal Engine 4 for Design Visualization** at informit.com for convenient access to downloads, updates, and corrections as they become available.

To start the registration process, go to informit.com/register and log in or create an account. Enter the product ISBN (9780134680705) and click Submit.

ACKNOWLEDGMENTS

I'd like to express my gratitude to Laura Lewin, Executive Editor at Pearson Education Technology Group, for the opportunity to publish this book. I'd also like to thank Sheri Replin, my awesome development editor, for her feedback and guidance; Paula Lowell for her exacting copy edit, and Lori Lyons for assistance. I'd also like to thank Olivia Basegio for her help putting all this together.

The technical reviewers on this book went above and beyond to provide in-depth feedback and an absolute font of knowledge and experience. I cannot thank David Sparks enough for his thoughtful advice and letting me lean on his years of experience as an educator and trainer. I'd also like to thank Tim Hobson and Sam Deiter at Epic Games for providing their time and effort to ensure the most accurate information possible.

I'd like to thank Epic Games for their vision and passion, and for bringing me along for the ride. It's an honor and a thrill to work alongside the world's best game developers, shaping the future of visual communication.

I'd also like to thank the team at Hoyt Architecture Labs and Imerza, specifically Dorian Vee and Gary Hoyt, for their generosity and support and for providing the readers of this book access to their source content.

Finally, I'd like to thank my wife for her endless support, encouragement, and inspiration; and my kids for their love, and for bringing joy and play into my every day life.

ABOUT THE AUTHOR

Tom Shannon is a UE4 expert/addict and technical artist with more than a decade of professional experience developing video games and visualizations using Unreal Engine. He is passionate about gaming and game technology as well as visualization and its importance and impact on the real world. He spends his days balancing between building the world alongside architects, engineers, and designers, and then destroying it with giant robots alongside programmers, animators, and effects artists.

Tom lives in Colorado with his beautiful and inspiring wife Serine and his amazing and humbling kids Emma and Dexter.

You can find his website at www.TomShannon3D.com.

PART I

UNREAL ENGINE 4 OVERVIEW

CHAPTER 1

GETTING STARTED WITH UNREAL ENGINE 4

Unreal Engine 4 is a powerful software development and content creation platform. Its graphical capabilities, robust tools, and unrivaled extensibility have made it one of the most popular development platforms available. Game developers, architects, scientists, hobbyists, movie makers, and visual artists are using UE4 to create stunning, interactive experiences that are redefining the state of the art. All of these people had to start their first UE4 project somewhere, and that was probably at www.unrealengine.com.

What Is Unreal Engine 4?

Unreal Engine 4 (UE4) is the latest version of the long-running Unreal Engine game development tool created by Epic Games. It is a premiere, professional video game development tool suite that combines cutting-edge, real-time physically based rendering (PBR) materials, reflections, and lighting with robust tools for creating compelling interactive experiences. These tools encompass physics simulation, lighting and shadowing, user interfaces (UI), foliage propagation and rendering, massive terrains, complex materials, visual scripting, character animation, particle simulations, cinematics, networked multiplayer, and more—everything a team of experienced game developers needs to make the next multimillion-dollar AAA blockbuster game. Any capability that UE4 lacks can be added thanks to access to the full, modifiable C++ source code.

Despite its power and complexity, UE4 is incredibly approachable. The UE4 Editor (see Figure 1.1) boasts a modern interface, great tools, well-maintained documentation, complete source code access, and a thriving, growing community. A single person can create astounding games, simulations, and visualizations at a professional level very quickly.

Figure 1.1 Unreal Engine 4 Editor Interface

Small teams can easily grow and work together on the same project, allowing them to pull off incredible feats once thought to be achievable only by huge studios with big budgets. Now, anybody with access to a sufficiently powerful computer can download Unreal Engine 4 for free and begin creating his own amazing, interactive worlds.

A Brief History of Unreal Engine

Since the late 1990s, Epic Games and other professional game developers have used the various versions of Unreal Engine to create an astounding number of top-selling and award-winning games and simulations. Games such as *Gears of War*, *Mass Effect*, *Batman Arkham Knight* and, of course, *Unreal Tournament*, have been developed using Unreal Engine.

Access to professional-level game engines has traditionally been a very technical and expensive proposition beyond the reach of most small game studios and simply unreachable for even the biggest, most technically adept visualization professionals and studios. This forced many small indie game studios and visualization developers to create custom engines or adopt less performing but less expensive and less technically challenging solutions. These solutions included early middleware renderers, physics libraries, audio systems, and other tools that could be cobbled together to create compelling projects, but generally lacked finesse and visual quality and were still often overwhelmingly complex to author.

Over the last decade, independent games—games developed by small studios that are mostly self-funded—have exploded in popularity and have often proven to be hugely financially successful. Thousands of individuals and small teams are now creating games and experiences for a massive audience of gamers.

Although many indie teams have developed their own in-house engines, many rely on middleware engines such as Unity 3D, DX Studio, and Torque. These engines have been developed to offer complete, integrated game development toolsets at significantly lower cost than professional game engines like Unreal Engine 3 and CRYENGINE. Even Epic Games entered this space with a free-to-use, binary-only version of Unreal Engine 3 called the Unreal Developers Kit (UDK).

Although these engines have proven to be huge successes, they have always played a game of catchup with the premiere game development tools available, leaving independent developers and small studios at a significant technological disadvantage.

Introducing Unreal Engine 4

After years of secretive development behind closed doors at Epic Games headquarters in Cary, North Carolina, Epic (with only a few, scant demos and a secret, closed beta) announced the release of Unreal Engine 4 (UE4), its next-generation game engine and successor to the enormously successful Unreal Engine 3.

The release was absolutely unprecedented and shook the industry.

UE4 is not some subset of the engine and not a demo; it is access to the entire C++ source code and tools, *everything* that had previously cost tens of thousands of dollars, all for a low monthly subscription fee. The engine also included robust documentation and direct access to the developers and their in-development code base.

The reaction from the game development community was immediate and hugely positive. Hundreds of developers downloaded the engine and began producing games and demos that quickly began to redefine how independent video games could look, sound, and play.

Unreal Engine 4 introduced an entirely new Editor built from the ground up to be cross-platform, extensible, and modern. The rendering pipeline had been completely overhauled using Physically Based Materials and Lighting to render incredibly lifelike and realistic scenes that rivaled the quality of ray-traced renders.

A new lighting and reflection system, combined with a fully linear rendering pipeline and advanced post-process effects, created film-quality visuals on par with the best in rendered cinematics—and all of this with an unmatched ease of use never before seen in a video game engine.

A new visual scripting language, Blueprints, was introduced, allowing almost anything in the game world to be scripted in-engine and tested on-the-fly without developers' needing to write a line of code. Entire games, including multiplayer and HUD, can be authored using only Blueprints, freeing developers from the burden of C++ programming.

Unreal Engine 4 was simply years ahead of its closest competitor at the time of its launch, even at the highest professional level and it was being offered for *anybody* to download for a small monthly subscription fee of just $20.

Less than a year later, Epic announced it was dropping the monthly fee and releasing the engine for anybody to download and use for free. The most powerful game engine on the market was suddenly also the lowest cost, easiest to use, most open and most well-supported engine available.

Epic Games has not rested on its laurels, either. Since the first release in 2014, Unreal Engine 4 has seen 16 major updates and counting. Each has brought hundreds of new features and thousands of improvements and bug fixes. Examples include major rendering features such as hair and skin shading to core engine features like VR integration and continuously updated support for almost all modern hardware. Thanks to source code access, UE4 is developed openly between Epic Games and community members who collaborate and contribute directly to the engine's development helping to ensure each feature is as robust, bug-free and useful as possible. Never has such a large piece of software been developed so openly and freely, and the results speak for themselves.

Not only have game developers big and small flocked to UE4 to achieve their visions, non-game developers of all kinds have begun to embrace the engine. Movie makers, musicians, architects, engineers, and more have harnessed the power and ease of use of UE4. Creative professionals and teams who would previously never have dreamed of using, or even had access to, a video game engine have begun using Unreal Engine 4 in increasing numbers to create their own unique, interactive, visual stories.

UE4 Highlights for Visualization

Unreal Engine 4 has everything you need to make a AAA video game or visualization. In fact, it offers dozens of tools, benefits, and features; however, the following are the ones most important to developing visualizations:

- **UE4 Editor**: Dynamic, modern, fun-to-use game development suite developed by professional game developers who rely on the engine to make their own games. The Editor is what ties all the Engine's tools together with your content to create amazing experiences.

- **Lighting and materials**: Amazingly realistic pre-baked global illumination using Lightmass or high-performance dynamic lighting with realistic shadows, reflections, and materials thanks to the advanced and easy-to-use physically based rendering (PBR) system.

- **Sequencer**: An innovative camera and object animation and sequencing tool that combines the easy-to-learn simplicity of a video editing application with the power of an interactive game engine.

- **FBX workflow**: The ubiquitous FBX file format is used almost exclusively for 3D geometry and animation data in UE4.

- **Blueprints**: Visual scripting that doesn't require a single line of code and compiles directly in the Editor for immediate feedback. Create user interactions, actor behaviors, user interfaces, and almost every other aspect of your visualization.

- **UMG (Unreal Motion Graphics)**: Based on Blueprints, develop easy-to-use, great-looking user interfaces, essential for successful interactive visualizations.

- **Virtual reality**: Once the thing of science fiction, VR is here and is transforming every form of media, visualization included. UE4 has VR integrated to its very roots and sets the standard for interactive VR content creation.

- **Platform support**: Develop once and release your application on PC, Mac, Linux, iOS, Android, VR, and more with very little if any modification to your projects.

- **Licensing and costs**: Liberal licensing terms and free access to the editor, support, and the amazing UE4 community combined with inexpensive hardware requirements mean almost anybody can get started developing in Unreal Engine 4 today.

Developing Interactive Visualizations with Unreal Engine 4

Unreal Engine 4 boasts one of the most realistic and flexible rendering pipelines available. You have no doubt seen the amazing games, visualizations, and VR experiences created with UE4 on the Internet and been inspired by the jaw-dropping quality on display.

Although these videos and images indeed push visual and artistic boundaries, the speed at which UE4 can render them is what gives UE4 its biggest advantage: interactivity. From the

Editor to the projects you create with it, UE4 allows the rendering respond directly to you and your Player's input in real time.

Rendering speed and the interactivity it imbues into your visualizations are the two most important differences between interactive visualizations in UE4 and traditionally rendered visualizations and affect almost every aspect of working with it.

What UE4 Brings to Visualization

Despite the effort involved, the time and technical knowledge it requires and the sometimes complex workflows, the reward of interactivity is more than worth it. It transforms how you look at creating visualizations and will likewise transform how your clients see their projects and how their customers can experience their visions. The creative limits are boundless for visualization studios and professionals who are willing to learn new tricks, shake old, bad habits, and begin thinking about visualizations as interactive experiences.

Unreal Engine 4 has proven itself as a powerful tool for all kinds of interactive visualization applications: automotive, aerospace, architectural, engineering, and scientific visualizations all come to life in real time. The tools UE4 offers are unmatched in the industry and the applications that are being developed using it are proof of the incredible capabilities of UE4 as an interactive visualization development platform.

Nonlinear and Real Time

An Unreal Engine 4 application runs in real time. Not only does this allow interactivity, it means that time passes in your world as it does in real life. In an image, time is stopped. In a video file, time is static and immutable. In Unreal Engine 4, time and space are variable and can move at your discretion. Entire world can be changed in the blink of an eye, revealing spatial and temporal relationships that couldn't be seen any other way.

You can author your interactive visualization to run the exact same way each time with pre-defined camera paths and pre-scripted actors, but the magic begins when you transform viewers into players by giving them control over time and space the way only an interactive visualization can.

Speed, Speed, and More Speed

Being able to render entire scenes in less than a second is a game changer. By incorporating input, physics, sound, UI, and interactions, you can create nearly any world you can imagine and any kind of player experience you want. Your only limits are your capabilities and the amount of processing power you have available.

Traditional visualizations typically rely on pre-rendered animations created by offline rendering: rendering a series of 2D bitmap frames using ray-tracing software such as V-Ray, Mental Ray, or Maxwell that are then compiled in a video editing or compositing application such as After Effects.

These renderings are extremely detailed, with accurate lighting and amazingly realistic materials that simulate glass, marble, water, and foliage with near photo-realistic precision. These frames are then edited together and visual effects, audio, and motion graphics are applied and then it's all rendered (once again) to a video or still image file. This file is then delivered to the client as a digital file.

Although each frame represents a discrete amount of time (typically 1/30 of a second each), frames can take hours to render, and animations can take days to complete. When complete, each frame often requires additional processing and editing time in post before a final deliverable is produced.

Unreal Engine renders each frame in real time, which means that it takes only 1/30 of a second to render at 30 frames per second. Not only does UE4 render the image in a fraction of a second, it also composites post effects and audio and simulates physics and gameplay logic along with player input each frame.

Interactive visualizations require a frame rate of at least 30 frames per second (fps). That gives each frame only 1/30 of a second or 33.3 milliseconds (ms) to render. Compared to a single rendered frame that takes 20 minutes, that's 36,000 times faster!

As an example, assume you are tasked with producing a three-minute walkthrough animation at HD resolutions. This gives you 5,400 frames to render. At 20 minutes a frame (an optimistic target for many visualizations), that's 108,000 minutes or 1,800 hours, or 75 days. Of course, most studios use a render farm that can harness the power of multiple computers to bring that animation time down to a fraction of that, but even a rather large render farm with 25 nodes will still need three full days to complete the three-minute rendering run.

Rendering Stills and Animations

In addition to using speed to allow interactivity, UE4 can be used to render stills and animations using pre-defined camera paths using either cameras keyframed directly in Sequencer or camera paths imported from your application of choice.

These animations render in almost real time, and you can use some rendering tricks to make the quality much higher than you would typically for an interactive scene; that is, you sacrifice rendering speed for additional resolution and quality. You can easily render high-resolution, high frame rate video in seconds per frame. It's so fast that UE4 may spend more time writing frames to disk than actually rendering the image being saved.

What You See Is What You Get (WYSIWYG)

Ray-traced renders can take hours to complete, and most of the time, the real-time viewport of the editor you author in presents a simplified, preview version of the scene that doesn't accurately reflect the final rendering. Lighting is approximated, and materials often do not display at all. Shadows and global illumination are very rarely ever shown in the viewports. Each change to your lighting or materials requires minutes of rendering for you to even begin to see a pre-view. In larger scenes, this workflow can quickly become time consuming and tedious. With the UE4 editor, you're almost always getting an accurate view of the scene's lighting, the camera's position, the post-process effects, and all the other scene elements—all at once, in real time. The viewport in which you edit your scenes runs the very game engine that runs in the final project. When you make a change, you see it in context in real time.

The WYSIWYG nature of UE4 unlocks a huge amount of creative freedom in the production pipeline. Directors and clients can now see final quality–style renderings at the very early stages of a project. This makes signoff and approval faster and much more reliable. Finding views and refining lighting and materials can take minutes with one-on-one, real-time input from the decision makers who then get immediate feedback and previews of the changes they propose.

Interactivity Makes Worlds Come Alive in UE4

Bringing viewers into the visualization and making them into players redefines what a visualiza-tion can be. There's simply no limit to what can be achieved. You can sit in any seat in a theater, or see the view from any room in any condo in your high rise at the touch of button. Custom-ize each aspect of your new car down to the grain of the leather, all rendered with remarkable accuracy and fidelity.

One of the most compelling uses for interactive visualizations is to explore designs through time or to compare alternatives and design alternatives in-context and in real-time. Turning the "viewer" into the Player is incredibly empowering and offers new ways of visualizing and com-municating complex datasets.

Even working and editing worlds in UE4 is fun, interactive, and visually pleasing. You fly through the world in the Perspective Viewport at interactive frame rates, seeing the lighting reflect off the materials as you do.

As you place lights you see high-resolution shadow previews showing you exactly what you will get in the end product. Blueprints let you interactively modify the world without coding, compiling, or having to exit the editor to try out new features.

Cameras can be set up on the fly, providing lens-accurate post-processing effects like depth of field and motion blur that render in real time. For visualization artists who have spent years struggling to get these expensive effects into their scenes, seeing such high-quality effects and being able to adjust them in real time is liberating.

The Wow Factor

Unreal Engine 4 produces visuals that make people say "wow." Visualization has always been a very technology-driven industry. Advances in computing, imagery, and modeling and render-ing are quickly adopted. Clients are always looking for ways to stand out, as are visualization studios. The use of game engines for visualization isn't new, but the ability for interactive appli-cations to wow people is. In my opinion, the surface has only just been scratched. People have only just begun to think about their designs and how to communicate them to their audience in an interactive context.

The Future

Virtual reality, augmented reality, mobile platforms—you name it—Epic Games, its partners, and the tens of thousands of UE4 developers are doing it. With nearly unlimited extensibility and an ever-growing feature set, no other single development or rendering platform is more poised to enable you to take advantage of what comes next.

UE4 Development Caveats

Unreal Engine 4 is a fantastic development platform that offers creative and artistic possibilities unimagined only a few years ago. Although there has never been a game engine like UE4, it's still a video game engine at heart, developed by a video game development company to develop video games with.

To fully utilize what UE4 offers and to author the most compelling visualizations possible, you must learn to think about your stories, content, and development workflows in new ways. You must also learn how to work with and sometimes around UE4's limitations, and how to avoid them altogether if you can.

Authoring Complexity

You might ask, "Why haven't we all been using game engines to render all along?" The simple reason is because it can require a good deal more effort. Authoring content to render so fast requires extremely aggressive optimizations, powerful hardware, and many clever workflows to ensure accuracy and fidelity.

Developers use level of detail (LOD), streaming, tessellation, precalculation, culling, and caching to make sure as little of each frame needs to be calculated as possible at runtime. Textures are pre-processed and stored as hardware-accelerated formats, reflections are pre-captured in reflection probes, and lighting and global illumination (GI) is calculated and stored in Textures using Lightmass.

All of this takes time, effort, and planning to ensure it works. Although traditional rendering requires much of the same optimization, the pressure to render in a fraction of a second isn't there and render times can be compensated for with additional hardware or well-planned schedules that allow for plenty of rendering time. Although a five-minute per-frame render time is great for offline rendering, even taking more than 1/15 of a second in an interactive visualization means a rough, stuttering experience for your players.

No Room for Error

With only 0.033 seconds (33.3ms or 1/30 of a second) to render each frame, no error or inefficiency is negligible. Trimming only .001 seconds off the time it takes to render an object seems like it might be too much effort for so little gain, but if you have only 30 of those objects (think trees, flowers, cars, buildings, or people) in your scene, you've already saved 0.03 seconds (3ms) or 2.5 frames per second. That's a tiny margin of error, and small inefficiencies add up fast.

When you begin to discuss VR, you're talking a minimum of 90fps spread across two views. That's only 11 milliseconds to render your entire scene—twice.

Requires Other Applications

UE4 offers an amazing suite of tools that you can use to accomplish amazing things with your content. What it can't do very well is author the content to be displayed. While UE4 offers dozens of cutting-edge tools, almost all of them require content created in another application to achieve the best results possible.

This "disadvantage" has one major advantage, by design. It allows you to do almost all your content authoring in the applications you use every day and to use the workflows you have developed. If your application supports a FBX workflow or can be imported by one that does, you can get your content into UE4.

It's Software Development

Interactive visualizations are software applications. They have logic and user interfaces and run in real time. That means they can also have bugs, need new features, and require support and maintenance that lives far past the delivery date of the project.

Even the most organized studios will find the structure, timing, and management of interactive visualization development with UE4 to be often incompatible with the offline rendering pipeline. Playtesting, programming, and bug tracking are a few of the new workflows you must incorporate to ensure successful project delivery.

If your application is bound for public consumption, the effort to fully test and fix your application will consume far more time than you would initially estimate. Be prepared for this and budget and schedule your projects accordingly.

Players Can Look Everywhere

When you're creating a static visualization or animation you have the advantage of knowing exactly what the viewer will see at every moment. Save for the inevitable last-minute camera path change, you can pick and choose what to focus your efforts on, ignoring anything that you can't see. If it's not rendered, it doesn't need to even be there.

In an interactive, 3D Viewport, the player can look in any direction at any time. They can get as close as they like to nearly every corner and fixture. Any mistake can (and will) be found. Accuracy, precision, and attention to detail are essential.

In virtual reality, this is made even more apparent when the user is using positional tracking. That means they can often get literally inside walls and other objects, seeing outside the world, revealing the wizard behind the curtain.

Identifying Great UE4 Projects

Some common project requirements can help you identify when a project will benefit from using UE4 as well as a few red flags to look out for.

To benefit from UE4, the project has to leverage one of Unreal Engine 4's strengths enough that it balances out the additional effort of developing an interactive visualization versus a traditionally rendered visualization.

Interactivity, speed, programmability, and the non-linear, real-time nature of interactive visualizations enable limitless possibilities, but sometimes, UE4 is just inappropriate for the project and can even be detrimental. Having a clear reason to use UE4 is essential before heading down this road.

Comparing Options

By far, the most common and compelling reason to develop an interactive visualization is the need to compare datasets or design options in 3D space and time.

Comparing alternatives has always been a challenging proposition for traditional visualization and linear media delivery. Even simple A/B comparisons can double the rendering time for traditional visualizations. Adding only a few more options can quickly multiply into tens or hundreds of variations and permutations. The non-linear nature of interactive visualization and the powerful user interfaces (UIs) you can develop in UE4 enable players to explore data in personal, meaningful ways.

Giving the player the ability to toggle alternatives, set variables, and control their view to fit their exact needs is hugely empowering. It also happens in real time. There are no frames to render, and no PowerPoint presentations to update; changes to the data can be integrated immediately.

Changing Datasets

Projects with constantly changing datasets, or ones that are likely to receive last-minute updates, are also great candidates for using UE4. By nearly eliminating rendering time, updates can be seen immediately.

A great example of this kind of project is a design proposal effort. It's essential for the designers, architects, and engineers to be able to work up to the last minute. Specifications for projects often change days before the due date, or solutions to key problems aren't figured out until days or hours before the presentation. With traditional animations, these changes can be a huge problem because render times often prevent the visualizations from representing the final proposed design, or worse, the requirements of the project. This can severely reduce the value of visualizations, and sometimes even be a liability. Having great-looking visualizations that the team can rely on in the eleventh hour is essential, and UE4's speed can give your team that capability.

Unreal Engine 4 Development Requirements

Developing with UE4 requires a combination of the right hardware, software, and, of course, the right people. The biggest challenge for most visualization artists and studios will assuredly be acquiring the new skillsets required for developing interactive visualizations. Hardware and software can be purchased and upgraded easily; acquiring new skills and people takes time and perseverance.

As an experienced visualization developer, you are already a skilled tradesperson with mastery of the art of visual storytelling, light and color, animations, and eliciting the emotional and cerebral responses that make visualization such a powerful communication tool. You likely won't be an adept programmer, audio engineer, or user interface designer, and your workflow is almost certainly not based around tracking and updating hundreds of pieces of content and source code.

Finding somebody who is passionate about creating interactive experiences is, in my opinion, essential for studios wanting to move past creating static visualizations. This person might already exist on your team and is clamoring to use UE4 or any other game engine to make his or her art with. Hundreds, if not thousands of professionals and students alike have also embraced UE4 and are in the community eager to join any team that is as eager as they are.

As for hardware and software, UE4 development requires a reasonably powerful computer with a good amount of hard drive space. The most important component is a strong "dedicated" GPU or graphics card. Workstations and laptops are often shipped without dedicated GPUs, instead relying on the "integrated" graphics chips that reside on the motherboard to CPU. Integrated GPUs are *not* recommended or supported.

For development, I recommend an overpowered GPU that is a good deal more powerful than your target. This allows you to bear the overhead of the editor plus any other applications you might be running while developing in UE4. I must warn, however, about getting the very top-of-the-line GPUs because they can give you a very inaccurate idea of your application's performance, making it difficult to judge how it will run on your target platform.

The software requirements for UE4 development vary mostly on your specific needs, and you likely already have everything you need to get started with almost no or for very little investment. The Unreal Engine 4 editor runs natively in Windows, Mac OSX, and Linux. You can use commercial applications like Photoshop, Maya, and 3DS Max or free alternatives like GIMP and Blender to produce the content for UE4. Unreal Engine 4 uses industry standard file formats to exchange data (FBX, TARGA, EXR, and so on), freeing you to adapt your tools and workflow to work with UE4.

Teamwork in Unreal Engine 4

How teams work together in Unreal Engine 4 is different from the type of workflow most visualization teams are used to. Unreal Engine's roots lay not in the animation and video production roots of most production software that's common in visualization, but in the software development–style production environment of video game development.

Source Control Overview

The typical file-server–hosted project workflow most visualization artists are used to—where all the project files are stored on a server and accessed simultaneously—is not recommended at all for Unreal Engine 4 projects.

Having several people working on the same files in a UE4 project can quickly introduce conflicts and errors and can break a project incredibly quickly. Anybody who's ever worked on a team has had the experience where two people have worked on the same file at the same time. In most circumstances, one person's work will get clobbered. In UE4 that conflict can not only mean lost work, but can also cause referencing errors that can cause complete failure of a project to run.

To avoid these conflicts and to provide backup and data security, you should always use a **source control** or file versioning system.

Although many "brands" of versioning software (Perforce, SVN, Git, and so on) are available, they all share a common workflow: Users update or download the latest version of the project from a remote server to their local machine, and then as they make changes to files, they are "checked-out." This tells other users that these files have been modified and are off limits. After the user finishes making changes, she can then "check-in" or "submit" her files to the server. Now, other users can "update" their copies of the files on their workstations.

It's important to note that none of the file transfer happens automatically as it might with a system like Dropbox. It is always initiated by the users. This ensures that no surprises occur; for example, no files accidently update while somebody's working or accidently update when they shouldn't have been saved.

Most versioning systems also require a comment each time files are modified. This allows everybody to easily see who did what work and what new features were added simply by glancing at the version log.

Unreal Engine 4 Versioning Support Integration

Unreal Engine 4 has support for several of the most common and suitable file versioning platforms built directly into the Editor. If you enable the versioning support in UE4, the Editor will automate many of the most common tasks such as checking out, renaming, and other file management tasks.

You must still manually submit your work to the server when you are done making changes, but even this process is integrated into the Editor.

This integration to the UE4 Editor is extensive and makes using versioning an integral part of developing with UE4. Having the Editor do most of the hard work frees users from the complexities of versioning, ensuring everybody on the team uses file versioning.

I highly encourage teams looking to develop UE4 applications to get up to speed with versioning systems as fast as possible. A single developer can also benefit from the security and convenience of having all his projects hosted on an external server.

Because of the large number of versioning systems available and the complexity of learning any new system, covering a step-by-step how-to for using versioning systems is outside of the scope of this book; however, some fantastic official and community resources can help you set up your own versioning server and begin using UE4 in a team environment within hours. Visit the companion website for this book at www.TomShannon3d.com/UnrealForViz for an up-to-date list and information about UE4 file versioning integrations.

Costs of Developing for UE4

For most visualization artists and studios, UE4 carries very little additional software or hardware costs to get started. The Editor is free to download, and the other tools needed are industry standard. Most of the tools, hardware, and software you rely on to create traditional visualizations will serve you well for creating content for UE4. Of course, you can expect to spend more time and money on some areas.

Hardware

The number one thing you need to run UE4 is a good video card—the faster the better. The good news here is that UE4 runs best on gaming-level video cards. Although professional cards such as Quadro and Fire GL cards can offer some reliability benefits, a high-end gaming card typically costs much less and provides far greater performance.

You also need a lot of fast, local storage. Whereas you might have stored a lot of your content and projects on a shared server, UE4 is designed to run off the user's local machine.

UE4 projects can balloon in size very quickly, with some projects clocking in more than 50Gb. Even smaller projects can eat up a lot of disk space.

Development Time

Although much of your workflow will remain unchanged—preparing the client data, organizing the scene, building and applying materials and lighting, making camera paths and views, and so on—as soon as you add interactivity, it's a whole new ballgame.

Programming is a requirement most traditional visualizations typically don't have much of and most studios and individuals don't have much experience with. Even the simplest interactive visualization requires some level of scripting and needs some logic and user interface. Player input has to be read and interactions have to be programmed. Programming and scripting will quickly become significant parts of most development budgets.

Development costs can quickly grow and multiply. The complexity of an interactive visualization increases in a seemingly exponential manner as features are added or developed. A bit of a Pandora's Box effect occurs during the development of interactive visualizations. One feature inevitably affects another, increasing both estimated development times. Identifying when features will interact and increasing budgets accordingly is hugely important and must be strongly considered when developing your project's scope.

Testing and QA

Along with the overhead of logic and programming comes an often hidden or overlooked cost: testing and (quality assurance) QA. As your visualization applications become more complex and/or when they are released to the public, finding, tracking, and fixing bugs can become an unexpectedly time-consuming part of your development cycle.

Be aware of these costs and don't sell yourself short when budgeting on projects using UE4. You must provide ample time for the software development part of interactive visualization. These costs can be as much if not more than the costs for generating the 3D models and the scenes, especially as you start out and have to develop your skills as a developer.

Cost Savings of UE4

Developing in Unreal Engine 4 can seem to be an expensive proposition, especially when factoring the time for you and your team to learn and adapt to a new way of working. However, some major cost savings occur based simply on the development pipeline and technology of UE4.

Freed from intense CPU-bound rendering and massive datasets generated by frame rendering, the need for either a dedicated or cloud-based render-farm is eliminated or greatly reduced. A single workstation can take the place of tens and sometimes hundreds of thousands of dollars' worth of rendering hardware, software licensing fees, maintenance, and upkeep or hosting costs. If you already have a render farm set up, you can harness it to accelerate Lightmass rendering using the Swarm Agent and Coordinator to distribute the rendering workload much like other distributed rendering tool you may be familiar with.

If you are not using UE4 to generate renderings, you can also see a massive savings on storage. When you render an interactive application, each frame replaces the last and is literally thrown away rather than being stored on disk.

Unreal Engine 4 simply doesn't require the massive rendering infrastructure required for ray-traced rendering. Without the need for render farms, huge storage solutions, or super-high-speed networks, you can achieve a lot more with less capital investment by developing in UE4. Like most aspects of developing with Unreal Engine 4, trade-offs exist, and the cost of developing in UE4 is no different. You'll be faced with increased production time and effort, but rewarded with real-time rendering and all the advantages that brings.

As you and your team become more comfortable with the tools and begin building your own robust workflows to accommodate your specialized visualization pipelines, data sources, client requirements, and expectations, the costs can come down dramatically. However, be warned: Like all visualization projects, each UE4 project you do will challenge you in new and unexpected ways. This is not a failing of the tools; it is because Unreal Engine 4 is so vast, powerful, and extensible that almost no limit exists as to what you can achieve with it. You and your clients' imaginations will be unlocked and you will push each other to achieve the next great thing, so budget accordingly.

Resources and Training

Two of the biggest differences between professional-level software and all other software are documentation and support. Without comprehensive, up-to-date documentation and access to a support system, adopting any software application can be challenging or downright impossible. The abilities to train your team, find timely solutions to problems, and track and contribute to the development of the tools you are using are essential for a smooth, predictable development cycle.

Unreal Engine 4 is one of the most well-documented applications I've ever used. The official documentation is comprehensive, well-written, and up to date, despite the enormous updates that occur to the application on a regular basis. New features are introduced with detailed documentation and example projects and often specific, live training sessions are held several times a week where the actual developers of the tools demonstrate them. During these live streams, the audience can ask questions, getting immediate, one-on-one training, and feedback on the engine directly from the developers.

Despite the enormous efforts of Epic Games to produce world-class documentation and training material, this book included, the projects that developers are working on are so unique that it's impossible to cover every use case without hundreds of people working to produce the documentation. That's exactly what's happened.

Community Support

From the very beginning, Epic Games has reached out to the development community to help with Unreal Engine 4, and the community has responded in a huge way. Immediately, community members began producing amazing training and demonstration materials to help bring new developers on as fast as possible. Epic Games has recognized this effort and has generated an enormous amount of support for the UE4 Development community in the form of marketing for developers, the Unreal Dev Grant program that awards community developers with cash grants, direct support for user groups around the world, and more.

Epic Games took a massive risk by releasing its most valuable asset to world for free. I believe one of the key reasons it has seen such success with UE4 is because it has not only just embraced and nurtured the community, but has also become a member of the development community.

Marketplace

An extension of Epic's community-focused business model is the Unreal Engine Marketplace. The Marketplace allows developers to sell content directly to other developers. Hundreds of assets are available in every imaginable category. 3D models, materials, full game source files, animations, music and sound effects, and particle systems can be purchased from the marketplace a single time per studio and used in any UE4 projects by that studio or individual from that point forward.

These assets, of course, vary in quality and level of support because they are not created by Epic Games; however, Epic Games has strict quality control standards and a community review system to ensure all the assets available are of good quality.

Marketplace assets can not only save hundreds of hours of development from your project, but can also be an amazing learning resource. You can take apart each asset you purchase from the Marketplace and study in-depth to learn how it works. As you learn more, you can modify these assets to fit your needs or integrate their features into your own technologies.

Community Events and Conferences

The game development community has always enjoyed gathering together to talk shop, sneak peeks at each other's new games, and learn from one another. Game development meetups and conferences happen in almost every major city in the U.S., Europe, and Asia. Game development is a massive industry. In the U.S. alone, players spend $25.3 billion a year on video games. A quick Google search can quickly reveal events near you. Although most might not be specific to UE4, they will certainly have some UE4 developers attending, and maybe even some interactive visualization developers will be in attendance as well. Stranger things have happened.

Official user groups supported directly by Epic Games are few, but the numbers are growing. If you are lucky enough to be able to access these groups, they are great resources for networking, learning, and getting directly involved with the UE4 development community. Thousands of Unreal Engine 4 developers also meet unofficially using tools such as meetup.com to find like-minded developers near them.

The largest game development gathering in the U.S. is the Game Developer's Conference (GDC). The week-long gathering held in San Francisco each year allows developers from all kinds of backgrounds to get together to learn, network, and exchange ideas. Talks, training, and roundtables from premiere and indie game developers fill the days whereas the evenings are filled with parties and events throughout the city. The GDC also has an extensive show floor with vendors and developers demonstrating everything from the latest mind-control software to the latest game engine or input device. A job fair attracts hundreds of eager artists, programmers, and designers looking for their first big break into the interactive entertainment industry. If you can afford to attend, I highly recommend it for every serious interactive visualization developer. Although not specifically geared to the visualization industry, it's never an unrepresented community on the floor or in the talks.

Wherever you live, I hope you can get to a community gathering of interactive application and game developers, and hopefully, a UE4-focused group. They are all a very passionate bunch and these events are always a great time.

Summary

Getting started with interactive visualization development and Unreal Engine 4 in specific is an undertaking with fantastic reward, empowering you, your team, and your clients creatively and giving your audience new ways to learn about and experience the stories you tell as design-visualization professionals.

You should now have a much better understanding of what Ue4 is, what it offers for visualization, and an overview of how UE4 differs from how you may be used to developing visualizations. You should also have some idea what kinds of projects are good candidates for your first UE4 project and understand some of the challenges you might face moving forward and how to avoid some of them.

It's a great place to see new things being done with UE4 and can be a fantastic source of exposure for your own projects. Epic Games is eager to help its developers succeed, and promoting content in the Launcher and through Epic's social media networks is one of the biggest ways the company accomplishes this.

There are also links to the forums, the online documentation, and other community and official resources like the Engine Road Map and the AnswerHub.

Learn

The **Learn** section is an absolute treasure trove of training resources, example projects, and content. Each of these projects is offered under the same liberal terms as the rest of the content included with the Engine; you can use any of the content provided in any of your personal *and* commercial projects for FREE.

The section has tutorials, wikis, videos, and downloadable content such as effects, materials, textures, and more. I encourage you to download and explore. You can learn an amazing amount from seeing how the people who built the Engine use it to bring their own visions to life.

Marketplace

The **Marketplace** is where developers and artists can buy and sell nearly any kind of content (3D models, animations, effects, and so on) and plugins to extend the capabilities of UE4.

Thousands of UE4 developers are making free and paid content of pretty much every kind imaginable on the Marketplace. More content is available on third-party websites such as Gumroad.com or the developer's own websites.

Before developing something in UE4 yourself, do a Google search on it; there's a good chance you can find something available "off-the-shelf" to use.

Library

The **Library** tab is where you manage, install, uninstall, and update your various Engine versions. You can also view and manage your UE4 projects within the Library and manage your Marketplace content.

> **note**
>
> The Launcher is actually an Unreal Engine 4 application! You can find it installed alongside the other UE4 installations in your Applications folder.

Other Epic and UE4 Content

Along the top of the Launcher are other Epic Games projects and featured UE4 projects. Some of these are commercial games, such as *Paragon* and *Fortnite*; others are UE4 games with modding components that are supported through the UE4 Marketplace.

Epic Games is developing a new version of *Unreal Tournament* and providing the public full source code access to the game as it's being developed. The community is actively helping develop the game down to the code and art level. If you've ever wanted to see how a professional video game development company makes a massive, AAA game, you can watch or even get involved with the project by contributing directly.

UE4 Engine

The Engine resides in your Applications folder and is the collection of code and resources required to run UE4 applications. The Engine is the base code upon which the Launcher and the Editor are built and contains all the rendering, physics, UI, and other code and tools required to build and run the applications developed with the Editor.

Engine Versions

Unreal Engine 4 is updated regularly with both major feature updates and minor bug fix updates. UE4 uses a decimal numbering scheme to describe each release. Version updates are denoted by the first decimal number. For example, Unreal Engine 4.13 represents a major upgrade from 4.12. New features, updated core components, and other big changes are typically included in these releases.

Hot-fixes and bug-fix releases are described using the second decimal number: Unreal Engine 4.13.1 contains small bug fixes and other minor changes to the 4.13 release.

> ### note
>
> The Launcher allows you to have more than one major version of UE4 installed simultaneously, but only a single instance of each version. That means you can have 4.10.3 and 4.11.2 installed at the same time, but not 4.10.3 and 4.10.2.[1]
>
> _____
>
> 1. This only applies for Launcher-managed Engine installations. Users on Linux and projects that require Engine modifications might require a specific Engine build that is typically compiled from source code and managed outside the Launcher. There is no limitation to the number, location, or version numbers of these Engine builds.

Upgrading Projects

Upgrading UE4 projects to newer versions of the Engine is supported, but downgrading is not. Files saved in a newer version of the Editor cannot be opened by older versions. You should usually start new projects in the latest version of the Engine available, and upgrade only as necessary. If it's not broken, don't fix it, because you might break it.

Upgrading projects and content from one Engine version to the next is typically a smooth process, but can have many unexpected hiccups. Third-party plugins, for example, often take a while to get updated to the latest version of the Engine.

Epic Games provides clear guidance in the release notes describing the changes made that will affect upgraded projects. Always approach the task of upgrading existing projects with caution and typically do it only if your project would see a substantial benefit from the features or fixes in the upgraded Engine.

UE4 Editor

The UE4 **Editor** is the main interface for creating, testing, packaging, and programming UE4 projects. The Editor is a collection of tools and interfaces for importing, organizing, optimizing, programming, and creating compelling interactive content.

It offers tools for creating particle systems, robust artificial intelligence systems, advanced vehicle simulations, networking, multiplayer, virtual reality, realistic lighting and materials, user interfaces, and cinematic sequences. It provides nearly unlimited functionality via visual scripting and—believe it or not—much, much more. The UE4 Editor is a *massive*, professional-level development platform.

> note
>
> Like the Launcher, the UE4 Editor is an application built with Unreal Engine 4 as a graphical interface to create other Unreal Engine 4 applications!

The Editor also gives you easy access to a slew of configuration settings, world-building tools and deployment, and debugging and performance profiling tools that can help you diagnose performance issues so you can make your visualizations look as good as possible.

UE4 Projects

Most applications used for traditional visualization use a single file to describe an entire scene. That file typically swells as the scene grows. A Photoshop file gets bigger as you add layers, and a Max file grows as you add geometry. This single file can be copied from drive to drive and can contain *everything* needed to render the scene.[2]

Rather than a single file, each **Project** in Unreal Engine 4 is a collection of source-code files, content asset files, plugins, configuration files, and other supporting files all stored in a single directory. This directory and the files it contains is the Project, not any one file (see Figure 2.2).

---

2. Of course, both Photoshop and 3ds Max allow linking to external files (textures, for example), but that structure is not enforced. You can have your textures stored on a separate drive or on a network location that's literally thousands of miles away.

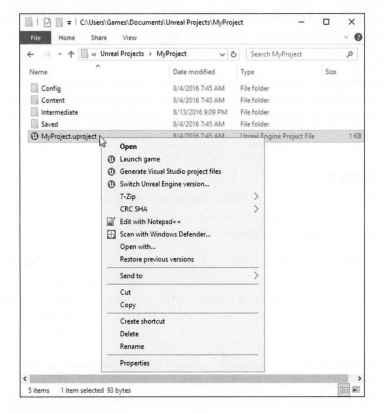

Figure 2.2 Unreal Project folder and context menu (Windows 10)

In the root of a project directory is a **.uproject** file that associates your project with a specific UE4 version and your plugin installations. This file doesn't grow or even get saved to or modified very often, if at all. It's actually just a text file that you can open and read using a text editor.

The following shows a typical .uproject file's contents:

```
{
        "FileVersion": 3,
        "EngineAssociation": "4.13",
        "Category": "",
        "Description": "",
        "Plugins": [
                {
                        "Name": "Substance",
                        "Enabled": true,
                        "MarketplaceURL":
"com.epicgames.launcher://ue/marketplace/content/2f6439c2f9584f49809d9b13b16c
2ba4"
                }
        ]
}
```

Double-clicking this file in your file browser launches the associated UE4 Editor version, if installed, or a prompt to be associated with a new Engine version.

Right-clicking the .uproject file presents you with some handy options, such as to launch the project without the Editor by selecting Launch Game from the context menu.

This is a great way of bypassing the Editor in your day-to-day work and is my preferred way of launching projects.

Source Art

Unreal Engine is amazing and capable of helping you create awesome worlds. However, its focus is not on helping you create most of the content that populates those worlds. You do that with the 3D and 2D applications you know and love (such as Photoshop, 3ds Max, and Maya). UE4 has no reason to compete with these applications' capabilities or to require you to learn a whole new way of doing things.

You will still create almost all your art assets in the programs you already know and love and others you might not be as familiar with, such as Substance Painter, ZBrush, and Blender. New tools are being developed every day; it's a very fast-growing ecosystem, and by outsourcing the content creation to these applications, Epic Games can focus on developing UE4's capabilities for creating compelling interactive worlds.

In visualization, your source art might also be CAD data, scientific data, or GIS information. Whatever the source application or format you can consider all of it as part of your source art.

You create, store, access, and modify source art files *completely outside* your UE4 project folders. Keep your existing, proven workflows and modify them to match the conventions and requirements of UE4. Unreal Engine 4 is agnostic about where data comes from, as long as it's exported or saved to format UE4 can import.

Project Folder Structure

The UE4 project folder structure is strictly enforced. A project cannot load or reference any file outside the project directory. Because of this, UE4 projects are portable and self-contained. Projects can easily be copied and synchronized across workstations easily and reliably.

Several folders are in each Project folder. Understanding what each one is and what you should and shouldn't do with each is important.

Config

The **Config** directory holds the settings for each project in text files with an **.ini** extension. Settings for every feature in the Engine are exposed in these files. *Thousands* of individual settings exist, and you can leave most as defaults.[3]

Almost all the most important configuration settings appear in the Editor's Preference panels (see Figure 2.3). You can directly modify the settings using a convenient user interface with helpful contextual tooltips that describe the function and often use cases for each setting. The .ini files are updated on the fly, and only a few settings require an Editor restart to take effect. If you change a setting that requires a restart, the Editor notifies you.

You should *always* include the Config folder when copying, sharing, or syncing your project with others. Having differing configuration files between project copies can cause a litany of difficult-to-diagnose problems.

Figure 2.3 UE4 Editor Project Settings dialog

Saved

The **Saved** folder is a temporary folder generated on the fly as the project is run. Screenshots, logs, and other files that are "saved" by the game appear here. This folder also contains the auto-backup files.

---

3. You can use several advanced settings to trade rendering speed for quality, but you must use them with caution. There's a reason they aren't exposed in the Project and Editor settings. I cover the most important tweaks and settings later in the book, so stay tuned.

This folder can become extremely large and is one of the main reasons to avoid hosting your project on a network or shared folder. Likewise, if you are copying your project or using source control (you are using source control, aren't you?), you should exclude this folder to save time and space and avoid configuration conflicts.

Plugins (Optional)

Many plugins are available for UE4 and while some are content based and only require a folder to be paced into your project's Content folder, others must be placed either into the **Plugins** directory and/or compiled from the Source folder.

Those plugins end up, predictably in the Plugins directory. Here the platform-specific shared files (.dll on PC, .so on Linux, and so on) that have been generated from C++ or downloaded are installed. These files are read by the Editor and game and can modify either in nearly any way you can imagine—examples include adding additional file import support or new rendering features.

Everybody on the team should have the full contents of this folder.

Content

The **Content** directory stores all the assets that are used to build the game. Only two types of files are typically stored in the Content directory: **.uasset** and **.umap** files. These files are generic wrappers and represent all the assets and Levels in the project.

> note
>
> *Never* modify the Content folder outside the UE4 Editor. Do *all* of your file management from within the UE4 Editor. Moving, renaming, deleting, or otherwise modifying the .uasset and .umap files *will* cause null references. That's bad. Double bad.

Seeing a folder full of files with the same extension and thinking of them as textures, materials, animations, 3D models, Blueprints, sounds, and more can be counterintuitive. We often use file extensions in our daily interactions with computers to differentiate file types and functions. Unreal Engine 4 uses data within each .uasset file to determine what it is and how it is displayed in the Editor and used in the game at runtime.

It goes without saying that this folder is essential to a project and should always be included when sharing the project.

Intermediate

The **Intermediate** directory is like the Saved directory in that the Engine generates it dynamically at runtime. It contains files required to compile and run the game or that speed up the day-to-day operation of the Editor, such as with shader and geometry caches.

Like the Saved folder, you should not include or share this folder when copying or versioning your project.

Understanding .uasset Files

UE4 requires almost all content—models, textures, audio, and animations—to be imported into the Engine to be stored in your project's Content folder as .uasset files. Each .uasset file is also referred to as a **Content Package**. In each package is the source file that was imported as well as a ton of other asset-specific information. The Engine converts these .uasset files on the fly to the correct format for the platform you are running on and deploying to.

This means a single .uasset file can be used to deploy content to Mac, PC, mobile, VR, or any other platform UE4 supports without any modification of the .uasset or access to the source file. The Engine does the conversion to the proper format for you in the background. You can even export the source file (image, model, and so on) back out from the .uasset file in the Editor to modify, and then reimport the modified file back into the project.

The UE4 Engine and Editor will ONLY read and display .uasset files in the Content Browser.

Unreal Engine 4 Content Pipeline

UE4 has polished and easy-to-learn workflows for almost every aspect and feature of the Engine. Although some of the workflows can be exacting or labor intensive, they are consistent. If you follow the rules and do things the UE4 way, you'll be rewarded with high frame rates, reliable deliverables, and amazing visualizations.

A typical UE4 project has a predictable workflow. Nearly every project requires you to complete several tasks to get it into your clients' hands.

Set Up a New Project

UE4 offers a few ways to set up a new project. You can create one by launching an Engine directly from the Library section of the Launcher. You can also create a new project from the File menu within the UE4 Editor.

> **note**
>
> I do *not* recommend using a network drive to host your project for individual or shared development. UE4 is not designed to run in this manner and will not be any fun to work with. Use **version control software** to allow multiple developers to work on the same project.

Store and work on your project on a fast, local drive. Using a hard drive makes even the biggest Level or asset load and save in seconds and decreases the time you spend importing and processing assets, making for much faster workflow.

Choose a single location to keep your UE4 Projects close to the root of your drive with a short folder name. I typically keep all my projects on E:/UE4/ProjectName. Long path names can cause issues when you go to package your projects.

Build Content

Before you can make much of a visualization, you need to build content. You're already a pro at this. Your existing workflows and systems will typically keep working for you with only minor modifications. If you're producing 3D geometry, you can probably get it into UE4.

Export Content

You must export nearly all the content you want to get into UE4 to a format UE4 understands. Unreal Engine 4 imports a growing number of industry standard file formats such as FBX, TGS, PNG, PSD, and more. However, UE4 does not support importing application-specific binary files such as 3ds Max files.

Many of these files are temporary, intermediate files and are simply used as an exchange between the various content creation tools and UE4. You should maintain your application-specific source files and re-export as required.

Import Content to UE4

After creating and exporting your content, you import it into UE4. This process creates a .uasset content package for each asset you import. This .uasset package typically contains a copy of the imported data along with a ton of other asset-specific metadata and other information.

You can automate much of this workflow using scripts and tools to generate your export files; importing is then a typically painless affair with support for batch importing.

Populate the Level with Content

After you import it, your content is displayed and organized in the **Content Browser**. You can then simply drag and drop your content from the Content Browser into the 3D Viewport and begin populating your world.

Each Mesh you add to the Level is an instance of the .uasset you imported that references the .uasset. If you drag a model into your scene 30 times, it doesn't create 30 copies of it—only 30 identical *references* of the asset in the library while only a single copy is loaded into RAM. If you modify that one .uasset, all the references to that asset will update to match.

You can also add lighting, atmospheric effects, animation, and other content, creating the look and feel you want. Post-processing effects are applied in real time: Bloom, Lens Flares, Motion Blur, Depth of Field, even Ambient Occlusion are all computed in a fraction of a millisecond and composited in real time, creating beautiful, final-quality images.

Add Interactivity (Programming!)

At this point, you can create static camera paths and render out your scene to frames to be delivered on video, and the quality of these renderings can be of very high quality.

However, you're really missing the boat if you're expending all that effort to get your content into UE4 without adding interactivity.

Even adding a simple orbit camera enables a user to manipulate a photo-realistic visualization in ways impossible with any other delivery platform.

In UE4 you can create amazingly rich, interactive worlds without writing a single line of code using the Blueprint script editing system. You can also use C++ or one of the many scripting integrations available.

Test and Refine

Because interactivity involves users, bugs inevitably occur. You're probably accustomed to visual bugs in your visualization work. From rendering glitches to modeling errors to data errors, your UE4 interactive visualization will have those, too. Plus, you will also encounter the fresh challenge of user interaction bugs.

Creating smooth-running, easy-to-use interfaces, scenes, and applications isn't as easy as it seems. Your users will have high expectations for the interfaces you create, and the process of fine-tuning your systems and interfaces takes far more time and resources than you might expect.

The more capabilities that you add, the more testing and iteration you must do, and the wider your audience, the more rigorous your testing needs to be.

Get your application in your client's/audience's hands as soon as possible and, if you can, watch them use it. Listen to them and get as much feedback on your application as you can as early along as you can. This is the best way of avoiding the development process from imploding in the eleventh hour.

Package

After your interactive visualization is tested and running like greased lighting with an interface so clean and absurdly useable that Apple takes notice, it's time to get it out of your development environment and onto the public's computers, tablets, and phones!

To do this, you need to **Package** your project. This is a multistage operation. First, UE4 "cooks" all of your project's content. Cooking simply takes all the .uasset files you made and processes them for whatever platform you are deploying to and removes any source content or other cruft, leaving only the most efficient file to be loaded by that system.

The cooked content is then merged with a version of the UE4 Engine that's had the Editor and other development tools removed from it. An executable is created, resulting in a self-contained, completely portable version of your project that can be installed to any machine capable of running it!

Distribute

Getting your application out to your clients or the general public is a bit more involved than emailing an image or uploading a movie to YouTube.

UE4 application installers are typically several hundred megabytes, often more than a gigabyte. A simple Dropbox link, while sufficient for sending files to a few people, can quickly become overwhelmed if even a few hundred people access it.

Provide Support

After your application is outside your walls, it will be tested and used in ways you never imagined. Your audience will find incompatibilities with an amazing array of hardware and software that you never even knew existed, much less tested against. Always plan for support time for any project and scale it appropriately the larger your audience gets.

Summary

Where you might have once considered a project done after your visualization scene has been populated and you click Render, developing interactive visualization in UE4 introduces a new second half to your visualization development process. You must account for it in your scopes, your personnel and their skillsets, and the timeframes you set forth for developing interactive visualization applications.

CHAPTER 3

CONTENT PIPELINE

Getting your existing scenes and content into UE4 is likely one of the first things you want to do after the Editor is running. It might also be your first major roadblock, especially if you're looking to convert large, existing ray-traced visualization scenes over to UE4. By understanding what you need to do to prepare your content for UE4, you can save a huge amount of time by doing it the "Unreal way" the first time and get the quality and performance you and your clients expect from Unreal Engine 4.

Content Pipeline Overview

You're probably used to working in a 3D application with an integrated modeler, material system, and renderer. After your data is in your 3D application, you can render your scene with a push of a button. You apply materials and lighting, create animations, and build your stories using the tools in your chosen 3D application. You might prepare textures and other data in external applications, but you do most of your day-to-day work in the 3D application of your choosing.

After your image or animation is rendered, you then load your image(s) into a post-editing application to add effects and titles, edit footage, and add audio. When it's complete, a final version is rendered to a video or image file and shared with your audience or client (see Figure 3.1).

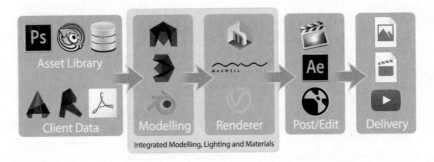

Figure 3.1 Traditional visualization workflow

UE4 is a standalone application and doesn't integrate directly into any 3D application. Instead, you use 2D and 3D applications to produce 3D models and textures that you must export to an exchange format (FBX, TGA, and so on) and import into UE4 (see Figure 3.2).

Figure 3.2 UE4 visualization workflow

After import into UE4, you build your worlds within the UE4 Editor: adding lighting, materials, and interactivity. There is no Render button; the Viewport renders everything in real time, producing final-quality images including post-processing effects like motion blur, depth of field, and color grading.

To add interactivity, you use Blueprints, C++, and Unreal Motion Graphics (UMG) to create user interfaces and other onscreen titling. Sequencer allows you to create Hollywood-quality cinematics using a non-linear editor, physically based cameras, and camera rigs.

After the project is complete, you can deliver your application on any number of platforms: Mac, Windows, VR, mobile, and so on. You can also render high-quality stills and animations.

Content Preparation

Take extra care when preparing content for use in UE4. Proper naming conventions, Lightmap UV coordinates, collision, LODs, and more are required to ensure a smooth, fast workflow, high performance, and quality rendering. Because there's so much more to do to prepare your scenes, automation and consistency are essential for keeping production nimble, keeping your project stable and performant, and keeping production costs down.

The UE4 workflow uses a lot more artist time than raytracing. Why? Remember those insanely fast render times (.016–.033 seconds per frame discussed in Chapter 1) One of the best ways of making things render faster is to do the processing work ahead of time and store it in various ways. Baking in lighting, recording details using normal maps, or even the lowly act of assigning UVW coordinates all free up processing resources.

The upside is that your downtime during the UE4 workflow is almost zero. Exporting, importing, and processing data in UE4 is *very* fast. The only processes that take extended periods of time are typically threaded and can run in parallel with the Editor, allowing you to continue working in-Editor while you bake lighting or compile the project to run on a different platform.

> note
>
> Several of the most time-consuming and processor-intensive calculations can not only be done in parallel with the Editor, but can also be distributed over a network. You can easily use your existing workstations or render farm to provide massive boosts to Lightmass rendering, content cooking, compiling, and more.

You'll also not be spending huge portions of your day waiting for renders. The Viewports in Max and Maya are notoriously terrible for conveying what the lit, rendered scene will look like, often failing to even show materials and textures properly. This forces you to render your scene to preview each of your changes, taking minutes, sometimes hours to get a good idea of how your final image will look.

UE4 is also fast at loading content. The Content Browser opens assets and previews them in real time, and the various editors open quickly even with complex content. Massive levels save and open in seconds, not minutes. The result is an interactive workflow that means you can do more in less time, and if you follow some simple guidelines, a lot of the work will be taken care of for you through automation and other magic.

3D Scene Setup

You should always conform your content to the standards and conventions presented by UE4. Most of these are technical in nature, many are stylistic, but all have good reasoning behind them.

You must start by organizing your source art files (your Max, Maya, and Photoshop files). Organization is the name of the game and taking the time now to get it right is important.

Changing names, scale, vertex count, pivot points, and so on are all very easy to do in Digital Content Creation (DCC) apps—just click, rename, move, and scale. These apps were made to modify Meshes and bitmaps and are good at it, and you're probably good at using them to do that. Doing these things is much more involved (if they are even possible) after you have your content into UE4.

Units

Unreal Engine 4 uses centimeters as the default scene **unit**. Ideally, always set your applications to work in a 1 unit == 1 cm unit scale. However, for a lot of visualization, this is not as easy as it seems. We are often beholden to source data limitations or other workflow imperatives that prevent us from easily doing that conversion.

A few ways exist to alleviate this issue. The FBX exporter enables you to apply a scale to Meshes while exporting, and UE4 offers an import scale (and rotation) setting for Meshes. These options might or might not work depending on your content and isn't recommended if you can help it. Instead, try to find a way to rescale your content prior to export.

Max also offers the option to set **Display Units**. This option does *nothing* to the data or scene. It is simply a conversion from the scene unit scale to the visual elements in the UI. This lets you keep your content in centimeters and continue to work with familiar units.

Statistics

Getting accurate **statistics** is essential for optimizing your content. The most important ones are Triangle and Vertex counts. Note that I said *triangle* not *poly* or *faces* or any other terminology. UE4 breaks down all geometry to triangles defined by vertices for rendering, so anything else is unimportant for our needs.

Backface Cull and Normals

Backface Cull is a rendering optimization where triangles aren't rendered if they are facing away from the camera. This can also be known as **two-sided** or **double-sided** rendering.

Many 3D applications have two-sided rendering enabled by default, showing both sides of objects. This can give you an incorrect view of the geometry because UE4 culls back-facing triangles by default. You can set individual materials and material instances in UE4 to be two-sided, but it's not an efficient fix and isn't intended to fix bad content, but is a feature to render specific surfaces such as foliage.

You should turn off two-sided rendering in your 3D applications to ensure you are looking at the same model that you will see in UE4. Fix any face and vertex normal issues in your 3D application before exporting to UE4.

Preparing Geometry for UE4

Unreal Engine 4 refers to 3D Objects as either **Static Meshes** or **Skeletal Meshes**. A single Mesh can have Smoothing Groups, multiple materials, and vertex colors. Meshes can be rigid (Static Meshes) or deforming (Skeletal Meshes). You export each Mesh as an FBX file from your 3D application, and then import it into your UE4 Project.

> ### note
>
> You will use Static Meshes exclusively in this book to build your scenes. Static Meshes, despite the name, are not incapable of moving or being moved in your applications. The "static" parts of a Static Mesh are the vertexes. Static Meshes cannot deform based on bones. That's what a Skeletal Mesh is for.

Architecture and Prop Meshes

I think of my Static Mesh assets in two broad categories: Architecture and Props. Each follows similar rules but both have considerations that can make dealing with each much easier.

Architecture

Architecture Meshes are objects that are unique and are placed in a specific location, such as walls and floors, terrain, roads, and so on. Typically, only one copy of these objects is in your scene, and they need to be in a specific location.

You will usually keep a 1:1 relationship between the objects in your source art, your Content folder, and your UE4 Level. (For example, you'll have one SM_Wall01 in each in the exact same place.)

You export these objects in place, import them, and place them into the scene at 0,0,0 (or another defined origin point). Keeping your UE4 content in sync with your scene using this method is easy because you can import or reimport Meshes or entire scenes without needing to reposition them.

Props

Prop Meshes are repeating or reusable Static Meshes that you place in or on your Architecture within your Level. An example is plates on a table. You could have a unique Static Mesh asset for each one in your scene or, because they are all exactly the same, you can reference a single asset and move it into position in the Viewport. The table would also be a Prop and could also be moved about easily.

Having multiple Props reference a single asset reduces memory overhead and makes updating and iterating on content easy.

Naming

Like all digital projects, developing and sticking to a solid naming convention for your projects is an important task for anybody developing with UE4. Projects end up with thousands of individual assets and they all have the extension of .uasset. Naming your objects in your 3D application is easy and fast—but this isn't quite the case in UE4.

You will undoubtedly come up with your own standards and system to accommodate your specific data pipelines, but it helps to be on the same page as the rest of the Unreal Engine 4 community as you will likely use and share content with them.

Basics

Don't use spaces or special/Unicode characters when naming anything (Meshes, files, variables, and so on). Sometimes you can get away with breaking these rules, but it makes things tough later when you encounter a system that won't accept the space or special character.

UE4 Naming Convention

A basic naming scheme for Unreal content has been used over the last 15 years by Epic Games and developers using Unreal Engine. It follows the basic convention of

Prefix_AssetName_Suffix

If you looked through any of the content included with UE4, you have already seen this convention.

> note
>
> The Engine and Editor do **not** enforce any rules upon naming conventions. You are free to name content whatever you like.

Prefix

The **Prefix** is a short one- or two-letter code that identifies the type of content the asset is. Common examples are M_ for Materials and SM_ for Static Meshes. You can see that it's usually a simple acronym or abbreviation, but sometimes conflicts or tradition require others like SK_ for Skeletal Meshes. (A complete list is available on the companion website at www.TomShannon3D.com/unreal4Viz)

AssetName

BaseName describes the object in a simple, understandable manner. WoodFloor, Stone, Concrete, Asphalt, and Leather are all great examples.

Suffix

A few classes of assets have some subtle variations that are important to note in the name. The most common example is Texture assets. Although they all share the same T_ prefix, different kinds of textures are intended for specific uses in the Engine such as normal maps and roughness maps. Using a suffix helps describe these differences while keeping all the Texture objects grouped neatly.

Examples

You could find the examples shown in Table 3.1 in any common UE4 project.

Table 3.1   Example Asset Names

Asset Name	Note
T_Flooring_OakBig_D	Base Color (diffuse) Texture of big, oak flooring
T_Flooring_OakBig_N	Normal map Texture of big, oak flooring
MI_Flooring_OakBig	Material Instance using the big, oak flooring Textures
M_Flooring_MasterMaterial	The Material that the big, oak flooring Material Instance is parented to
SM_Floor_1stFloor	Static Mesh with the MI_Flooring_OakBig Material Instance is applied to

There are dozens of content types and variations in UE4, each with a different possible naming scheme. You can go to www.TomShannon3D.com/UnrealForViz for a direct link to a community-driven list of all the suggested prefixes and suffixes.

Although this list is exhaustive, none of these naming rules are enforced in anyway. What's most important is consistency. Develop a system and stick to it.

UV Mapping

UV mapping is a challenge for all 3D artists and even more so for visualization. Most visualization rendering can make do with some very poor UVW mapping, and sometimes none. UE4 simply cannot.

UVW coordinates are used for a litany of features and effects; from the obvious such as applying texturing to surfaces to the less obvious but equally important things such as Lightmap coordinates.

All of your 3D assets will need quality, consistent UVW coordinates. For simple geometry, this can be as easy as applying a UVW Map modifier to your geometry; more complicated geometry will be a more involved, manual process. Don't fear; most of the time you can get good results easily. Just keep an eye on your UV coordinates when you are working with UE4. If you have rendering issues that are difficult to diagnose, check your UV coordinates.

Real-World Scale

Many 3D applications can use a real-world scale UV coordinate system, where the texture is scaled in the material, rather than the UV coordinates. Although this is completely possible to accomplish in UE4, it's not the best option.

If your scenes are already mapped to real-world scale, you should scale your UV coordinates using a modifier (Scale UVW in Max) or manually scale the UV verticies in a UV Editor.

World-Projection Mapping

A common "cheat" for visualization is to use world-projected textures (textures projected along the XYZ world coordinates) to cover complex, static models quickly with tiling textures. This method doesn't require well-authored UV coordinates for good results. UE4 has methods for doing this and I rely on them heavily in my own projects.

It's important to note that if you are planning to use pre-calculated lighting with Lightmass, you still need to provide good, explicit Lightmap UV coordinates, even when using world-projection mapping. This is because the Lightmass stores the lighting information in texture maps that need unique UC space to render correctly.

Tiling Versus Unique Coordinates

Most visualizations make extensive use of tiling textures. In truth, the texture does not tile; rather the UV coordinates are set or being modified by the material to allow tiling. A tiled UVW coordinate set allows UV faces to overlap and for vertices to go outside the 0–1 UV space. By the nature of UV coordinates, going outside the 0–1 range results in tiling. Essentially, 0.2, 1.2, and 2.2 all sample the same pixel.

Unique UV coordinates are defined by having no coordinates outside 0–1 and each face occupies a unique area in the UV map space without overlaps. This is useful when you are "baking" information into the texture map, because each pixel can correspond to a specific location on the surface of the model (see Figure 3.3).

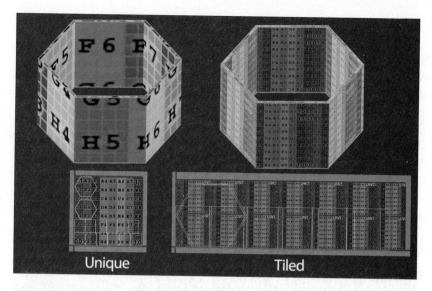

Figure 3.3 Unique versus tiled UV coordinates

Common examples of baking data into textures are normal maps generated from high-polygon models using reprojection or, in UE4, using Lightmass to record lighting and Global Illumination (GI) information into texture maps called **Lightmaps**.

Multiple UV Channels

Unreal Engine 4 supports and even encourages and requires multiple UV channels to allow texture blending and other Engine-level features such as baked lighting with Lightmass.

3D applications can often have trouble visualizing multiple UV channels in the Viewport, and the workflow is typically clunky and often left unused in favor of using larger, more detailed textures. This isn't an option; massive textures can consume huge amounts of VRAM and make scenes bog down.

Instead, make use of multiple UV channels and layered UV coordinates in your materials to add detail to large objects.

> **note**
>
> UE4 uses a base 0 for UV coordinates. Many applications use a base 1. In other words, if your application (Max, I'm looking at you!) uses 1 for the base UV channel, UE4 will import that as coordinate index 0.

Lightmap Coordinates

Making Lightmap UV coordinates can seem like an onerous task. Have no fear: Lightmap coordinates are easy to author and are simply a second set of UV coordinates that enforce a few rules:

- If your project uses dynamic lighting exclusively, you probably don't need to worry about Lightmapping coordinates at all!
- Coordinates need to be unique and not overlap or tile. If faces overlap, Lightmass can't decide what face's lighting information to record into the pixel, creating terrible-looking errors.
- A space must exist between UV charts (groups of attached faces in the UV Editor). This is called **padding** and ensures that pixels from one triangle don't bleed into adjacent triangles.
- The last major rule is twofold: Avoid splitting your Lightmap UVs across smooth faces because this can cause an unsightly seam and split your coordinates along Smoothing Group boundaries to avoid light bleeding across Smoothing Groups.

> **note**
>
> Sometimes, you will have no choice but to place a UV seam on a smooth face. Do your best to author it facing away from where the viewer will most likely be (the back or the bottom of the object are common choices).

Auto Generate Lightmap UVs

The Auto Generate Lightmap UVs import option is one of the biggest timesavers for preparing models for lighting with Lightmass. I can't recommend it enough. It generates high-quality Lightmap coordinates quickly on import (or after) and is artist-tweakable for optimal results (see Figure 3.4).

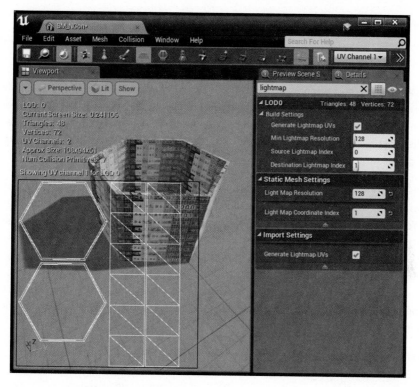

Figure 3.4 Autogenerated UV coordinates with Lightmap UV coordinates overlaid (note the efficiency versus Figure 3.2)

In a broad sense, the Auto Generate Lightmap UVs system is simply a repack and normalization operation that takes a source channel and packs the existing UV charts into the 0–1 UV space as efficiently as possible. It also adds the correct amount of pixel padding between the charts based on the intended Lightmap resolution as set by the Source Lightmap Index. (Lower resolution Lightmaps have larger pixels requiring larger spaces between charts; higher resolution inversely has smaller pixels requiring smaller spaces.)

This only requires that the coordinates in your base UV channel follow the rules about being split along Smoothing Groups and don't have stretching. They can be any scale, be overlapped, and more, if they are cleanly mapped to begin with.

> ### tip
> You can often Lightmap geometry easily by applying a simple box mapping or using UV tools within your application to perform quick-and-dirty mapping to the object(s) before export (splitting by Smoothing Groups or by face angle, for example). Combined with world-projection mapping, your UV mapping workflow can be fast and easily automated.

Level of Detail (LOD)

UE4 has fantastic **LOD** support. LOD is the process of switching out 3D models with lower-detail versions as they recede into the distance and become smaller on-screen.

If you are developing content for mobile or VR, LOD and model optimization are incredibly important. Even if you're running on high-end hardware, consider creating LOD models for your high-polygon props. For Meshes like vehicles, people, trees, and other vegetation that are used hundreds of times each in a large scene, having efficient LOD models will mean you can keep more assets on-screen, creating a more detailed simulation.

UE4 fully supports LOD chains from applications that support exporting these to FBX. That means you can author your LODs in your favorite 3D package and import them all at once into UE4. You can also manually import LODs by exporting several FBX files and importing them from the Editor.

Automatic LOD Creation

UE4 supports creating LODs directly in the Editor. Much like Lightmap generation, these LODs are specifically created by and for UE4 and can produce great-looking LODs with almost no artist intervention needed.

To generate LOD Meshes in the Editor, simply assign an LOD Group in either the Static Mesh Editor or by assigning an LOD Group at import. I recommend taking a look at it for your higher-density Meshes, especially if you are targeting mobile or VR platforms.

Several third-party plugins, such as Simplygon (https://www.simplygon.com) and InstaLOD (http://www.instalod.io/), can further automate the entire LOD generation process and have more powerful reduction abilities than UE4's built-in solution.

If you regularly deal with heavily tessellated Meshes, I recommend considering integrating these plugins into your UE4 pipeline, because they are far more robust than the optimization systems in most 3D applications, and the time saved using automatic LOD generation can be significant, not to mention the obvious performance benefits of reducing the total number of vertices being transformed and rendered each frame.

Collision

Collision is a complex subject in UE4. Interactive actors collide and simulate physics using a combination of per-polygon and low-resolution proxy geometry (for speed) and various settings to determine what they collide with and what they can pass through (for example, a rocket being blocked by a shield your character can pass through).

Fortunately, because most visualization does not require complex physics interactions between warring factions, you can use a simplified approach to collision preparation.

Architecture Mesh Collision

For large, unique architecture you can simply use per-polygon (complex) collision. Walls, floors, roads, terrains, sidewalks, and so on can use this easily without incurring a huge performance penalty. Keep in mind that the denser the Mesh the more expensive this operation is, so use good judgment, and break apart larger Meshes to avoid performance issues.

Prop Mesh Collision

For smaller or more detailed Meshes, per-polygon collision is too memory and performance intensive. You should instead use a low-resolution Collision Proxy Mesh or Simple collision.

You might opt to generate your own, low-polygon proxy **Collision Meshes**[1] in a 3D package, or in the UE4 Editor using manually placed primitives (boxes, spheres, capsules). You should also take a look at the automatic collision generation options the Editor provides.

Convex Decomposition (Auto Convex Collision)

UE4 also offers a great automatic collision generation system in the Editor called **Convex Decomposition**. This feature uses a fancy voxelization system that breaks down polygon objects into 3D grids to create good quality collision primitives. It even works on complicated Meshes, and I highly recommend it for reducing the polygon count on your props.

Do not confuse convex decomposition with the option to automatically generate collision during the import process. That system is a legacy system from UE3 and is unusable for most visualization purposes because it doesn't handle large, irregular, or elongated shapes well.

Convex Decomposition is not enabled on import because it can be very slow for large Meshes or Meshes with lots of triangles. For these, you should author a traditional collision shell in your 3D application and import it with your model.

You can find more information about generating collisions in the official documentation and at www.TomShannon3d.com/UnrealForViz.

Pivot Point

UE4 imports pivots differently than you expect. UE4 lets you choose between two options for your **pivot points** on import via the Transform Vertex to Absolute option in the Static Mesh importer. You can either have the pivot set where it is in your 3D application (by setting Transform Vertex to Absolute to false) or you can force the pivot point to be imported at the scene's 0,0,0 origin, ignoring the defined pivot point completely (by setting Transform Vertex to Absolute to true).

---

1. Low-polygon primitives exported with your Meshes that follow a specific naming convention. For more information, see the Static Mesh documentation at https://docs.unrealengine.com/latest/INT/Engine/Content/FBX/StaticMeshes/index.html#collision.

You might wonder why in the world you would want to override your object's pivot point, but doing can be a huge time saver. By using a common pivot point, you can place all **Architecture Meshes** in your scene easily and reliably by putting them into the Level and setting the position to 0,0,0; they will all line up perfectly.

This works because you don't typically move your Architecture Meshes around, so where they rotate and scale from is irrelevant. What's important is their accurate position in 3D space.

Prop Meshes are the opposite. As you place props in your scenes, the pivot point is essential for moving, rotating, and scaling them into place.

To get the pivot point in UE4 to match your 3D application, you have a couple options. You can model all your props at 0,0,0, or move them each as you export. Newer versions of UE4 (4.13 and up) allow you to override the default import behavior and use the Meshes' authored pivot point as well. This is usually the best bet to ensure your pivot points match.

FBX Mesh Pipeline

After preparing your geometry assets, you need to export them to FBX. This format has a long, history that eventually led to its being one of the most common interchange formats available for 3D data.

UE4 uses FBX extensively for both Mesh and animation data so knowing what Unreal Engine 4 expects from your exported geometry is important.

Export Settings

Be sure to select Smoothing Groups and Tangents and Binormals and to Triangulate your Mesh in your export options, if available (see Figure 3.5). These options ensure that your Mesh is triangulated and shaded exactly the same way in both your 3D package and UE4.

If your scene is in a scale other than centimeters, you can easily rescale all of your assets as you export by explicitly setting **Scene units to converted to:** to *Centimeters*.

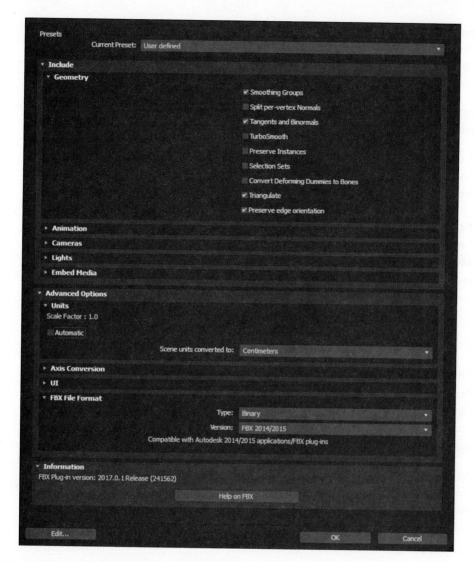

Figure 3.5 Suggested FBX export settings for static meshes (3D Studio Max)

Exporting Multiple Meshes

You can employ several workflows to export multiple Meshes. Each has drawbacks and advantages.

Single FBX File

You can include multiple Meshes in a single FBX file. When you import into UE4, you are offered an option to combine those Meshes into a single Mesh or to import those Meshes as individual Meshes.

I'm not a huge fan of this method. Several issues can make this workflow clunky and sometimes unstable.

A common issue is that you need to export the exact same set of Meshes each time you update any single one. This task is very hard to maintain, and failing to so can cause crashes and other issues.

Scene Import

Later versions of UE4 have additional workflows to help alleviate the aforementioned issue. **Scene Import** takes a single FBX file, imports all the Meshes, and places them into a Level. This promising feature can also import cameras, lights, and animation; however, it needs to mature some to become a solid workflow.

Keep an eye on this feature as the engine improves over time. Try to apply it to your data. It could make exchanging data between your 3D application and UE4 much easier.

Multiple FBX Files

Exporting multiple FBX files is my favorite option. Although most 3D applications don't natively support exporting in this manner, several scripts and tools are available that enable you to batch the export process. You can find a selection of these scripts at www.TomShannon3D.com/UnrealForViz.

UE4 can quickly import entire folder structures of FBX files. With this workflow, if you need to update a single asset or a group of assets, you can easily and reliably replace their FBX files and reimport into UE4. This fine-grained approach gives you a great deal of control, and it is the least risky and least technically complicated of the options.

Reimporting

An easy iterative workflow is to simply overwrite your existing, exported FBX with the updated geometry. This allows you to select the file in the Content Browser and reimport it, updating the asset in UE4.

Auto Reimport

I frequently use the auto reimport feature in UE4. It enables you to define a directory and, any time you update or create a new, importable file, the Editor detects the change and automatically updates existing assets or imports and creates new ones.

To enable this feature, open Editor Preferences, and define a folder to watch and a corresponding folder in your Content folder (see Figure 3.6).

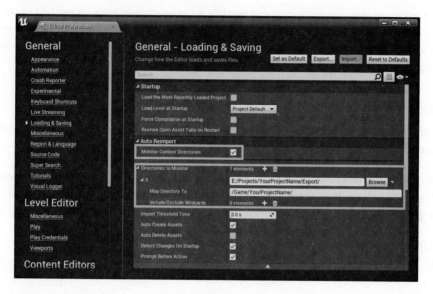

Figure 3.6 Setting up Auto Import in the Editor Preferences

note

By default, the Auto Import feature is enabled for the Content folder. Although this is easy to understand and use, I don't recommend putting your source files here. Never modify the Content folder outside the Editor—UE4 does not like this and it can cause project corruption.

Where to Put Your FBX Files

Typically, you do not need to maintain your exported FBX files, and can be considered temporary. You can save them wherever is most convenient for you. Being consistent is important so you can use reimporting features.

Texture and Material Workflow

Just like any time you move from one rendering software to another, you must face the requirement to re-author your materials to take advantage of the new renderer's features, and UE4 is no different.

UE4 allows you to import materials with your Meshes, but the options for import are limited and require your source Materials to be authored in a very specific manner.

This is not to say that importing materials into UE4 is not worth your time—it can be a huge time saver for prototyping and assigning well-authored UE4 Materials. Don't spend too much time working on your materials in your 3D application, however. A simple diffuse map or color will suffice (and is about all that will come in!).

Textures

UE4 imposes some strict rules and limits on textures. Some rules are strictly enforced and cause textures to fail to import; others might simply degrade quality or performance in your project.

Most of the rules are technical limitations imposed upon Unreal Engine 4 by the hardware and software UE4 runs on. The Graphical Processing Units (GPU) on graphics cards are specific about how textures are stored, accessed, and rendered, and UE4 is beholden to these limitations.

Supported Formats

UE4 supports a range of image formats:

- **.bmp**
- **.float**
- **.pcx**
- **.png**
- **.psd**
- **.tga**
- **.jpg**
- **.exr**
- **.dds**
- **.hdr**

The most commonly used are BMP, TGA, and PNG.

TGA files are the game-industry standard for 8-bit images. This is due to the explicit control artists have over the content of the image on a per-channel basis. UE4 accepts 24-bit (RGB) and 32-bit (RGBA) TGA files.[2]

PNG files are most widely used for UI elements because they use a pre-multiplied alpha that lets them blend properly. This alpha, however, isn't typically suitable for other textures.

I recommend using TGA or BMP for all textures being used in materials.

---

2. Image formats can be confusing. A 32-bit TGA file consists of four 8-bit channels (RGBA), rather than a 32-bit image format like HDR or EXR that represents 32 bits per channel.

Mip-Maps

Mip-Maps are reduced resolution versions of textures that are pre-calculated and stored as part of the texture. These allow the GPU to use the smaller texture sizes as objects get farther away from the camera. This avoids aliasing and can help performance.

Resolution

All textures should be scaled to a power-of-two resolution, such as 64, 128, 256, 512, 1024, and so on. With a maximum dimension of 8192 x 8192, higher resolution textures require source code modification and might not be supported on all video cards.

Textures can be non-square, but should still be a power of two on each dimension; for example, 128 x 1024 is fine.

You can import textures that are non-power of two, but they will not produce Mip-Maps, which introduces various visual artifacts in the project. You should almost always take the time to scale your textures to an appropriate size before importing.

Alpha Channels

You can include alpha channels in many of the formats; however, be aware that alpha channels double the memory footprint of your texture, so include them only if they are being used.

Another option is to include an alpha channel as a separate texture. This can help when you need to share alpha info between different textures or want to have a lower resolution alpha map than the other channels.

Compression

UE4 uses hardware-level texture compression. In most cases, this is a DDS format with some significant block compression artifacts, so having quality source images is very important (that is, avoid using compressed source images).

You can override compression on a per-texture basis, but you should only do this as required. Uncompressed textures can be up to eight times the size in memory.

Multiple Materials

UE4 fully supports multiple materials on a single Mesh. In your 3D application simply assign materials to your individual faces and use the usual FBX workflow. The only caveat is that each material increases the rendering overhead for that Actor. For actors that are used infrequently, such as architecture or buildings, this is fine. Author assets that get used liberally in scenes (vehicles, vegetation, props, and so on) to have as few materials as possible because not doing so will quickly present a performance issue in your project.

Importing to the Content Library

Importing content is a much less technical and involved process than preparing and exporting your assets. A few options are of particular interest if you're working with visualization data.

Initiating Imports

You have a few simple ways to initiate an import:

- Drag-and-drop assets from your file browser into the Content Browser. You can drag multiple files, even entire directories into the Content Browser to import.
- Right-click in the Content Browser and select Import.
- Use the prominent **Import** button in the Content Browser.
- Auto import assets by defining a folder to watch and a destination directory in your project.

Depending on what type of file you are importing, UE4 presents you with a different set of import options.

Mesh Import Options

The options you choose will vary slightly depending on your specific needs, but the following will serve you well most of the time (see Figure 3.7).

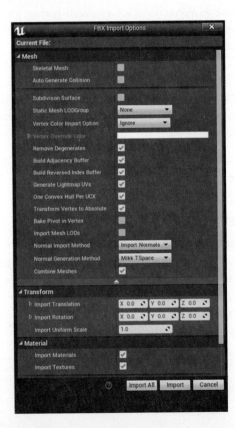

Figure 3.7 Suggested FBX import settings for Static Meshes

Auto Generate Collision

I do not recommend using the **Auto Generate Collision** option for most Meshes. This is a legacy system and produces bad results for content that isn't specifically authored for it.

You should make your own collision (either in your 3D application or in the Editor by placing Primitives), rely on per-polygon collision (slow on high-poly Meshes), or use the Convex Decomposition Collision generation in the Editor.

Generate Lightmap UVs

I recommend using the **Generate Lightmap UVs** option and forgoing creating your own Lightmap channel. Rather, you should focus on making your base UV channel clean and allowing the Editor to work its magic on your content.

Import Materials and Textures

Usually, I leave **Import Materials and Textures** on because having a head start on creating and assigning materials and getting the various textures that have been applied to be imported is very convenient and offers a good starting point for building and assigning materials later.

If you're not careful, however, this option can cause a huge mess. To avoid this, you should ensure your materials are well-assigned in your 3D application before exporting. You can also use the Material Instance assignment system to create Material Instances rather than Materials. This is fantastic for those with established UE4 workflows and Material systems, but can be too complex for beginners.

Transform Vertex to Absolute

When the **Transform Vertex to Absolute** option is *true*, UE4 will replace the authored pivot point with one at the scene's 0,0,0. If *false*, the Mesh will use the authored pivot point. As mentioned in the earlier section "Preparing Geometry for UE4," this setting can be a huge time saver for placing and maintaining your Architecture Meshes.

Texture Options

When you import textures, you aren't presented with import options; however, you should ensure that your textures have the proper flags set. This can have a dramatic effect on the performance and visual fidelity of your projects.

After importing, open the Texture Editor by double-clicking a Texture asset in the Content Browser. The following settings are of the most importance:

- **Texture Group:** Most of your textures can simply be left in the World Group. Normal Maps, HDR Images, UI Images, and other specialty textures like LUTs and vector maps should be set to their appropriate groups. This sets many internal flags to ensure these textures are read and display correctly.

- **Compression Settings:** Setting the Texture Group will often correctly set the Compression Settings; often it won't. Most textures use the Default setting. Normal maps should always use the normal map setting. UI textures should be set to the User Interface setting to allow proper alpha blending and scaling.

- **sRGB:** The sRGB flag should be true for almost all textures that contain color information. This tells the rendering engine to gamma adjust this texture to display accurately in the scene (UE4 uses a linear rendering pipeline and requires textures to be gamma corrected to match the linear colorspace). Textures used as masks or other "data" maps like normal maps and vector maps should be set to false to ensure the data is read accurately without having a gamma curve applied to it.

Camera Workflow

You are an expert at creating amazing visualization animations with sweeping, smooth camera animations highlighting each aspect of the project. You have spent years honing your craft and have developed tools and techniques that set you apart from the competition.

UE4 offers an amazing cinematics and animation system with Sequencer, but learning an entirely new system can be daunting and unnecessary. UE4 offers a robust suite of tools to import and export cameras to and from your application and the Editor, allowing you to iterate easily using familiar tools.

Simply select your Camera object in your 3D application and export it as an FBX. You might need to bake out the animation if your camera is attached to a spline or uses any other non-standard transforms (being attached to other objects, using Look-at controllers or modifiers, or being part of a rig, for example).

In UE4, create a new Level sequence by clicking the Cinematic button of the Editor toolbar and selecting Add Level Sequence and select a location to save the Sequence asset (see Figure 3.8).

Figure 3.8 Adding a new Level sequence

After the new sequence opens in Sequencer, right-click the dynamically spawned Camera Actor in the Sequencer window and select Import.

Your animation is brought in and applied to the camera. I have experienced some inconsistencies with camera types other than the application defaults such as rotated pivot points or incorrect positioning. You might have to rework your cameras or convert them to standard types to fully utilize this feature.

You can also export the camera's animation from Sequencer back to an FBX file and import into your 3D application or even a post-editing suite like Nuke to complete a shot rendered in UE4.

Summary

Preparing your content for exporting and importing into UE4 is the largest hurdle many will face. However, spending the time to prepare your content for UE4 will pay big dividends as you reconstruct your data in the UE4 Editor. Even massive datasets can be smoothly brought into UE4 and into your scenes when you set yourself up for success.

CHAPTER 4

LIGHTING AND RENDERING

One of the most compelling features of UE4 is the amazing visual quality it can achieve. By leveraging physically based rendering (PBR), UE4 achieves staggering realism. Surfaces react to light and shadow in amazingly realistic ways. The Material Editor uses a visual graphing system that empowers you to bring complex, dynamic, physically based Materials to life while Material Instances and Functions let you reuse your Materials and modify them in real time. You might never want to go back to your old renderer again.

Understanding Unreal Engine's Physically Based Rendering (PBR)

In the last decade, computer graphics have seen a renaissance of quality and fidelity. This is in large part due to the development of physically based rendering (PBR). PBR replaces traditional Phong/Blinn specular shading with a more accurate representation of how actual surfaces react to light based on surface parameters such as roughness (see Figure 4.1).

Figure 4.1 The same materials in four different lighting environments

Unreal Engine 4's renderer takes the PBR technology created for Hollywood blockbusters and presents a powerful, artist-friendly, easy-to-learn material and lighting system, combining physically based materials, lights, and reflections as a unified system to create nearly ray-traced quality images in real time.

Those who have been using physically based renderers such as Maxwell should be able to grasp the concepts in UE4s renderer very quickly. To others, this change is a bit confusing at first, but after you see how good the materials and lighting look, how straightforward they are to set up, and how remarkably well they hold up in almost all lighting conditions, you'll have a hard time going back to your old, specular-based materials.

Base Color

The **Base Color** simply defines the color of the material with all the shadows and highlights taken out (UE4 assumes it will fill in that lighting information).

These values are almost never fully black or fully white. Charcoal and Fresh Asphalt are around .02 (on a scale of intensity from 0 to 1), whereas Fresh Snow should be around .81, with Fresh Concrete and Sand somewhere in the middle at .51 and .36, respectively.

Roughness

UE4 almost completely abandons the Specular channel. Although you can still access the specular value, its use is only for special cases where the PBR system doesn't quite hold up.

Instead, you use a single, grayscale or float value to determine both the brightness and tightness of the specular reflections: **Roughness** (see Figure 4.2). You can drive the Roughness either through a single value or by using a texture. In Figure 4.2, note that only the Roughness values have been modified. Notice how the specular highlights and reflections are both blurred as roughness increases.

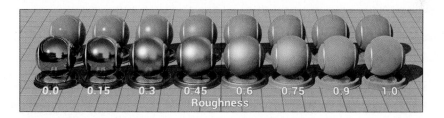

Figure 4.2 Roughness as it appears on Nonmetal (top row) and Metal (bottom row) Materials

In the real world, the rougher a surface is, the more diffuse or blurred the reflected light is. This is because of microscopic imperfections on the surface. These imperfections scatter the light that hits them whereas smooth surfaces without these imperfections don't scatter the reflections, resulting in a sharp, mirror-like reflection.

> **note**
> You might be tempted to reduce a material's specular value to remove highlights, but don't! Make your material rougher instead.

Metallic

The **Metallic** input sets how much like metal your material is (see Figure 4.3). This is a grayscale or **scalar**[1] input (0.0–1.0); however, almost all surfaces will either be at or near 0 or at or near 1. Only a few cases ever have a Metallic value that's between 0 and 1; for example, cases such as lightly dirtied metal, fancy pottery glazes, and so on, or when you are using a mask to define areas that are metallic or not.

Figure 4.3 Metallic variation. Reflection color is controlled by the Material's Base Color

Getting the Most from PBR

PBR requires good input data. Tons of resources are now available for downloading very good-quality PBR textures complete with Roughness, Normal, and other PBR maps.

Tools such as Substance Bitmap 2 Material (B2M) can help you prepare your existing Diffuse textures for PBR rendering.

You can also generate these maps manually in Photoshop or other image-editing software, but tools such as Substance, Quixel Suite, or Substance B2M can generate far better-looking map sets much faster.

These tools use image processing techniques to generate Normal, Roughness, and Base Color maps by analyzing the shapes and lighting in the source images.

Put Detail into Roughness

A Roughness Texture map is your key to the best PBR materials possible. Look around. The variations in roughness tell you everything you need to know about a surface and everything has some variation. This is where the scratches and dirt and blemishes of your materials should live.

---

1. Scalar values are just material shader language for floating point numbers.

Keep Base Color Maps Simple

Keep your Base Color map simple. It should contain no lighting or shadow information, only the color information. Let the renderer fill in the shading and lighting.

Lights in UE4

Lighting in Unreal Engine 4 is a lot like lighting in any other 3D package. You place spot, directional, sky, and point lights, and control brightness, falloff, and color. How they differ is in the strict limitations placed on you by UE4 to balance quality and features with performance.

> ### note
>
> UE4 does not have a built-in dynamic GI lighting solution. The ONLY production-ready global illumination system in UE4 is Lightmass, which relies on pre-calculated light and shadow maps and is calculated offline in the Editor.
>
> **Light Propagation Volumes**
>
> UE4 does offer limited real-time GI in the form of Light Propagation Volumes, an experimental feature that you can enable through the project's settings. As it's experimental, it's not exactly production ready and lacks support, but many have used it to stunning effect.
>
> **NVIDIA VXGI**
>
> NVIDIA also offers a GI solution for UE4 called VXGI. This requires you to download and build a custom build of the engine as modified by NVIDIA, which is outside the scope of this book. This solution can provide very high-quality results, but is not directly supported by Epic Games.

Lighting in a ray-tracing engine is slow, but typically very dynamic. You can easily move sunlight around, modulating the color to simulate a sun setting. Flawless GI fills each nook, corner, and crevice with rich light and shadow. The price you pay is time. Even a simple scene with a few basic primitives takes several seconds to render. Most real-world scenes take minutes to hours. To achieve real-time frame rates, we only have a fraction of a second to render the frame.

By restricting what lights can and can't do, massive performance benefits have been realized. These restrictions can be difficult to cope with at first, but by knowing what to expect and what you can and can't do, you can avoid some costly blunders.

Understanding Light Mobility

Each Light and Mesh Actor you place into your Level has a **Mobility** parameter. The three mobility modes of lights in UE4 are Moveable, Stationary, and Static. Each state has specific capabilities and limitations that you must carefully consider when lighting your scenes.

Moveable Lights

As its name implies, if you want a Light or Mesh you can move, you'll want a **moveable** one. Use Moveable Lights cautiously. Although UE4 can render hundreds of unshadowed, Moveable Lights at a time, they are one of the most performance-intensive effects to render in UE4, especially if they *are* casting shadows.

Shadows

Moveable Lights can directly light and cast shadows onto and from Moveable and Static Meshes. This is hugely important. If your scene geometry needs to be dynamic—for instance, with lots of moving people or cars or moving or changing scene geometry—you will need to rely on Moveable Lights.

Shadowing is expensive[2] for Dynamic Lights, so use it sparingly. The larger a light's radius, the more expensive it is to render and the more Actors it will need to generate shadows for.

Dynamic shadows are low resolution and are generally very crisp edged. You cannot easily get soft attenuated shadow edges as you would with pre-calculated static shadows (see Figure 4.4).

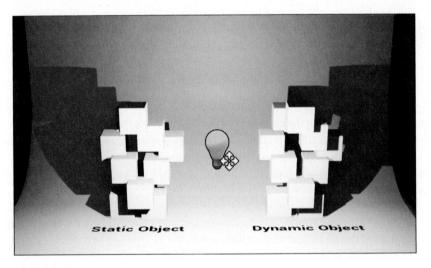

Static Object   *Dynamic Object*

Figure 4.4 Moveable Light Shadows on both Moveable and Static Objects with a dynamic shadow (also with no GI contribution)

---

2. The term "expensive" is often used to describe the performance penalty of an effect. Each frame is often thought of as having a specific "budget" and each light, polygon, and shadow has a cost against that budget.

Global Illumination

Lights that move do not contribute to global illumination (GI). Some third-party plugins and integrations can achieve this, but the use and integration of those is beyond the scope of this book.

Specular Reflections

Moveable Lights contribute direct specular reflections onto surfaces. This gives them a nice-looking highlight on PBR surfaces and can help your materials really pop.

Stationary Lights

The middle child of the UE4 lighting family, Stationary Lights use both the Static and Dynamic lighting paths together to create a light that cannot move, but that *can* cast dynamic shadows and modulate their color and intensity at runtime. They can contribute to GI, but changing the intensity of the light only affects the direct lighting term, not the static GI lighting stored in Lightmaps.

Stationary Lights are useful for statically lit scenes because they can add detail and allow dynamic Actors to cast dynamic shadows; however, you must use them carefully to avoid causing some severe performance penalties.

Shadows

Shadows from and on Static Meshes are baked into Shadow maps by Lightmass, but the direct lighting and shadows from and on Moveable objects is calculated dynamically (see Figure 4.5).

Figure 4.5 Stationary Light shadowing the Static Mesh on the left with a static Shadow map, and dynamic shadows shadowing the Dynamic Mesh on the right

Although Stationary Lights can provide the best of both worlds, there is a serious limitation to this magic. Each statically lit Mesh can only be influenced by *four* Stationary Lights at a time.

If more than four Stationary Lights affect a single Mesh, additional Stationary Lights will revert to Moveable Lights with dynamic shadows and have an extreme performance penalty.

To help avoid this situation, UE4 alerts you with both descriptive icons in the Editor Viewport and warnings when you build your lighting.

You can preview stationary Lightmap Overlaps by choosing the appropriate view mode in the Editor. In Figure 4.6, the four Spot Light Actors are all set to Stationary as is the Directional Light sunlight coming in from the window. The additional Spot Light cannot be rendered as a Stationary Light and will instead be rendered as more expensive Moveable Light.

Figure 4.6 Stationary Light Overlap view mode on the left

Global Illumination

Stationary Lights can contribute to GI, but if you change the color or intensity of the Light, the GI will not change with it. You can control the amount of GI using the **GI Contribution** value in the Light Actor's properties.

Specular and Reflections

Because the Stationary Lights direct lighting component is rendered dynamically, it can contribute a specular highlight to surfaces like a Moveable Light does.

tip

Stationary Lights make the perfect sunlight in your statically lit visualizations.

Static Lights

Static Lights, as the name suggests, are completely static. They cannot move or change in real time at all. All of their lighting and shadow information is baked into textures. Static Lights are used exclusively by the Lightmass GI system.

> note
>
> Static Lights are used extensively in architectural visualization, where lighting quality is more important than flexibility. You can have a basically unlimited number of Static Lights in your scenes because the static lighting path has a fixed rendering cost after Lightmass has baked the lighting information into Lightmaps.

Shadows

Static Lights use Lightmass to render **Lightmaps**, textures that contain lighting and shadowing information. Because of this, Static Lights cannot directly light or shadow dynamic objects (see Figure 4.7).

You can adjust the softness of Static shadows by changing the Light Source Radius property of the Light Actor. You won't see the effect until you render the lighting in Lightmass.

Figure 4.7 Static Light Shadowing a Static Mesh with a baked Lightmap (left); no shadow on the Dynamic Mesh on the right

Global Illumination

You also won't see any GI effects until you build your lighting with Lightmass. Static Lights also store their direct illumination and their GI information in Lightmaps.

Specular and Reflections

Static Lights do not cast specular highlights. They are, however, very well-supported by the Reflection Capture system that uses pre-captured HDR cube maps to apply specular reflections to the PBR materials.

Real-Time Reflections

Reflections have long been one of the most sought after and difficult to achieve visual effects for real-time graphics. Hundreds of techniques and tricks have been used to try to mimic the look and quality of ray-traced reflections.

Reflections are essential for a PBR system to function. Without scene reflections, materials lose depth and are forced to rely on direct specular highlights to show surface information. This leads to the plastic, shiny look we've all come to associate with computer graphics.

Reflections are something that ray-tracing is great at, but incredibly slow at, especially when you start blurring those reflections. How does UE4 manage it? Mostly by faking it.

The two main reflections in a UE4 scene are static cube maps generated by Reflection Capture Actors and a screen-space reflection Post Process Effect. Both are automatically applied to materials and modulated appropriately. This helps with authoring materials *and* lighting scenes because you won't have to customize materials specifically for scenes as you might have had to do with previous game engines or other renderers.

Reflection Probes

UE4 uses **reflection probes**, called Reflection Capture Actors, manually placed around the scene to create most surface reflections. These probes take a high dynamic range (HDR) cube map of their surroundings and apply it to any material that enters their radius.

They also contribute to ambient lighting on both Dynamic and Static Meshes, making them essential for high-quality lighting.

Reflection Capture Actors cannot be updated in any way at runtime.

Post Process Reflections

Screen Space Reflection (SSR) is an amazing post-process technique that uses the G-Buffer information to reconstruct reflections from the already rendered, 2D scene. This has some serious limitations such as causing dithering noise and the inability to display information that is off-screen, but it does provide sharp, dynamic reflections that look fantastic most of the time and have a relatively low rendering cost. However, at higher resolutions such as in 4K displays and VR, SSR can become a performance issue. If you are having performance issues, this is a good option to try turning off first.

Post-Processing

Unreal Engine 4 relies heavily on post processing for everything from anti-aliasing to reflections to ambient occlusion to motion blur.

With traditionally rendered visualizations, you typically apply these effects to your rendered frames in a video editing or effects package such as After Effects or Nuke.

In UE4, you apply Post Process Effects in real time by defining them either in a scene Actor called a **Post Process Volume** or with the Post Process settings in a Camera Actor. These settings can have a dramatic effect on the scene's look and quality and are essential for making your visualizations look as good as possible (see Figures 4.8 and 4.9).

These settings can inherit from and override each other using a priority system and can blend seamlessly from one to another.

Post Process Effects in UE4 are screen-space, meaning they only exist in the pixels being rendered onscreen. They cannot produce effects or react to anything that isn't being directly rendered.

Figure 4.8 UE4 scene with no post processing applied (other than the tone mapper)

Figure 4.9 UE4 scene with heavy post processing (bloom, ambient occlusion, screen-space reflections, and anti-aliasing)

Anti-Aliasing

Anti-aliasing is one of the slowest rendering operations. Most renderers use a form of super or multi-sampling (rendering a single pixel at a higher resolution to resolve the average color more accurately, smoothing out edge aliasing). This method is simply too slow for real time because each pixel rendered decreases the frame rate.

Unreal Engine 4 uses a custom-built temporal anti-aliasing (TAA) system that produces almost perfectly anti-aliased images at the cost of some image sharpness and some possible ghosting artifacts in motion[3]. TAA samples multiple rendered frames in succession and compares them to create an average.

A less effective FXAA screen-space anti-aliasing effect is also available that while better than no anti-aliasing is usually too rough to be used in visualization.

The softness of TAA, when used in conjunction with other Post Process Effects can help give your image a filmic, realistic look and gives the highest overall quality (see Figure 4.10).

---

3. Ghosting most often happens with high-frequency or noisy areas that change from frame to frame. Avoiding noise in your scenes helps hide this artifact.

Figure 4.10 Anti-aliasing methods comparison showing the change in quality of the edges

Bloom, Glare, and Lens Flares

Because most displays can't display luminance over 1, **Bloom** was developed to allow over-bright pixels to be bloom or **glare** to help increase the apparent dynamic range of the image. Bloom is effective because it simulates the effect camera lenses and our eyes exhibit when exposed to very bright light.

Lens flares simulate the interlens reflections that are captured when cameras are exposed to high-contrast lighting conditions.

UE4 renders the scene using a linear workflow and uses that information to determine luminance to create high-quality specular blooms and lens flares. These effects if used sparingly can help accentuate the HDR lighting in your scene and elevate the quality of your visualizations.

Eye Adaptation (Auto Exposure)

A common effect used in film and games is to adjust exposure as cameras enter and leave dim and brightly lit areas. This creates a dramatic bloom of light and is typically tricky to pull off in a traditionally rendered visualization (see Figure 4.11).

Figure 4.11 Creating dramatic effects by allowing the camera to overexpose as lighting intensity changes

UE4 features high-dynamic range rendering, allowing both dark and very bright areas to exist within a single scene. As the player moves from indoors to outdoors, his view will adjust brightness smoothly, simulating the human eye and/or cameras using auto exposure.

Depth of Field

DOF (depth of field) is another effect that's extremely time consuming to render with most ray-tracing renderers, but can be achieved in real-time with UE4 (see Figure 4.12).

Figure 4.12 Physically correct depth of field with circle DOF

A few different types of DOF exist in UE4: Gaussian, Bokeh, and Circle.

Gaussian

Gaussian DOF is fast, but has a lot of artifacts. It is blurry, unrealistic, and not physically accurate.

Bokeh

Bokeh is also blurry and inaccurate, but looks better thanks to the inclusion of a Bokeh (aperture mask) shape for high-contrast pixels. Each Bokeh shape is a particle being rendered for each pixel that's brighter than the threshold; as such, this effect can get *very* expensive to render.

Circle

Circle DOF is a relatively new feature and that Sequencer and cinematic cameras leverage heavily to achieve physically accurate depth of field based on camera aperture and field of view.

This effect is fast and gives your images a realistic, filmic look. You can use it in almost all of your visualizations with a minimal rendering cost.

Film Effects

Film and video both have a lot of interpixel noise and other lens effects such as vignette and chromatic aberration. UE4 offers a wide range of filmic post-process adjustments and effects to help you achieve a photorealistic or stylized look with almost no performance hit.

Motion Blur

Motion Blur is another effect that is traditionally very expensive in ray-tracing. Interpolating an object across time and space is inherently slow. Once again post processing comes into play. UE4 renders a velocity G-Buffer that allows it to apply a very high-quality but very fast motion blur to the entire scene as well as moving objects (see Figure 4.13).

Figure 4.13 High-quality motion blur

Screen Space Ambient Occlusion (SSAO)

Screen space ambient occlusion is one of the most important graphical techniques available for video game engines and one that almost all 3D game engines use. SSAO is created using the depth and world normal G-Buffers to determine where edges and objects are close, rendering an AO map and compositing it in real-time each frame.

In scenes with dynamic lighting, SSAO provides an enormous visual boost. Objects gain contact shadows helping them read as connected to the surfaces they sit on and it increases the depth of shadowed areas immensely. Although SSAO is no substitute for ray-traced or pre-calculated AO, it's a huge improvement.

Screen Space Reflections

By transforming and distorting the rendered image based on G-Buffer information such as World Normal and Depth, UE4 can produce a fake, but good looking and fast-to-render reflection.

Screen-space reflections help complement the Reflection Capture Actors by providing dynamic, high-detail reflections (see Figure 4.14). This helps to ground objects and provide the most accurate looking and dynamic reflections possible.

Like all other screen-space effects, these reflections cannot render anything off-screen. This can create some transition artifacts and other strange effects as you move through a scene. Whether to use them is an artistic choice.

Figure 4.14 Sharp screen-space reflections work in harmony with captured cube map reflections from Reflection Capture Actors

Screen Percentage

Although UE4 doesn't offer multi- or super-sampling anti-aliasing[4], it does, kind of. UE4 has a very high-quality image scaler and the capability to render at any resolution, independent of the screen.

Screen Percentage controls how many pixels are being rendered for each pixel onscreen. For example, 100% is a 1:1 ratio; 80% indicates an 80% reduction in rendered pixels; and 140% is a 40% increase. You can use this setting in two ways: To reduce the resolution of the image to allow more graphically intense scenes to run on slower machines *or* to increase the resolution past the screen resolution, allowing the scaler to return a very crisp image. By combining Screen Percentage with TAA you can get amazingly clear image quality, approaching ray-traced quality.

---

4. UE4 offers a Forward Rendering pipeline that allows the use of MSAA while trading many of the benefits of a deferred rendering pipeline like Dynamic Lighting.

As you increase the project's resolution, Screen-space effects become increasingly slow to use. Users on high-resolution monitors will be more acutely impacted by this setting.

Post Process Materials

UE4 exposes the G-Buffers it uses to render and composite its final image to the Material Editor. UE4 allows you to create custom Post Process Effects that extend the rendering capabilities of UE4 using the same Material Editor and Material Instancing system used in the rest of the Engine.

These can range from the simple, such as creating your own vignette system, to the complex, such as writing your own cell-shading and outlining effects (see Figure 4.15). The sky is your limit thanks to the flexibility of the Material Editor.

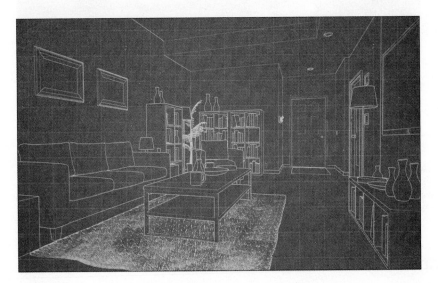

Figure 4.15 Example of using Post Process Materials to completely change how UE4 renders scenes

Although they are called Post Process Effects, they actually happen while you're running the project, not after. They are rendered at the end of each frame, while the next frame is beginning to render. They run in real time, reacting to a dynamically changing scene and point of view.

Post Process Effects can make your scene look like an art student's first photo-editing assignment with gaudy blooms, vignette, and lens flares dominating the view. If used wisely, they can also give it the most filmic, realistic look possible.

Summary

UE4 has one of the most robust rendering systems available. The realism and ease of use is simply unmatched and the quality speaks for itself. Most of the systems are based on techniques and systems you've been using for years, making them familiar and easy to understand.

PBR introduces a whole new way of looking at and defining material surfaces that are artist friendly and look great. Combined with an arsenal of lighting tricks and tools, you can achieve near-ray-traced images in real-time.

CHAPTER 5

MATERIALS

Materials in UE4 are like visual programs that run on each pixel (pixel shader) and vertex (vertex shader) in the scene. Using the visual Material Editor, you can create a bewildering array of surfaces using only a few parameters and textures. Even very simple Materials look astounding thanks to PBR. As your skills grow, you can build on those Materials, making them more flexible and dynamic and incorporating interactivity and programmability.

Materials Overview

Materials are one of the most essential elements for creating compelling, interactive content. Materials define how every single pixel in your scene reacts to light, shadow, and reflection.

Creating Materials for real time can be very different than creating Materials in 3D applications and renderers. Like most of the UE4 workflow, the Material workflow centers around interactivity and performance.

UE4 features WYSIWYG, real-time Material previews and—by way of the visual Material Editor—the ability to program, literally on a per-pixel and per-vertex basis, how your Materials behave. Thanks to the interactive nature of UE4, you also get instant, in-scene feedback on how your Materials look (see Figure 5.1).

Figure 5.1 Materials being previewed in UE4

Creating Materials

Materials in UE4 are assets, like Meshes and Textures, stored in the Content folder. They are created exclusively in the Editor and cannot be edited outside the Material Editor. The Material Editor is a visual, node-based scripting editor that lets you make extremely performant High-Level Shading Language (HLSL) shaders using a simple, artist-friendly interface.

To create a new Material asset, right-click in the Content Browser and select Create Material or click the **Add New** button in the Content Browser and select Material from the menu that appears.

Applying Materials

You can apply materials to Meshes in various ways: Dragging and dropping from the Content Browser onto Meshes in your scene, through the Static and Skeletal Mesh Editors, or through Object Property dialogs.

You can choose the method that works best for you, but I highly recommend applying Materials directly to your assets (rather than their scene references) using the Static and Skeletal Mesh Editors. This ensures that each time you place your Mesh into a Level, the proper Meshes will be applied.

Modifying Materials

Changing Materials at runtime is an essential tool in the UE4 visualization artist's tool belt. The flexibility of the Material Editor is unmatched and enables you to create a near-endless array of visual effects that can bring life, interactivity, and realism to your scenes.

Blueprints take that flexibility even further by giving you the ability to add logic and interactivity to Materials by setting Material Parameters dynamically at runtime.

UE4 Material Editor

The Unreal Engine Material Editor is a bit of engineering magic and user interface brilliance rolled together to create an artist-friendly way of authoring complex pixel and vertex HLSL shaders without your having to write a single line of code.

Using a visual scripting–style visual editor, you construct Materials via a network of Material Expression nodes. Each node represents a snippet of HLSL code and as you connect them, the Engine writes the HLSL code in the background. You can preview this code in the Material Editor to see in real time what the code being written looks like.

The visual nature of the Editor makes it approachable and easy to use, and PBR rendering makes creating compelling Materials very straightforward. You can also author complex, dynamic interactive Materials that incorporate advanced techniques like tessellation, parallax occlusion mapping, and vertex deformation and animation.

Opening the Material Editor

You can only access the Material Editor by double-clicking on a Material Asset in the Content Browser. If you don't have a Material in your project, you will need to create one as described earlier in the "Creating Materials" section.

Editor UI

The Material Editor consists of the usual menu bar and toolbar that are common to most UE4 Editors (see Figure 5.2). You can also see a real-time preview of the Material in a Viewport, a dynamic Details Panel that presents available Parameters and options for selected Expression nodes. A Palette pane shows a list of available Expressions.

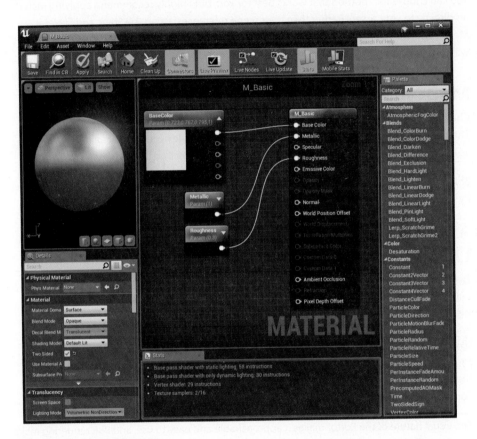

Figure 5.2 The Material Editor UI

In the center is the **Graph Editor**. This is where the magic happens. In each Material is a Base Material node. This node has inputs for each aspect of the Material that you can modify by connecting other nodes to them.

Placing Nodes

There are a few ways to place nodes into the Graph View. The most obvious is the **Palette**. From there you can simply drag and drop Expression nodes into the Graph Editor.

You can also right-click in empty space in the Graph Editor to open a contextual palette, giving you access to the available Expressions.

A lot of Expressions are available for you to create your Materials with. In both palettes, you can you can easily filter the nodes by name by using the Search field to rapidly narrow down your search.

Using the Preview Viewport

The preview is one of the Material Editor's best features. You get immediate feedback on almost every modification to your Material and real-time playback of time-based effects such as panning textures and rippling waves.

The Preview Viewport is a live game Viewport with all the same post processing and rendering features. This means you get a 1:1 representation of what your Material will look like in your project.

The Preview Viewport also allows you to choose standard primitives like cubes and spheres to preview your Material. You can also load your own custom Mesh by first selecting your desired Mesh from the Content Browser, and then clicking the teapot icon in the Material Editor's Preview Viewport.

The default preview Meshes are 500 cm tall, so Meshes much bigger or larger might be hard to see at first. If you're having trouble seeing your Mesh, you can press F while the Viewport is active to center the view on the Mesh and zoom to its bounds.

Notice that the Material uses an orbiting camera that behaves a little differently than the typical Viewport camera. Simply click and drag to rotate around your object, and use the mouse wheel to zoom in and out. If you need to change the light angle, hold down the L key while left-dragging with your mouse.

Although the Viewport provides an excellent preview of your Material, you should always test it in your scenes because variations in lighting, post processing, and more can affect how your Materials look.

Compiling Shaders

As you place and connect nodes in the Editor, you will see the Preview Viewport update in real time. This preview recompiles relatively quickly as you make changes. You will notice that changes do not happen on your scene Meshes that might have the Material applied until you click the Apply button in the toolbar to compile your Material. You can also use the Save button to save your Material, which forces a compile if it's necessary.

Compiling creates the HLSL code and caches the platform-specific hardware shaders that are used to display the Material on Meshes in your scene. This step is required because some Materials can take more than a minute to compile based on how they are used and how many Material Parameters they contain.

As you apply Materials to different kinds of Meshes (Static, Skeletal, Particle, Foliage, Terrain, Instanced, and so on) you will increase the number of shader permutations of your Material that are required, increasing the compiling time.

While your Material is compiling or if there are errors, the Material applied to in-scene Meshes will display as a default gray Material. Be sure to keep an eye on the Material Editor after compiling to make sure there are no errors. If there are, they will appear in the Output window of the Material Editor.

Saving

You're not done yet! Save that Material! Seeing your Materials applied to your scene can give you the false sense that they have been saved. Compiling does not save your Materials; you must manually save your Materials (which then compiles the shader before saving).

How Unreal Materials Work

UE4 Materials are an extension of the PBR rendering pipeline and are tightly integrated into the lighting and reflection pipelines. Materials define how every surface in the world reacts to light, reflections, and shadow.

Pixel and Vertex Shaders

The first thing to understand about how Unreal Materials work is how pixel and vertex shaders are used to render images. It's similar to how most images are rendered, but there is a tighter integration with the rendering hardware (your GPU) and the materials expose this hardware interface more readily.

As each frame is rendered, it first passes through a vertex shader. This shader transforms the vertices of the scene in 3D space, assigns materials, and prepares the scene to be evaluated by the pixel shader. This is where UV coordinates are transformed and rotated, displacement and tessellation are applied, and any other vertex and geometry level calculations are performed before being sent to the pixel shader.

After the vertex pass is finished, the image is then rendered pixel by pixel by the pixel shader. As each pixel is rendered, it is provided information by the vertex shader such as the surface normal direction, the UV coordinates, and material and texture data required to render the pixel.

The pixel shader uses this information to sample Textures, perform math operations, and return a single, linear HDR pixel value. After all the pixels for a single frame are rendered, the image is passed to the post-processing chain to be tone-mapped and have other effects applied to it. This image is then presented onscreen as the final image.

Materials Are Math

You will quickly notice that most of the Material Expression nodes available in the Material Editor are math terms. Expressions exist for nearly all common math operations: adding, subtracting, sin, square, power, and so on.

At its core, each Material is a complex math expression. Pixel color values are added, subtracted, and modulated in other ways based on input such as light positions, world position and direction, the UV coordinate of the pixel, the color of the vertexes, and so on.

Colors as Numbers

You're probably not used to thinking about the numbers behind your images in your daily work. For most artists, an RGBA Texture means a color image with opacity. To the UE4 artist, RGBA images often mean four grayscale values that can be accessed and modified.

This concept might seem confusing, but it's how you've been working in Photoshop and other image editing software for years. Layer operations like Add, Multiply, and so on are all pixel math operations that UE4 just exposes more directly.

Linear Color

Materials in UE4 are rendered internally in floating point, so although textures might be limited to 0–255 values for each channel, the Material it's being rendered in can have floating point values from 0 to 1 and higher. If something is possible with numbers, it's possible in the Material Editor.

However, your monitor probably can't display information above or below a luminance of 0 to 1. For example, a color value below 0 would just render black, and a value above 1 might render as white (possibly with some post-process bloom applied).

Normal Maps

Nothing exemplifies "Materials are Math" more than Normal maps (see Figure 5.3). Normal maps are 3D vectors (X,Y,Z direction values) stored in each pixel as Red, Green, and Blue values. XYZ=RGB. The Engine uses this information and modifies each pixel's apparent world-space direction to change how it reacts to the lighting environment around it.

In Figure 5.3, the purple color is a neutral normal that doesn't modify the pixel normal at all at render time; the Red channel modifies the X direction and Green modifies the Y.

> ### note
>
> Did you ever notice that the Transform Gizmo in UE4 and many other 3D applications use Red for X axis, Green for Y Axis, and Blue for Z? RGB = XYZ = UVW
>
> These values are interchangeable and are treated as generic number arrays by materials and can be magmatically evaluated like such.

As each pixel is rendered, the value of the Normal map at that location is literally added (+) to the tangent-space vertex normal of the model's surface as returned by the vertex shader, returning a new normal and therefore a different color after lighting is applied to it.

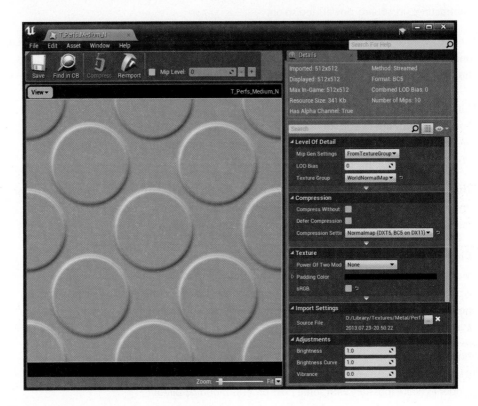

Figure 5.3 Normal maps store direction data

note
> note
>
> Normal maps generated by different software packages produce slightly different results and can require some adjustment. For instance, Maya outputs Normal maps with the Green channel flipped from UE4's standard. You can easily fix this in the Texture Editor dialog by setting the Flip Green Channel option to true.

Like all data-style maps, you should not store Normal maps with an sRGB correction on them.

Packed Mask Textures

Just like you might store your opacity mask in a Texture's Alpha channel, a common technique used in UE4 is to utilize the other three channels (RGB) to store three additional masks instead of color information (see Figure 5.4).

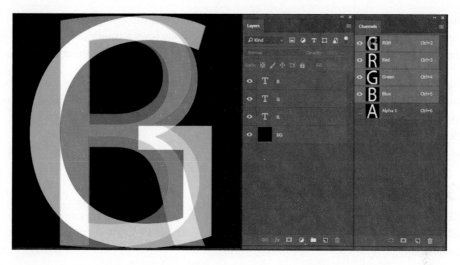

Figure 5.4 An RGB image used to contain four masks, conveniently named RGB and A

In this figure, each Text layer is simply set to Additive. Although the combined image is useless, there are four clear, grayscale images.

Because each mask only needs to be a value between 0 and 1, a popular method for reducing Texture reads and memory is to combine several mask Textures into a single RGBA image. This means you can have four masks in a single Texture. This can be a little tricky to author, but can reduce memory and help performance in complex scenes and Materials.

Modern GPU raw rendering power and the relatively light memory and texture requirements for most visualizations means this technique is mostly unneeded. However, for long-term or very large, organized projects, packing textures can save significant amounts of memory and render times.

> **note**
>
> Data-style textures like masks and Normal maps should not have an sRGB gamma adjustment applied to them. You should ensure this option is set to false in UE4.

Material Functions

You will often want to create functionality in your Materials that you want to reuse in other Materials. Material Functions allow you to collapse Material code networks into assets that can then be added to any Material in your project as an Expression node.

You can add inputs and outputs allowing Material Functions to process data and return transformed data. A common function might be as simple as taking several color inputs and returning their average value or as complicated as applying tessellated waves to an ocean surface.

Functions can even return entire Material definitions, including textures and other parameters and values. By placing two Functions into a Material, you can blend them together with a mask to define where one function or another will render, keeping your Material Graph Editor code clean and readable.

Surface Types

UE4 Materials use several different "Surface Domains" or Types. Each Type is a completely different rendering codebase than the others and often has wildly different capabilities and parameters.

Understanding when and why to use each Type is as important as how and is likely more difficult to understand.

Opaque

Opaque Materials make up the vast majority of the Materials you will use in your projects. Opaque Materials, you guessed it, are opaque! You can never see a pixel that's behind an opaque pixel. It will simply never be rendered.

Opaque Materials are the most efficient, fully lit, most robust Materials available. Use Opaque Materials for most of your Materials.

Masked

Masked Materials are like Opaque Materials, but can have a form of transparency applied to them in the form of a 1-bit opacity mask. That means they can either be fully opaque or fully transparent with a hard edge delineating the two.

Masked Materials look great and are almost as fast to render as Opaque Materials, but can incur heavy overdraw[1] where they are transparent. Masked Materials are most often used for foliage in UE4 allowing very high lighting quality while providing some level of transparency.

---

1. Overdraw is where more than one surface is rendered in a single pixel. When an opaque surface is rendered, the objects behind it will not be evaluated, so only that one pixel is rendered. Transparent surfaces must also render any pixels behind them in addition to their own. This has the result of increasing the complexity of that pixel to render.

Translucent

Translucent Materials render using a completely different rendering path than most of the Materials in UE4 and are composited onto the final image. This presents several challenges for their use in scenes.

Translucent surfaces receive very approximate lighting information and are not physically accurate. They are mostly intended for effects such as smoke and fire and while you can make glass, water, and other translucent surfaces with them, they will never come close to the quality of these Materials in ray-traced renderers.

Opacity

When you set your Material to Translucent, you enable the Opacity input. This input takes a value from 0-1 and simply determines how much the surface will blend with the pixels behind it. Surfaces with an opacity of 1 will look opaque but will still render the pixels behind it, causing overdraw and incurring a performance penalty.

Refraction

Translucent Materials allow the use of **refraction**. This effect is a screen-space effect and is limited in UE4 but, if used sparingly, can add a lot of visual interest to transparent surfaces in your scenes.

Refraction uses the pixel's screen normal and offsets the pixel sample behind it by that normal direction multiplied by the refraction amount. It's a little counterintuitive, but 1.0 is no refraction, .9 distorts the pixels by –10%, and 1.1 is a 10% distortion.

Values between 0.95 and 1.05 are enough for most purposes to get a realistic distortion.

Material Instances

The key to dynamic, manageable Materials is **Material Instances**: lightweight, instanced versions of Materials with inheritance not unlike the child-parent relationship between classes in programming languages (see Figure 5.5).

Material Instances don't require the compiling process that full Materials do when they are modified. By using **Material Parameters** in your materials, you can dynamically update your Materials on the fly both in the Editor and at runtime in your project.

Modifying the properties of Material Instances while editing your scenes provides amazing, real-time feedback on the look of your scenes. While you're perfecting your Materials' settings, you see them update instantly in your scene with final lighting and post-processing effects applied.

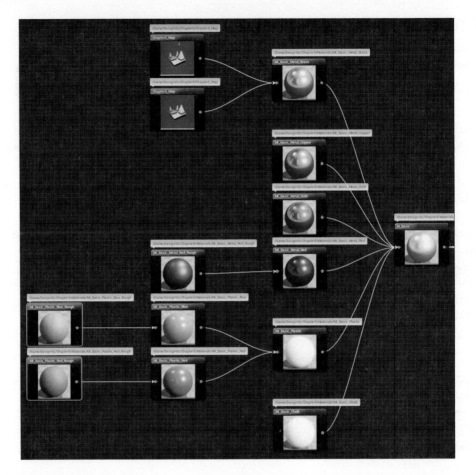

Figure 5.5 Inheritance graph showing how various Material Instances are parented to a single Material (M_Basic on the far right)

Material Parameters

Parameters are special input nodes in Materials that are exposed to Material Instances. These can be colors (vectors), textures, or simple Scalar (float) values. These appear in the Material Instance Editor as individual line items that can be overridden or can inherit the property of its parent. This allows you to author materials that can be reused and modified extensively.

Inheritance

At a high level, Material Instances are lightweight Instances or referenced copies of Materials. They cannot be edited with the Material Editor, rather they are edited using a special Material Instance Editor that opens when you double-click on a Material Instance asset.

Material Instances inherit all the parameter values of their parent material or Material instance.

This means two things: If you modify a property in an Instance, its parent Material is always unaffected and, if you modify a parent Material, all Instances parented to that Material will update.

You can also make Instances of other Material Instances, creating complex Material inheritance chains. This can get overwhelming and messy if you're not sure exactly why you're making Instances of Instances. Be sure to have a good plan before going down that road. Often, simply duplicating an Instance and modifying a single property is often better than creating too many Instances of Instances.

Overriding Parameters

Overriding a Material Parameter in an Instance allows that Instance to have a different value than its parent. You must explicitly define each property you are overriding by clicking the checkbox next to it, thus allowing it to be edited. Any children of that Instance will also update when these values are modified.

Organization

Each Parameter has a Group value that you can set. This is used to organize the Material Instance Editor's Parameter list. Parameters that do not have a group set are put into the Default group.

When you have Materials with a lot of parameters, making a habit of assigning groups to your inputs is important because they can easily get messy and hard to use.

Master Materials

Using Material Instances, creating a single Material that can handle every single surface type in your project is entirely possible. Although this might seem like a good idea at first, several good reasons exist to create multiple Master Materials for a variety of Surface and Actor types.

For instance, you probably don't want to have the same Master Material handle rendering wood floors and rendering smoke drifting from a candle.

Although you theoretically could create a single Material with enough parameters to handle all eventualities, that single Material would become a problem, generating long compile times and huge shader caches as the engine creates too many shader permutations to handle the shader's complexity.

Create Master Materials that are simple but that can create the widest possible number of variations without being overwhelming.

A Simple Material

You can achieve great quality and variety with very simple Materials in UE4. In this section you see how a simple Material is set up with Parameters for Material Instances. We'll then look at building an array of those Instances, demonstrating how even a few parameters can create a wide array of surfaces.

Figure 5.6 shows the most basic Material setup practical in UE4. Only a Vector Parameter (RGBA) called Base Color, a Scalar (float) named Metallic, and another Scalar called Roughness have been placed in the Material graph. They are connected to the inputs of the same name.

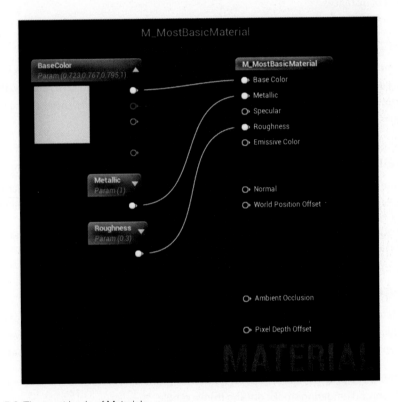

Figure 5.6 The most basic of Materials

Placing Parameter Nodes

You can see all the available Parameter expression nodes available by searching for the word "Parameter" in the node pallets. There are quite a few available, but we'll only need to use the Scalar and Vector types to make this material.

When you create a Parameter, you need to provide it with a Name and a default Value. You can also assign a group to each parameter if you need to organize a lot of parameters.

Then simply drag a wire from the output node on each parameter and connect it to the appropriate input node on another—in this case, the Material attributes inputs of the Material.

As you add more nodes to your material, you'll start to discover that there are times when you want to convert a static value like a Texture Sample or a scalar value to a Parameter. By right-clicking on certain node types, such as Vectors, Textures, and Scalar Material nodes, and selecting **Convert to Parameter**, you can quickly covert to and from static and dynamic parameters.

You can also place many nodes using keystroke shortcuts. You hold down a specific key, such as **T**, and click to create a Texture Parameter node. Hold **S** and click to place a Scalar Parameter, or hold **V** and click to place a Vector.

With these three simple parameters, you can create a huge assortment of Material Instances. Even these simple Materials will look fantastic in UE4, obeying the physical laws of lighting as per the demands of PBR.

Making Material Instances

Making Material Instance can be done a few ways. One way is to create a Material Instance by using the Add New or right-click menu in the Content Browser, and selecting Material Instance from the Materials & Textures group. You then need to open this asset and manually assign the Material you want as the parent.

An easier way is to right-click on the Material you want to create an instance of and select **Create Material Instance** from the menu. This will create a new instance, name it, and assign the parent for you.

After you have a parent material assigned to your Material Instance, you will see the parameters that were defined in your Material listed in the Details panel (see Figure 5.7). Checking the box next to a property declares it overridden, and now the Instance will no longer use the parameter as defined in the parent Material, even if that parameter is changed in the parent Material. You can see in Figure 5.7 that M_Basic is defined as the Parent. The Base color has been overridden as well as the default Roughness, resulting in a very different Material than you started with (Figure 5.8).

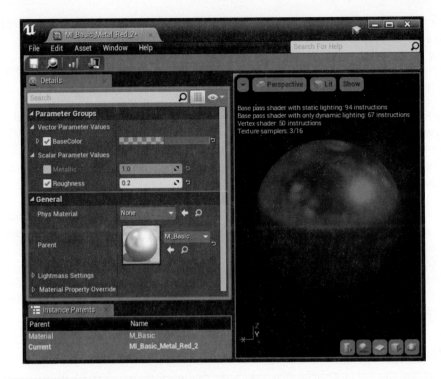

Figure 5.7 Material Instance created from M_Basic

Figure 5.8 Array of Material Instances created from M_Basic showing a lot of variation

Adding a Roughness Map

Simply adding a Roughness map to your Material (see Figure 5.9) adds an enormous amount of depth and detail to the surface, as you can see in Figure 5.10.

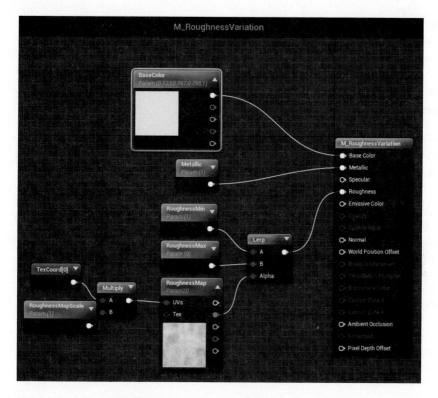

Figure 5.9 Adding a RoughnessMap Parameter to the Material for even more possibilities

Figure 5.10 Material Instances with Roughness maps

Creating a Texture Parameter

In addition to the previously described methods for adding parameters, you can also create a Texture Sample node by dragging a Texture into the Material Editor from the Content Browser. When you do this, the Texture is not a Parameter yet, and if compiled, cannot be modified by Instances in any way. To convert it to a Parameter, right-click the Texture node and select **Convert to Parameter** from the menu.

The Editor will give it ... a unique name; but you should probably give it a more thoughtful name. Now, Instances of this Material can define their own Texture map or modify them at runtime through Blueprints.

Lerping It

One of the most important features of Material Instances is the ability to adjust the look of the material on the fly. One of the best ways of doing this is by using a Lerp (Linear Interpolation) node.

Adding Min and Max Scalar Parameters allows artists to dynamically modify the values of the Roughness map on a per-Instance basis.

This is one of my favorite nodes for creating easy-to-tweak Materials. You can even easily invert the Alpha value by setting the A input to 1 and the B to 0. Lerp works with all kinds of inputs, including RGB colors, and is a great way to blend between two values.

> ### note
> The A and B inputs in a Lerp node can be almost any data type (Scalar, Vector, and so on); however, the Alpha input can only be a single, grayscale channel. You might need to use a Component Mask node to select what channel you are sending to this input.

Scaling the Texture Map

To scale Textures and create tiling in UE4, you don't scale the Texture, as you might be accustomed to doing; rather, you scale the UV coordinates by multiplying them by a scalar value.

Making Material Instances

As you can see, we now have many more parameters listed in our Material Instance Editor, including the ability to completely override the Texture being used to modulate the Roughness (see Figure 5.11).

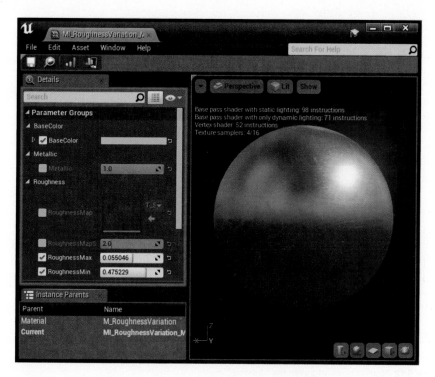

Figure 5.11 Material Instances Editor showing the Roughness Parameter group

Adding a Normal Map

The Normal map is much like a bump map, but far more efficient and flexible. Normal maps define an angle in space that helps add surface detail to otherwise flat polygons (see Figure 5.12).

Adding a Normal map to the Material adds another layer of visual depth and richness (see Figure 5.13). Scaling the normal and using a FlattenNormal Material Function allows artists to tone down the Normal map if it's too strong.

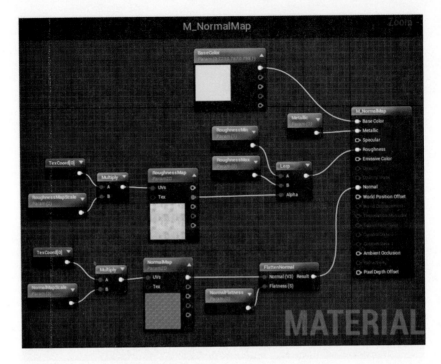

Figure 5.12 Normal map added to the Material

Figure 5.13 Instances of the NormalMap Material showing various Normal maps applied

Objects

UE4 is an object-oriented application. Object-Oriented Programming (OOP) is a way of thinking of your program in real-world terms and breaking down the work of programming into logical units. Rather than a single, huge script that runs the entire application, each element or **object** contains its own code and capabilities and communicates to other objects in the program to exchange information or trigger events.

Objects can be any part of an application: A button or a dropdown menu is a distinct type of object. A particle effect is an object that produces other objects.

A real-world example is a bowl of apples. The components, a bowl and several individual apples, are each completely independent (objects), but are interacting together form a whole.

Classes

The properties of each object are defined by its **class**, a set of programmatic rules, functions, and variables that define its behavior.

Objects are copies, or **instances**, of a class. Each object contains its own unique parameters or variables (like position and rotation) that it has inherited from its **parent** class. All objects of the same class share the same instructions and capabilities as the other instances of the object's class in the scene.

The apples example has two classes: Apple and Bowl. There is one instance of the Bowl class and several objects instantiated from the Apple class.

A single class can have hundreds of objects instantiated from it, each with its own unique data and properties.

Actors

Actors are a special kind of object. These objects can exist in the 3D world of your Levels and be rendered. Common examples are Static Mesh Actors and Point Light Actors. Actors can have collision, physics simulation, materials, animation, and scripted logic.

In the example, the bowl and the apples it contains are all Actors. Each occupies a distinct place in space and has a 3D Transform (Position, Rotation, and Scale).

In UE4, Lights, Sounds, Particle Systems, and Cameras are all different examples of Actor classes.

> note
>
> If you can see, place, or interact with it in the game world, it's an Actor. Lights, volumes, triggers, teapots, and rockets are all examples.

The Player

Most visualizations are linear and immutable. They are typically delivered as images, animations, or other linear formats that will almost never change in any significant way. Each person who views it (the **viewer**) will have the same experience and, for the most part, see the same things as anyone *else* who views it.

An interactive visualization is non-linear. Each **player** (the human behind the controls, providing input) has the freedom to explore the world in any way she pleases. You, as the designer, can limit and control what the player can do; but ultimately, the player will determine how the story proceeds. The player is the center of the UE4 universe. Everything UE4 does, it does it for the benefit of the players and their experience.

The Player Controller

A Player Controller or **PC** is the class responsible for modifying the world based on the player's input.

For each player in your application, a single PC will be spawned. A PC is automatically created by the world when a player joins the game and destroyed when he leaves.

The Player Controller has no form and can't be seen (it's an object in the world, not an Actor). You might think of the PC as the player's virtual representation in the world—its spirit or ghost, if you will.

A single PC can possess a single Pawn at a time. When the PC possesses something, it has direct access to that object and can forward commands along to it or otherwise modify it.

This lets a single player drastically change how she is playing the game from one moment to the next by possessing different Pawns with different capabilities.

Input Handling

The PC is the first place the input system forwards inputs after processing them. PC Blueprints have access to a massive input array from mouse and keyboard events to VR motion controller inputs and touch inputs for mobile devices.

Although Pawns and other Actors can also receive input events themselves, the PC is often used to forward those player inputs to the Pawns and other systems that might need those inputs, reducing the possibility for conflict between the various classes.

Although good reasons exist to have other objects handle some player inputs (a button in a UI detecting it's being pressed, for example), I try to keep almost all my input handling in the PC.

Player Data

One of the great things about the PC is that it's always there. If there's a player, there's a PC. That means that any time a system needs to interface with a single, reliable object, the PC is there.

All Actor Blueprints have fast, easy access to the PC through simple Get functions. This makes it a great place to store player data like name, team color, and so on. More complicated games might make use of specialized classes (inventory classes and so on), but these are usually created by and managed using the Player Controller.

Rotation

One of the most important roles of the Player Controller is to keep track of the player's rotation. The PC has no 3D position—no camera or other 3D representation. It does, however, have a Controller Rotation variable.

Keeping track of the player's rotation separate from the position has several advantages, especially when it comes to the player's view and presenting a consistent and smooth player viewpoint. Having a single view rotation is also easy to program for because there is a single variable to track and modify as needed.

Mouse Interface

The Player Controller class has a few important settings for visualizations. The most prominent is the ability to display the mouse cursor.

By default, UE4 and most video games do not show the mouse cursor. However, many visualization projects rely on robust user interfaces and having the cursor is essential.

You can also enable mouse-over and mouse-click events for your scenes here, letting you directly interact with the 3D Actors in your world. This can have a performance impact and affect how the player interacts with the HUD and other elements so only enable mouse events if they're needed for your project.

Other Controllers

You can author or add other Controllers to your applications. The most common is an AI (artificial intelligence) Controller. These Controllers act just like the Player Controller, but rather than using player input, they rely on programmed rules and sequences to simulate human behavior and inputs.

Pawns

Pawns are Actors in the world that can be possessed[1] by a Controller (player or AI). When possessed, the Controller sends input and other commands to the Pawn instructing it to move or launch rockets at enemies.

Pawns can be any sort of character, animal, or vehicle that can be controlled. The Controller gives the Pawn simple commands, like "move forward," and the Pawn interprets those in appropriate ways to simulate the kind of movement and interactions you're after.

By using the PC and Pawn together, you can ensure the Player has both the consistent set of abilities that are managed by the PC and specific interpretation of those inputs by each Pawn. This allows a single PC, and therefore player, to possess any kind of Pawn imaginable.

> ### note
> You can spawn and possess new Pawns at any time. It's a great way to create a new view mode or control method for a single game. For example, you could switch between a Walking Pawn and a Flying Drone Pawn, each with vastly different capabilities, looks, effects, sounds, and even User Interface elements.

The World

The **world** is where all the objects, Actors, and data in a UE4 application live. When you load a **Level** (also called a **map**), a new world is created and the Actors and objects that have been placed are spawned into it.

Everything that lives in the world (objects) can access and be accessed by any other thing in the world. Objects can also spawn and destroy other objects and Actors.

The world, like almost everything else in UE4, can be scripted using Blueprints and can also spawn, destroy, and modify Actors and objects in the world.

---

1. Possession is the term used when a controller takes control of an Actor. You can think of a controller like a ghost that can jump from Actor to Actor, or even exist without a possessed Actor.

Levels

Each level in UE4 is like a self-contained mini-application. Each level can have vastly different rules, geometry, and so on. In fact, each level could be a completely different game entirely. You might have seen this in games you have played where one level is a driving sequence and the next is an on-foot chase with very different controls, models, and gameplay.

> **note**
>
> Levels are often referred to as maps. The two terms are, for the most part, interchangeable.

A level can have multiple sublevels that it can stream in. This system is a great way to load specific content at specific times in your application. You can easily load, unload, and set the visibility of entire levels from Blueprints. This is a great way to manage information, both in the Editor and at runtime.

Components

Blueprints Actors can have any number of **components**: Special classes that are spawned with the Actor and can interface directly with it. Common examples are Static and Skeletal Meshes, Lights and Particle systems.

Components can be inherited from parent to child. They can be spawned at runtime or in the Construction Script. They can also be defined in the Blueprints Editor as Component Parameters.

Components are a great way to reuse code. For example, you can make a component that moves a specific speed along a path. You can attach this component to any Actor in your project to give it that ability.

Variables and their Types

All objects can store data using **variables** (also called **properties**). Variables can hold values like numbers and strings, or even references to other objects, classes, or Actors.

Variables in Blueprints are type strict, which means that each variable is of a certain class and cannot be changed. If you are coming from a purely scripting background this can be challenging, but it allows for more sophisticated compiling, error checking, and variable handling. One of the coolest things about it is that each type can have its own functions and variables!

Common variable types are

- **Boolean**: Simple true or false variable
- **Float or Scalar**: Numbers with decimals like 0.984, 4356.234, or −34.2
- **Integer**: Numbers without decimals such as 23 or −2354
- **String**: Alphanumeric characters in a list such as "Hello World"
- **Text**: Text is like String, but is primarily for localization
- **Vector**: An array of three float values representing X, Y, and Z values often used to record position, scale, or direction in 3D Space
- **Rotator**: An array of three float values that represent Roll, Pitch and Yaw rotation in 3D Space
- **Transform**: Combines Position (vector), Rotation (rotator), and Scale (vector) data
- **Object**: Reference to an object or Actor in the world, including Static Meshes, Cameras, Lights, and Player Controllers

The Tick

Each frame rendered in UE4 follows an exact order of operations. That set of operations is often referred to as the game loop or main loop. In UE4 it's referred to as a **Tick**.

On each Tick, player input is captured and forwarded to the scripting system where it can trigger events and functions. Characters move, guns fire, or cabinets change materials. The various systems in the game can then respond to that input: Physics, lighting, and artificial intelligence gather information about the world around them and perform their own actions as defined by their programming. After all the input and logic is processed, the scene geometry is updated and can be rendered and presented to the player.

Delta Seconds

The time it takes to render a single frame or Tick is referred to as the **Delta Seconds** or **Delta Time**. A game running at 60 frames per second has an average Delta Time of 0.0167 seconds.

Delta Time is important because each Tick can take a different amount of time to render from the last (scenes can change dramatically from one frame to the next) or from one computer to the next.

Tracking this value and applying it is essential when performing any task that takes places over time and space.

For example, if you wanted to rotate an Actor at a consistent rate you might think to simply add a rotation value on each Tick. A computer running at 30 fps would rotate the Actor 360 degrees per second if rotated 12 degrees per Tick, while a computer rendering at 120 fps would cause a rotation at a blistering 1440 degrees per second.

This is where Delta Time comes in: You can simply multiply the intended transform by the Delta Time to ensure that your movement is time based rather than framerate based.

In this example, multiply your intended degrees per second time by Delta Seconds. On the 30 fps machine, this looks like 360*0.033 degrees per Tick (about 12 degrees per Tick) while at 120 fps it's 360*0.0833 or 3 degrees per Tick. Even if the framerate fluctuates wildly, the Actor will rotate at exactly the same rate.

Class Inheritance

Each class can serve as a template (**parent**) for another class (**child**). The child **inherits** all the functionality and capability of its parent class. Any changes in the parent class are also inherited by the child class(es).

Returning to the earlier apple example, the Apple class might have several child classes: Red Delicious, Granny Smith, and so on. Each inherits the apple's functionality and description (crunchy, sweet, round), but overrides specific properties such as the color, size, and flavor parameters.

Child classes can override the functions of the parent class, adding or refining the functionality. For example, both PointLightActor and SpotLightActor are children of the LightActor class. Both classes have many of the same properties such as brightness, color, and attenuation.

Rather than both classes defining each of those properties, the parent class (LightActor) defines them and the child classes inherit them. Each class can then extend upon their parent to introduce new functionality and extend its abilities.

The Apple class also has a parent class: Fruit. The Fruit class encompasses apples, oranges, grapes, pears, and more. Although each is distinct and you can't make an apple from a grape, they inherit many shared properties and methods from the Fruit class.

UE4 leverages the concept of **inheritance** in almost every aspect of its design (material instances are a great example). Understanding it is essential for being able to develop more complex systems and applications. It's also a great way to avoid duplicating work that's already done.

Spawning and Destroying

Every object in your game world enters that world by **spawning**. When an object is spawned, it is instantiated from its defined class entering the game world, which allows it to be "seen" by everything else in the world.

Objects can be spawned at runtime using Blueprints. Pretty much any other object in the world can spawn a new object.

You can spawn Actors into your game world in the Editor before runtime by dragging and dropping them from the Content Browser into the game world.

You can also destroy Actors, removing them from the world. This can cause a problem in Blueprints that reference the destroyed Actor, so be careful to validate your references. Blueprints functions returning "none" can cause instability or make the project fail to build.

Spawning is an expensive operation, and spawning a lot of Actors can slow down your application. If you find yourself spawning and destroying many Actors of the same class, you might want to take the time to recycle those Actors rather than destroy and re-create new ones.

Construction Script

Actor objects do something special when they are spawned either in the Editor or at runtime: They run a Construction Script.

This feature is very powerful because it allows a Blueprint Actor to perform scripted actions before the game runs in the Editor (if it is being placed in the level) or before it's visible (if it is being spawned at runtime). This can include modifying itself, spawning new Meshes and other components, and doing other processing.

You can define variables in your Blueprint Actor classes as editable parameters. You can edit exposed parameters on the placed Blueprint Actors and the Construction Script will run, updating instantly.

You can build complex Construction Scripts that can build entire structures or systems based on the parameters. Some examples would be creating an Actor class that places Meshes along a spline (lamp posts, railings, roads) or that scatters objects over a Mesh (grass, foliage, and other props) or a time-of-day system that updates its various components based solely on the angle of the sun. The possibilities are endless.

Begin Play Event

After the Construction Script runs, the object is initialized and added to the world. As soon as it's available in the world and can see the world around it, the Begin Play event is fired.

This is where you want to set up any behaviors or interactions that need to be established before the first frame renders or just before the actor is visible onscreen. Actors at this stage will not have been rendered but will have access to the world and the objects it contains.

Begin Play only fires after all Actors and objects have been spawned for that Tick, so it is safe to access other objects that have been spawned that frame (as opposed to the Construction Script that runs before the object is initialized).

Blueprint Communication

Getting your Blueprints to talk to each other and the world is essential. UE4 provides several ways to get your objects, Actors, and the worlds they populate to exchange information and create rich interactions.

Direct Blueprint Communication

When you want one Blueprint to talk directly to another Blueprint on a one-to-one basis, you most often want to use Direct Blueprint Communication. This method requires you to explicitly define what object in the world is being referenced.

For example, a player clicks on a Light Switch Blueprint Actor that has a specific Light Bulb Blueprint Actor in the level assigned to a variable. The Light Switch then tells the Light Bulb to turn off and on directly. Only that Light Bulb is affected.

Event Dispatchers

Event Dispatchers allow you to have multiple Blueprints listening for a single event and have each react individually when it happens.

In the Light Switch example, the Light Bulbs could listen for the OnSwitch event of the Switch Blueprint and modify themselves accordingly when that event is triggered by the player's interaction with the light switch.

Blueprint Interfaces

Blueprint **interface(s)** are for when you have events that are common across different classes, such as being clicked on by a mouse or pointed to with a motion controller, but each class needs to do something different or nothing at all.

Interfaces are simply lists of expected events. When a Blueprint implements an interface, you can choose to implement any, all, or none of the listed methods.

You should use interfaces when you have some functionality that is *similar* in several Blueprints but needs to execute *differently* in each.

Interfaces are the least used method of communication between blueprints and isn't typically recommended for most use cases. Instead, use Event Dispatchers.

Blueprint Casting

Casting uses special nodes in the Graph editor. These nodes take an input of one class then attempt to access that node as a specific class. If the attempt is successful, you can access the variables, events, and functions in the target object directly.

This lets you query a generic set of Actors and classes. And if they are of a specific class, they will successfully cast to that class, giving you access to all the variables and methods available in that class.

For example, the Light Bulb Blueprint might extend the Actor class it's based on to have a ToggleLight function. The Switch Blueprint can query each actor in the scene and try to cast them to the Light Bulb class. If successful, it can run the ToggleLight function directly.

You can also use casting to trigger events and modify properties to all Actors of specific classes in a level. Using the Get All Actors of Class node, you can access an array of Actors that you can easily modify at once.

Compiling the Script

Before you run a Blueprint, you must compile it. Compiling converts your node graphs into the code that runs in the Editor and at runtime in the game.

Compiling also error-checks your code, attempting to find errors before the game even runs. It doesn't catch everything, but it typically gets the most dangerous types of errors before a crash can happen.

To compile a Blueprint, simply click the Compile button in the toolbar. Any errors found appear in the Compiler Results and typically include a handy link that takes you directly to the problem.

Summary

The terms and concepts presented in this chapter are pervasive in the UE4 interface, documentation, and community. You should have a better understanding of how a UE4 application runs "under the hood" and should be able to begin exploring Blueprints and building applications in UE4 with a bit more confidence.

In upcoming chapters, you will encounter these concepts often, even in systems outside Blueprints. Concepts like Inheritance and Variables and Properties are found throughout UE4 and inform almost every aspect of its design.

YOUR FIRST UE4 PROJECT

CHAPTER 7

SETTING UP THE PROJECT

Your first project in UE4 focuses on getting acclimated to the UE4 Editor, the Content Browser, and the level viewport. This chapter focuses on defining the scope of the project and getting everything set up to start building your first interactive world in UE4.

Project Scope

Before working on any interactive application, it's important to first define the goals of the project and write them down. A solid scope and well-defined minimum requirements ensure you develop your projects in a focused and methodical manner.

For your first project, you will keep it simple. UE4 includes a lot of sample content that's easily accessible and a great way to start learning the basics of UE4. You'll use that content to build a simple level, populate it, and set up a custom Pawn that can walk smoothly through the level, colliding with walls and floors giving the world a solid, immersive feeling.

Finally, you'll test the application using Play-In-Editor (PIE). After you're satisfied, you'll package and prepare your application for distribution as a stand-alone application.

By the end of this chapter, you'll have a good grasp of how to develop a simple UE4 application from the ground up. Let's break that down into a list:

1. Develop an application that allows a player to walk through a virtual environment.
2. Use Starter Content to build a simple environment with a light, door, and switch to toggle the light.
3. Use Dynamic Lighting.
4. Make the view first person and walking at a slow and steady pace.
5. Ensure the view height is appropriate for architectural visualizations.
6. Enable the player to collide with walls and floors, giving the simulation a feeling of solidity.

Creating a New Project from the Launcher

If you have not created your account at UnrealEngine.com, downloaded and installed the Epic Games Launcher, and installed engine version 4.14 or later (this book uses 4.14 in all examples), you need to do so before beginning.

The easiest way to make a new UE4 project is to use the New Project wizard. You can access it by launching the Engine from the Launcher (see Figure 7.1).

After the **Unreal Project Browser** launches, follow these steps:

1. Click the **New Project** tab along the top showing the New Project template selector (see Figure 7.2).

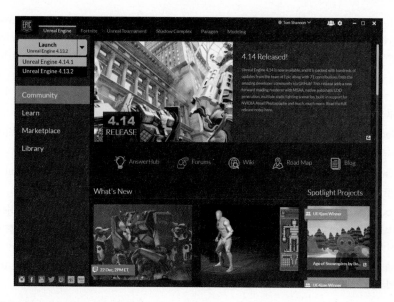

Figure 7.1 Launching the Engine from the Launcher using the Launch button in the upper-left corner of the Unreal Engine tab

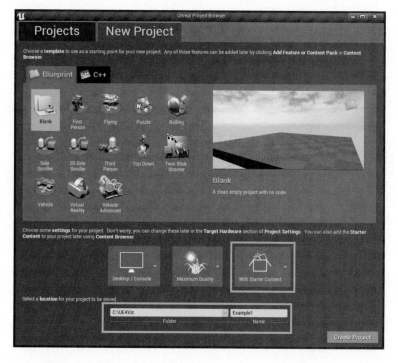

Figure 7.2 The New Project template setup panel in the Unreal Project Browser showing the settings for your first project

Here, you can choose from a wide array of starter **templates**. Each is well authored and can be a good starting point for many projects. They are also a great and easy way to play with different game modes and styles (First Person, Flying, Side Scroller, and so on) in UE4.

You won't use any of these for your project. Although they are great starting points, they are all game-centric and introduce things that you would have to undo and other things that you should know how to set up on your own.

2. Select the **Blank** Blueprint project template. This project template contains no content or code at all—in other words, it is a completely blank slate.

3. Click **Starter Content**, which adds some simple pre-made assets to the project that will help you quickly build your level.

4. Choose a location to store your project and give the project a name. I keep my projects outside my user folder; however, where you decide to keep your project is your decision. Just remember to choose a fast, local hard drive or SSD with plenty of free space.

5. Click the green **Create Project** button. The Engine creates a new folder and builds the folder structure required to run your project.

After your project files are created, a new instance of the UE4 Editor launches (see Figure 7.3) displaying the name of your new project.

Figure 7.3 The project loading for the first time

CHAPTER 8

POPULATING THE WORLD

Getting content into your Level is straightforward and artist friendly. The UE4 Editor offers many tools and features to help you place, modify, and organize your Assets in 3D space. In this chapter, you use the already-built Starter Content Assets you included with your project to build a simple Level in which to walk around.

Making and Saving a New, Blank Level

In my opinion, starting with a new Level and building a Level from scratch is the best way to get the desired results. Visualizations have different goals than most games, and most of the templates available just aren't suited for the types of interactions needed when making interactive visualizations.

In the File menu, select **New Level** and select the **Empty Level** option.

Save your Level by selecting **Save Current** from the File menu or by clicking the **Save Current** button in the toolbar. When the **Save Level As** dialog (see Figure 8.1) appears, name the Level **MyFirstMap** and click **Save** to save the map to disk.

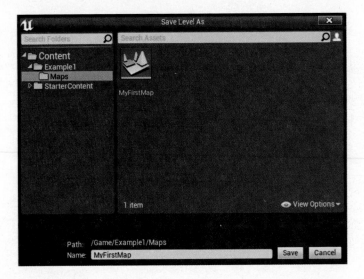

Figure 8.1 Save Level As dialog

As you can see in this example, I created a folder at the root of the Content directory called **Example1**. You can create a new folder by right-clicking in various logical places in the Content Browser or by using the Add New button in the Content Browser. Remember that you can and should do all of your file management from within the Content Browser.

If you make a mistake and need to rename your map or the folder, you can use the right-click menu or by selecting the Asset or folder and pressing F2 on your keyboard.

Making a project-specific directory within the Content folder is a common practice in UE4, because it ensures all content created for this project is self-contained within its own directory, while content from third parties or other projects can be merged into your project without fear that the two will conflict.

Remember that Levels and maps are the same thing and the terms are used interchangeably to represent UMAP files.

Placing and Modifying Assets

The most common method for getting Assets from the Content Browser into the Level is simply to drag and drop the Asset(s) from the Content Browser into the Viewport in the Editor (see Figure 8.2).

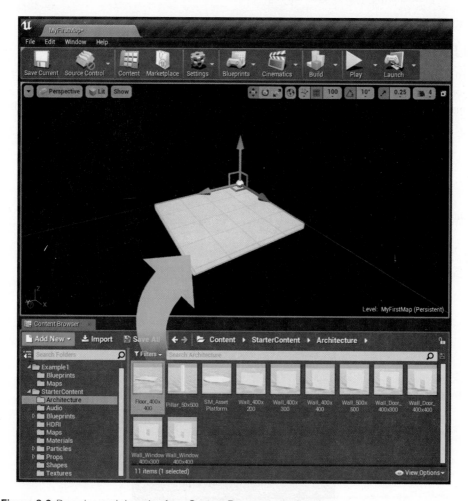

Figure 8.2 Dragging and dropping from Content Browser to the Level

Moving, Scaling, and Rotating

After placing the Actors, you can easily move, scale, and rotate them using familiar gizmos. You can easily switch between Move, Rotate, and Scale modes using the spacebar or the icons at the top of the Viewport.

> **note**
>
> You can also use the W, E, and R keys to switch between Move, Scale, and Rotate, or press the spacebar to cycle through each of the modes.

Using the Details Panel

The Details Panel is where all the properties for each selected Actor display (see Figure 8.3). Here, you can directly set the Location, Scale, and Rotation properties for Actors along with the Class-specific settings such as Lightmap Resolution, Shadow options, and Material assignment overrides.

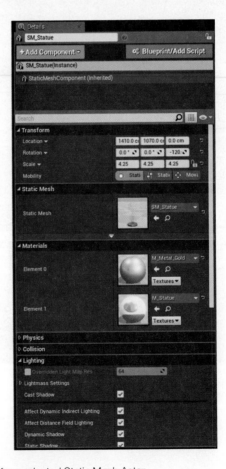

Figure 8.3 Details Panel for a selected Static Mesh Actor

Snapping

The Assets in the Starter Content are built with a grid size of 100 units. For this reason, enabling Snap in the Viewport and setting it to 100 units is a good idea. That way, when you move Actors around, they snap to a 100 x 100 x100 unit grid.

You can also set snapping for Rotation and Scale in the Viewport settings using toggle buttons located in the upper right of each Viewport (see Figure 8.4). Each displays the snapping interval to the right. You can adjust this setting by clicking on the interval.

Figure 8.4 Snap options in each Viewport

Duplicating

You have several ways to duplicate Actors. Doing a Copy-paste or using the Duplicate command in the right-click and Edit menus are good options.

I often use the keyboard shortcut Alt+Drag to instantly create copies of the selected object. Hold Shift while you duplicate an Actor to have the camera follow the Actor as you move it. You can also Alt+Drag multiple Actors at once. You need to grab onto the transform gizmo in the Viewport to do this, not just anywhere on the model. You can also clone Actors like this with the rotate and scale gizmos as well.

Adding Actors from the Class Browser

The Content Browser is for placing generated or imported content into the Level, but you will place many things into your game worlds that are not available in the Content Browser.

You place Classes such as Lights by dragging and dropping them from the Class Browser using Place Mode. Both methods create a new Level Actor that instantiates from the Class selected.

The Modes window is located in the upper left of the default Editor layout. You can also reveal the Class Browser by going to Window in the menu bar and selecting **Modes**.

The first tab in the Modes Panel is the Place Mode. The Place Mode contains the Class Browser.

Let there Be Light

Before you can start placing Actors in earnest, you need some light in the scene. Unlike in Max or Maya, there isn't a built-in default scene or Viewport light. You must author the lighting systems manually.

If no lights are in your scene it will use the Unlit view mode. This view mode only displays the unshaded Base Color of the objects. This is workable, but ultimately difficult to work with in the long term because you cannot easily see depth, and objects tend to blend together.

UE4 boasts great real-time lighting and shadows. Whether you're using Lightmass for high-performance, static GI lighting or using the dynamic shadows and lighting systems for direct lighting, a couple key lighting Actors are essential to achieving the best results from UE4.

Sun

For your sun, let's use a Directional Light Actor. To add it, use the Modes Panel and switch to Place Mode (Shift+1). Click on Lights and drag a Directional Light into the scene.

Set the sun to Moveable in the Details Panel. This allows it to move and change properties dynamically and forces it to use dynamic shadows.

In most architectural visualizations, you would use static lighting with Lightmass, but I get into that topic in the next section. For now, focus on the basics. Dynamic lighting offers a fast, easy-to-edit WYSIWYG way to experiment and learn without the complexities of Lightmass.

Atmospheric Fog

UE4 includes **atmospheric fog simulation**, or a mathematical way of shading the sky and attenuating and tinting light over long distances. This is akin to the effect of purple mountains' majesty when viewed from miles away as light is scattered in the atmosphere.

You place the Atmospheric Fog Actor like the Directional Light, using the Place Mode.

As soon as you drop the Fog Actor into the scene, a basic sky and horizon immediately generate, and if you're facing the right way you'll see a sun disk (see Figure 8.7, later in this chapter).

Right now, you'll note that the sun is at the wrong location and the sky looks as if the sun is setting. You can either set up the sun position and sky colors manually or you can assign your Directional Sun Light to define these settings, giving you a nice dynamic sky.

Assign the Sun to the Atmosphere

You must manually define what Directional Light Actor is being used to determine the sky colors. You do this in the Directional Light Actor's Properties with the **Atmosphere Sun Light** checkbox (see Figure 8.5).

This checkbox is slightly hidden in the advanced properties of the Light Actor. To access it, select the small downward arrow in the Light properties in the Details Panel (see Figure 8.5). You can also use the search bar in the Details Panel to quickly filter the properties list (see Figure 8.6).

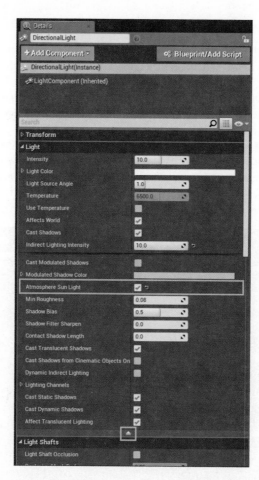

Figure 8.5 Directional Light details with the advanced properties displayed and Atmosphere Sun Light set to true

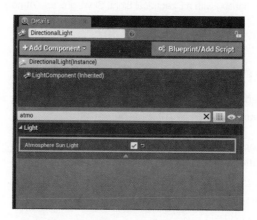

Figure 8.6 Directional light details filtered using the search bar

Sky Light

The Sky Light Actor is the third and final Actor you need to add. This Actor captures an HDR cube map of the scene or uses a defined HDR CubeMap Texture to light the scene.

After you add this Actor, set the Mobility to Moveable. Your shadowed areas should fill with blue color from the sky. If it's too bright, turn down the Intensity of the SkyLight.

Your scene should look a bit more like what's shown in Figure 8.7. The Directional Light, Sky Light, and Atmospheric Fog Actors are each set to Moveable to use the dynamic lighting pipeline. The Editor layout has been customized to allow for a larger Viewport and more room to modify the properties.

Figure 8.7 Basic scene lighting with a Directional Light, Sky Light, and Atmospheric Fog Actors

Moving Around the Scene

Now that there's something in your scene, you'll probably want to move and orbit your view a bit to take a look around.

UE4 features a great combination of Viewport navigation methods derived from both games and 3D design applications.

Game Style

The most common way to move around the scene is to use the game-style navigation system.

Holding down the right mouse button in the Viewport enables Game Navigation Mode. Dragging your mouse around (while still holding down the RMB) rotates your view. Pressing **W** on the keyboard moves you forward and **S** moves you back; pressing **A** and **D** moves you left and right, respectively.

You can also move up and down with the **E** and **Q** keys.

To adjust your movement speed, you can use the mouse wheel to speed up and slow down how fast you move around the Level.

Object Focused

You can also focus the camera on any Actor (or group of selected Actors) using the **F** keyboard shortcut. This key centers and zooms the camera to the selected objects. When it does, you can orbit around the selected Actors by holding down Alt and dragging with the left mouse button.

The orbit view is great for inspecting objects in the 3D view.

You can easily zoom in and out on the focused Actors by using the scroll wheel on your mouse (this time without holding down the right mouse button).

Building the Architecture

Using the various Static Meshes in the Architecture folder in the Starter Content, let's build a simple apartment or house.

If you have Snapping on, set your interval for 100 units. This makes each Mesh in this folder snap into the scene like building blocks.

You'll need a floor, some walls, and whatever else you come up with; have some fun.

Be sure there's a door that connects rooms and some room to walk around. Each floor piece is 400cm x 400cm so each room should be at least 2 x 2.

Figure 8.8 shows what I came up with after having some fun putting together a bunch of blocks. I tried to make something that would contain the player in a small area but be open enough to explore. It only uses the walls and floor Static Meshes from the Starter Content snapped to the 100 x 100 grid. I have exposed the Orthographic Viewports using the Maximize/ Minimize button in the upper-right corner of each Viewport. I've also set up a second Perspective view allowing me to see the scene from several 3D views.

Your area certainly doesn't need to be as complex or could be much more complex—it's up to you. However, make sure you have a floor for your Player to stand on and some walls so they can't walk off into the void.

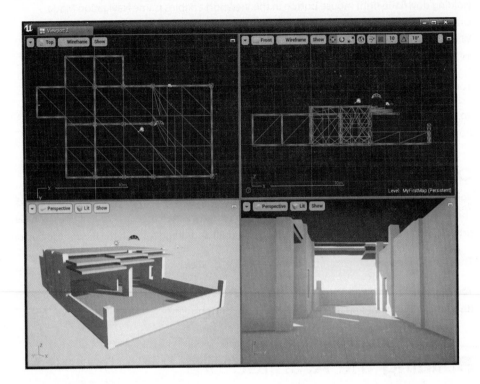

Figure 8.8 House floating in the endless void

Adding Details to Your Structure

Now that you have a structure, let's get some details into it. Let's place some Static Mesh Actors from the Content Browser then add some Spot Light Actors with Lighting profiles and various colors to add some fun lighting effects.

Placing Props

Props are the Static Mesh Actors in your scene that make up the decorations and other non-architectural elements. The Sample Content comes with a good selection of Meshes to play with.

Like all other Meshes, simply drag and drop them from the Content Browser to place the first one in your Level. Copy and paste, and then move and scale to taste.

You can also place Materials and Particle Systems in your Level. Go nuts, keep it minimal—it's up to you. All you really need are a floor and some walls; the rest is up to your imagination.

Here's what I came up with after a few more minutes dragging-dropping, copying-pasting, surface snapping, and dragging-cloning (see Figure 8.9). I spent some time making my floating house a home by placing various props from the Content Browser, and duplicating and manipulating the Meshes. The rocks help anchor the structure visually.

Figure 8.9 My scene after a few minutes of placing meshes

This is a great time to try out different snapping options. I encourage you to explore the Surface Snapping option to help you place Actors directly on other Actors.

Placing Lights

Like you did with the Directional Sun Light and Sky Light Actors, use the Class Browser to add lights to the scene.

Clicking the Lights tab in the Class Browser presents you with a list of the available light Classes (see Figure 8.10). Simply drag and drop the Light Class you want into the Viewport to place a Light Actor into your Level.

Figure 8.10 Light Classes listed in Placement Mode

Like with Static Mesh Actors, you can rotate and move Lights using gizmos or using the Details Panel's transform controls. You can also copy-paste and duplicate the same way.

Light Properties

Take the time to explore the Light Actor properties in the Details Panel. It offers options for brightness, shadow casting, and color. Many of these options are purely visual while many are tied closely to performance.

Dynamic Lights and Performance

Because you are using dynamic lighting, be careful how many lights you use. Although the deferred renderer of UE4 allows for many more dynamic lights than previous generation rendering techniques, they are expensive effects, especially when it comes to shadowing.

Shadows

Dynamic shadows add a lot of rendering overhead and you should use them sparingly. Shadowed point lights are the most expensive kind of light to render and should be used the most sparingly.

Attenuation Radius

You can also reduce the Attenuation Radius of your lights as much as possible to improve performance. Actors outside the radius will not be affected by the light and won't calculate lighting and shadows from that light.

Adding IES Profiles

UE4 supports 2D IES profiles for spot and point lights. IES profiles modulate the light's brightness using a Texture generated from an imported IES file. UE4 ships with several IES profiles, or you can import your own into the Content Browser as you would with any other content type.

Here's my scene after placing a few lights (see Figure 8.11). I've also added some IES profiles to the spot lights to make them a bit more interesting. You can find the IES property in your Details Panel when you select a Light Actor in your Level.

Figure 8.11 Final scene in the Editor with all four Viewports set to Perspective, allowing me to see the Level form multiple perspectives as I work

Summary

You've seen how easy it is to populate your Levels with Assets. Lights, Materials, and Actors can easily be dragged and dropped, copied and moved, and rotated and scaled as easily as in our favorite 3D application. Building Levels in UE4 is fun and interactive and getting a great lighting setup is very easy using the Atmospheric Fog and Skylight.

It's fun to have complete create control over a virtual space and to create something without any real constraints other than the simple requirements of walls and a floor.

I have included this scene at www.TomShannon3d.com/UnrealForViz for you to open on your own and play with.

CHAPTER 9

MAKING IT INTERACTIVE WITH BLUEPRINTS

You've set up your first project, populated the world, and set up some lights and props to make it look nice. That's all well and good, but to make your project extraordinary, it must be interactive. In this chapter, you learn how to author your first Blueprint Classes, set up your first Game Mode, and get your Player moving around the world using the Input system.

Setting Up the Project

The project requirements call for a first-person view and walking-style movement. Fortunately, getting a first-person character view and walking movement is something Unreal Engine can do really well.

You'll first create a Pawn, a Blueprint Class that receives the inputs processed by the Player Controller Class you'll learn to make after that. Lastly, you'll make a custom Game Mode Class to define these Classes as your project's defaults.

With these items in place you'll be able to easily place a Player Start Actor to define where your Player will spawn when she loads this Level.

At the end of the chapter, your Pawn will be able to walk smoothly around the Level, exploring and looking freely about.

The setup process for creating a new Game Mode, complete with Player Controller, input mappings, and Pawn is fairly lengthy, but in the end, you will have a good understanding how UE4 processes inputs and expects you to move your Players around. You'll also be able to migrate this content to new project, letting you build on your work as you add capabilities to your own interactive visualizations.

Press Play

You've probably already clicked the Play button in the Editor before this point. It's okay; it's hard not to. It's the whole reason UE4 exists: to be played!

Clicking the Play button in the Editor launches your game in a special mode called **Play in Editor** (PIE) that uses the already-loaded Assets to instantly start up the world and get you playing as fast as possible. It's a fantastic way to test out your application without your having to load it from scratch each time.

Play Modes

You can select the Option button to the right of the Play button to reveal some additional Play Mode options (see Figure 9.1).

Figure 9.1 PIE options

The default mode is to launch the game in the currently **Selected Viewport**. You can also launch into a **New Editor Window**. This is useful if your Viewport is obscured or you want to test in a specific resolution or aspect ratio.

Selecting **Standalone Game** launches an uncooked build of your game from the command line. This takes longer to launch than PIE (which is almost instant), but presents a more accurate representation of how your final application will behave outside the Editor.

Simulate is an interesting mode that launches the game but does not spawn the typical Player Controller and Pawn, leaving you free to explore the Level as it runs without the limitations placed on typical Pawns.

After you select one of these options, the Play button changes to match the Mode you selected last.

If you want to modify the resolutions and other launch behaviors, select **Advanced Settings**. This launches the Editor Settings dialog where you can modify them.

Default GameMode

Clicking Play in your Level at this point spawns the default UE4 PC and Pawn and allows you to fly around the Level using a flying character with game-like controls. This is the default **GameMode** in UE4.

The GameMode is a Class that defines what Player Controller, Pawn, and other Classes will be used when the game starts.

Notice that, in this mode, you are a proper Player with collision and physics responses, unlike the Editor viewpoint, where you are treated as a ghost. However, you can also fly and move very fast. This is not how you want to explore your space.

You must create your own Pawn, PC, and GameMode and then assign them to your project. After doing this you should be able to walk around your Level as defined in the project scope.

Creating the Pawn

The Class that represents your physical presence in the world is the **Pawn**. The Pawn handles physics, collision, and interaction with the world and other Level Actors.

Pawns are Blueprint-style Classes. They contain Components, Variables, and Event Graphs. To create one, follow these steps:

1. Select **Add New** in the Content Browser and select **Blueprint Class** (see Figure 9.2).

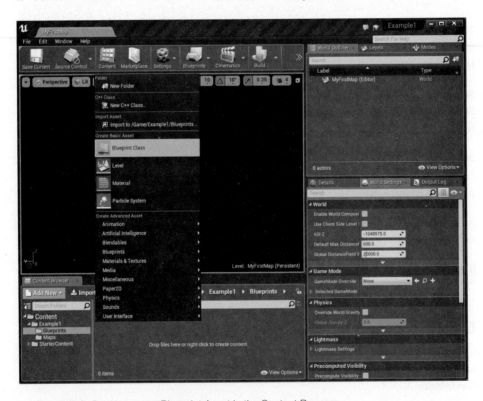

Figure 9.2 Creating a new Blueprint Asset in the Content Browser

2. Select the **Character** button in the **Pick Parent Class** dialog that opens. The Character Class is an advanced Pawn Class that works for a wide range of first- and third-person character applications, so it's perfect for the needs of this project and saves a lot of effort on your part. (There's no need to *always* reinvent the wheel!)

3. Name your Asset. I chose BP_Interior_Pawn, following commonly accepted UE4 naming conventions (see Figure 9.3).

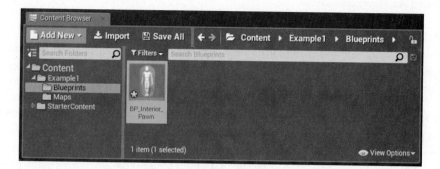

Figure 9.3 Created and named BP_Interior_Pawn Blueprint Asset in the Content Browser

4. Double-click the Asset to open the Blueprint Editor.

5. Select the BP_Interior_Pawn component from the Components list, and ensure the Class Defaults button is selected in the toolbar (see Figure 9.4).

Figure 9.4 Pawn Class defaults displayed in the Blueprint Editor

Setting the Player's View Height

To get the Player's viewpoint to a reasonable height you need to adjust the Base Eye Height parameter along with the Capsule Component's Half Height.

The Player's eye level is set by adding the Base Eye Height property of the Character with the Half-height property of the Capsule Component. You need to adjust both to achieve the right height and Player collision.

Adjusting the Capsule Component

The Pawn uses the Capsule Collision Component to simulate the Player's body in the world. You can see the Capsule Component in the Blueprint Editor's Viewport tab and in the Components list (see Figure 9.5 later in this chapter).

Select the Capsule Component from the Components list to access its two variables, Radius and Half-height. As the name implies, the Half-height represents the distance from the floor to the middle of the Capsule Collision Component. This defaults to 88 cm, or 176 cm (about 5'9") from the bottom to the top of the capsule. That's short for most people, but it's better to err on a bit shorter than to have the Player's head get caught on door frames and light fixtures. You can keep this default as is.

Setting Base Eye Height

UE4 calculates the character's view height by adding the Capsule Half-Height property of the Capsule Component to the Base Eye Height to get the final eye height.

The default Base Eye Height value of 64 gives an eye height of only 152 cm, which feels too short for most people. The average eye height for men is about 175 cm and is about 160 cm for women. Aiming for 168 splits the difference, leaving a difference of 80 cm for the Base Eye Height.

To return to the default properties of the Character Class, click on the root component (BP_Interior_Pawn) in your Components list and set the Base Eye Height to 80.

Using Controller Rotation Yaw

The next setting in your Class Defaults to know about deals with how the Player's view rotation will be determined. The yaw is the world Z rotation of the Player, controlling how she turns left and right.

Although you'll keep this at the default, it's important to know what's going on here. The movement component doesn't manage the rotation; the Player Controller does. Also, because you don't want the entire Capsule to pitch up and down as you look up and down, you only use the yaw (world Z rotation), leaving the pitch to be applied to the camera that's parented to the Pawn.

Having two components handle pitch and yaw independently avoids an interactive camera issue commonly known as **Gimbal Lock** where the camera doesn't maintain horizontal stability as it rotates around.

Enabling Controller Rotation Yaw automatically matches the Pawn's yaw with the Player Controller's Control Rotation Parameter.

Setting Up the Movement Speed

The **CharacterMovement Component** is responsible for moving the Character around the scene and managing movement states. It's also where you'll find the default settings pertaining to your character's movement such as walking speed, default movement mode, and so on.

Find CharacterMovement Component in the Components Panel and select it to see the default properties in the Details Panel (see Figure 9.5). You can filter Details panels using the Eye icon near the search bar at the top of the Details tab panel.

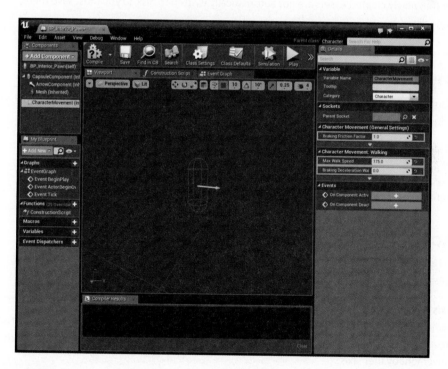

Figure 9.5 Modified CharacterMovement Component properties

There's not a lot you need to modify for this simple project, but notice the options are extensive and you can use them to create a ton of different movement types, from flying to falling to swimming and climbing.

Max Walk Speed

By default, the Player is set to move at 600 cm per second (13 mph). That's maybe a bit fast for most people to move around a room. Set it to somewhere in the 150–175 range for a slow, interior walk.

Braking Friction and Deceleration

Two settings are available for slowing down the character and both are defaulted to some high values (presumably for high-action games where people are walking around at 6m per second).

Set the Braking Friction Factor to 1 and the Braking Deceleration Walking setting to 0.0.

This lets the Player come to a smooth stop, rather than the abrupt stop needed in most games for precise control. This is a personal preference and a demonstration of how you can really tune the "feel" of your character using the Character Class.

Now that you've created and modified your Pawn Class, save it before you continue. Remember that newly created Assets are not automatically written to disk so you must save them manually.

Input Mapping

Input Mappings are project-wide settings that allow you to set up generic input events such as mouse clicks or key presses and access them from Blueprints.

To access the Input Mappings, go to Edit in the menu bar and select Project Settings.

Select Input from the left column (see upcoming Figure 9.6) to see the Input Mappings preferences.

Action and Axis Mapping

Action Mappings are one-time events triggered by single-action events such as button presses and mouse clicks. These mappings fire for a single Tick.

Axis Mappings represent things that can have a value numeric value and can persist from frame to frame. This would be like how fast you want to move forward or turn left or right. They are called *Axis Mappings* because they traditionally referred to game joysticks that defined their movement by their axis.

In modern interfaces this might be how many pixels the mouse moved in the last Tick, a key being depressed and held, or the position of an analog joystick on a gamepad.

For your Player movement and rotation, you'll exclusively use Axis Mappings.

Setting Up Mappings

The Axis Mappings array consists of a list of Mappings. Each Mapping has a Label and an array of inputs, each with a Scale value.

The Label is what the Mapping is referenced as in Blueprints. You can name this Label whatever you want: "Walk," "Turn," "EatShrimp." There is no set standard. Whatever you assign to this field becomes available as an Input Event and an Axis Value variable that's easily accessible by the Player Controller.

Each named Input Axis can have several inputs. For instance, the Mapping named "MoveForward" can have both the W and S keyboard presses assigned. The S key carries a **Scale** of –1, whereas W is set to +1. This means that when this event is called by the Player pressing W, it will return an Axis value of 1, and the Player pressing S it will return an Axis value of –1. In this way, you can group inputs further to avoid too many events in your game code.

Set up your Input Mappings to look like Figure 9.6 before continuing. The settings in the Project Settings dialog are automatically saved to your project's Configuration files. You don't have to click a Save button when you are done; you can simply close the Preferences window.

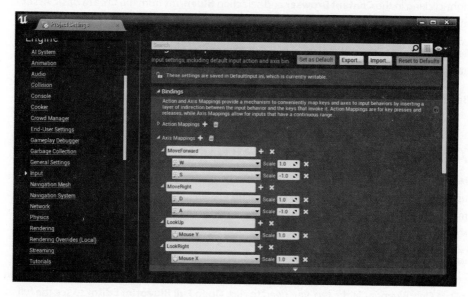

Figure 9.6 Input Mappings dialog with Mappings defined

Input Device Flexibility

Another advantage to setting up your input this way is the ability to use input from multiple devices in a generic manner. Pressing Enter can issue the same Event as pressing the X button on a gamepad or right-clicking. It's entirely up to you.

Because of this flexibility, UE4 doesn't come with defaults set up. You are free to make input mappings exactly fit your input system's needs. These settings are stored in your project's Saved/Config/DefaultInput.ini file and you can easily import and export using the buttons in the Project Settings interface or by copying and pasting the text contents from other input files.

Creating the Player Controller Class

Now that you have a Pawn and Input Mappings, you need to get the two together. Although you *can* put your input and movement logic directly into the Pawn Class, it's not the intended design pattern.

For that you have the Player Controller. As the name suggests, one of the primary functions of the Player Controller is to process Player input. Remember, there's *always* a Player Controller when a UE4 application is running, so it's a great place to put code that *always* needs to work, like input processing.

Create your Player Controller exactly like the Pawn and GameMode Assets you made before by right-clicking in the **Content Browser** and selecting **Blueprint** from the **Create Basic Asset** menu.

Select the **Player Controller** Class in the **Pick Parent Class** window and name the newly cre-ated Asset **BP_UE4Viz_PlayerController**.

Be sure to save your Asset, committing it to the disk for the first time.

Adding Input with Blueprints

Now that you have your inputs defined, you can begin using them to drive events in your game using Blueprint scripting! Let's begin by opening the Blueprint Editor. You do this, like with many of the Editors in UE4, by simply double-clicking your Player Controller Blueprint Asset in the Content Browser.

With your PC open, you need to get to the Event Graph to begin wiring your input processing code. If your Blueprint Editor window lacks an Event Graph and displays a message about being a Data Only Blueprint at the top, you need to click **Open Full Blueprint Editor** to see the full Blueprint Editor interface.

When it's available, click on the Event Graph tab.

Adding Axis Events

You need to detect the Input Axis Mappings you set up earlier. When one of the Input Axis Mappings is triggered (typically when the Player performs the action you selected), it fires an event that can be accessed from Blueprints. This is called an **Axis Event** and it returns a single variable: **Axis Value**.

The Axis Value represents the value of the input multiplied by the Scale value you set in the Input Mappings dialog (refer to Figure 9.6). So, pressing W fires the input event, returning 1.0 during each Tick the key is held down, and pressing S fires the input event as well but returns a value of –1.0 because the Mapping assigns it a Scale value of –1. Also, these values are cumulative, so if the Player presses both W and S at the same time, the input axis value would return 0 because the inputs cancel each other out.

Keys on the keyboard are, of course, digital and can only return 1 or 0. However, the Axis Value can work with an analog device such as a gamepad that can return any value between –1 and 1 in each axis or with the mouse input, which returns the number of pixels the mouse moved since the last time the input was sampled (sometimes called an **input delta**, or the difference between two samples). This setup lets many different types of inputs use the same axis and corresponding event, simplifying the input processing code.

To add an Axis event to your Player Controller, right-click in the Event Graph's Graph Editor and search for the Axis name defined in the Settings (see Figure 9.7). Simply begin typing and the list will be filtered dynamically.

Figure 9.7 Searching for the Move Forward Axis Event using the context menu available when you right-click in the Blueprint Event Graph

Add an event for each of your movement Axis Mappings: MoveForward and MoveRight (see Figure 9.8). Add two more for the Rotation Mappings: LookUp and LookRight.

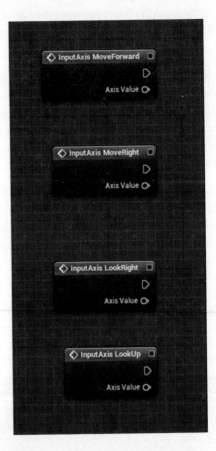

Figure 9.8 Added Axis Events

Notice the Axis value pin in Figure 9.8. This returns a float value that represents the Player Input value scaled by the Input Scale assigned in the Input Mapping.

Rotating the View (Looking)

Rotating the view is really straightforward. Thanks to the Character Class you have based your Pawn on, you simply need to rotate the Player Controller (remember that your Player Controller handles the view rotation) and the view will follow.

Because this is a common use case, UE4 offers some great shortcuts. **Add Yaw Input** and **Add Pitch Input** are two pre-made functions that take a simple input value and handle adding the rotation values to the PC's Control Rotation variable.

Follow these steps to create these nodes:

1. Right-click in the Event Graph and search for Add Yaw Input and Add Pitch Input.

2. Wire the **Exec Out** pin (the white arrow on the right of the node) from the InputAxis LookRight Event and connect it to the Add Yaw Input node's **Exec In** pin (the white arrow on the left of the node) by dragging and dropping from one to the other. You can drag pins in either direction.

3. Wire the **Axis Value** pin from the InputAxis LookRight node's **Axis Value** to the **In Val** node of the Add Yaw Input node.

4. Repeat for the LookUp axis and the Add Pitch function (see Figure 9.9).

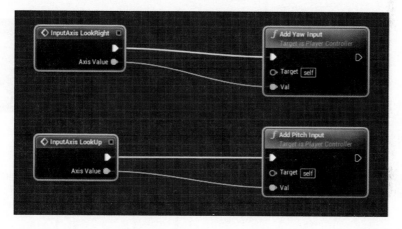

Figure 9.9 Completed Rotation Input script

Player Movement

Player movement is a little trickier to set up than the view rotation. The Player Controller needs to tell the Pawn to move. To do that you need to use a form a Blueprint communication to pass the player's input data to the Pawn so it can move about.

Referencing the Pawn

When the Player presses one of the Input Axis Mappings and triggers these events, you want the Pawn to move. To do this you must communicate with it and the first step is to get a **Reference** to the Pawn.

The base PC Class you based your PC on conveniently has a **Player Character** variable that is populated automatically with a Reference to the Character Pawn that it is possessing at any given time. This lets you directly access your Character and easily add movement input.

You can get a reference to the Player Character by right-clicking in the Event Graph and searching for **Character** in the Actions List that pops up. Select the **Get Player Character** function.

Is Valid

Because the Player Controller can possess almost any type of Actor in the world, the Player Character variable might return **none** if it's not controlling an Actor or Pawn based on the Character Class.

To avoid this, you use an **Is Valid** branch to make sure this doesn't happen (see Figure 9.10). The script will only continue if the Player Character value is valid and won't return an error if accessed.

Figure 9.10 Getting a reference to the Player Character and checking whether it's valid

Always using a validation check when you "get" other Actors or Objects that don't reliably exist in the world is a good idea.

Add Movement Input

The Character Class already has functions for moving the Player around the scene using the Movement Component. The function is called Add Movement Input, but you need to access it a different way than you've been doing.

So far, you've been right-clicking in the Viewport and using the contextual menu to create nodes. This menu only displays the nodes available to the Blueprint it is within. Functions, Events, and Variables that are stored in other Blueprints need to be referenced to be accessed.

To do so, drag a wire from the blue Return Value pin on the Get Player Controller out into the Graph Editor and release. A context menu populated with the Functions, Events, and Variables associated with the referenced Class appears (see Figure 9.11). Notice the context menu says "Actions taking a(n) Character Reference." This tells you that you are successfully referencing the other Blueprint Class.

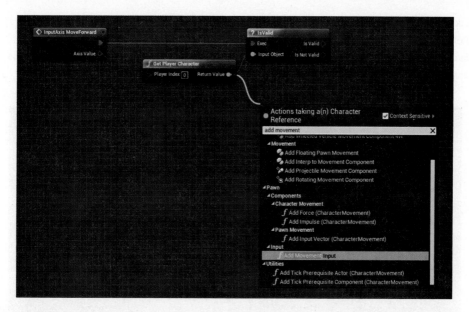

Figure 9.11 Adding the Add Movement Input from the Character Class Reference

Search for Add Movement Input and click it to place it on the Event Graph, connecting as shown in Figure 9.12.

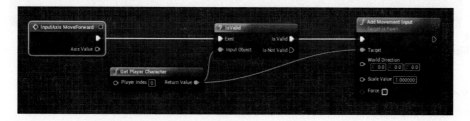

Figure 9.12 The placed Add Movement Input function

Notice in Figure 9.12 the blue wire connecting the Get Player Controller node to the Target input of the Add Movement Node. This wire represents a reference to the Player Character.

Get Forward and Right Vectors

The **AddMovementInput** function uses a world vector to move your character around. This vector changes based on which direction the Player is facing, so you need to figure that out and use it to determine the direction to move.

That's where the **Get Actor Forward Vector** and **Get Actor Right Vector** functions come in. They convert the world rotation into normalized XYZ vectors for each direction.

Like the Add Movement Input node, you must drag a reference from the Get Player Character's Return Value node to access the functions list. Search for the nodes and place them on the Event Graph (see Figure 9.13). You can see references to the Components of the Character Class as well; ensure you're selecting the root component as shown.

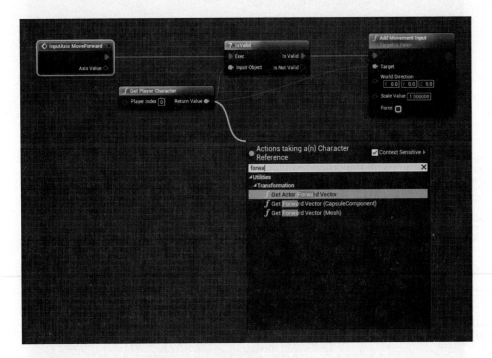

Figure 9.13 Adding Get Actor Forward vector function

Scaling Input

Without getting too much into vector math, you can then simply multiply the Vector (three float number values like X, Y, Z) by the Axis Value of the InputAxis Events to scale each direction by the input amount.

Dragging a wire from the Return Value pin of the Get Actor Forward Vector node into the Event Graph and releasing enables you to see the methods available for a Vector Reference. Search for * (an asterisk) to see the multiplication functions available and select **vector * float** from the list (see Figure 9.14).

You can then feed that scaled Vector value to the Add Movement Input function's World Direction input pins, completing your forward movement code. You need to repeat this process for the Move Right InputAxis Event as well. The only difference is you replace the Get Actor Forward Vector function with a Get Actor Right Vector node (see Figure 9.15).

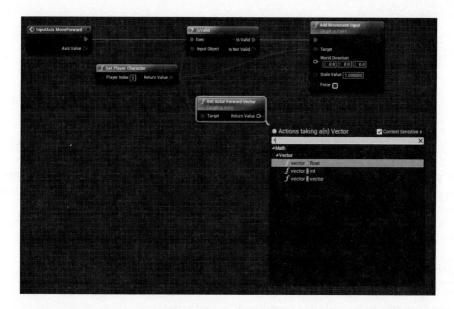

Figure 9.14 Adding a **vector * float** Math node

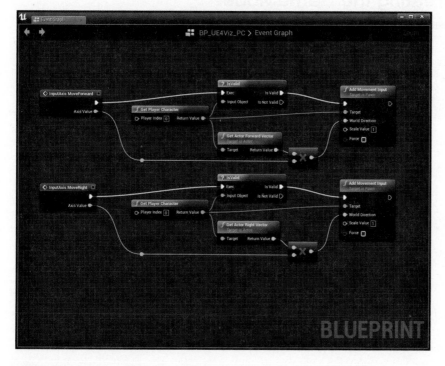

Figure 9.15 Completed movement input script

> **note**
>
> You can copy and paste nodes in the Blueprint Editor using standard keyboard shortcuts as well as the context menu when you right-click on selected nodes in the Graph Editor. This can be a big time saver when setting up similar code blocks.
>
> However, if you find yourself copying and pasting the exact same code over and over, consider creating a reusable Function instead.

Congratulations. That's all you need to do to get your Player's input to rotate the PC and move the Player's Pawn. Now you need to get the game world to use your Classes when you click Play, and you'll be ready to go.

GameMode

The **GameMode** Class is where the Engine looks when loading a Level to determine what Player Controller, Pawn, and other supporting Classes to spawn.

Creating the GameMode

Create a new GameMode Asset by following these steps:

1. Click the Add New button in the Content Browser and select Blueprint Class.
2. Select the **Game Mode Base** Class and name your Asset **BP_UE4Viz_Interior_Game**. Press Enter to create the Asset.
3. Open your newly created GameMode Asset by double-clicking it in the Content Browser. You'll see a list of Classes that you can define for this GameMode. In this case, assign the Pawn and Player Controllers you have created (see Figure 9.16).
4. Close the Blueprint Editor and save your progress by choosing **File > Save All**.

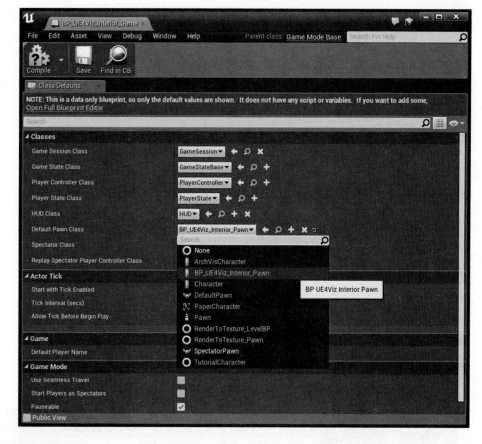

Figure 9.16 Assigning the Pawn and Player Controller to the GameMode Class

Assigning the GameMode to the Project

You have two ways to define what GameMode Class is used in a UE4 Level: as a project-wide default using the Project Settings dialog or through a per-Level override. Because you want your new GameMode to run on any Level you create in this project, set it up as a project default.

Open the Project Settings dialog by choosing **Edit** > **Project Settings** (see Figure 9.17). The Edit menu is available from almost all Editor windows.

Figure 9.17 Navigating to the Project Settings dialog

Select Maps and Modes under the Project heading. In the Default Modes section, select the
newly made BP_UE4Viz_Game Class (see Figure 9.18).

Figure 9.18 Assigning the BP_UE4Viz_Game Class to the project defaults

Placing the Player Start Actor

If there's one thing that's easily forgotten and essential, it's the Player Start Actor.

Without the Player Start Actor, the game will not know where to spawn your Pawn class when loaded as standalone or a packaged build. When you're in-Editor and use PIE without a Player Start, your Pawn will spawn at the default current camera position in the active Viewport. This can make it easy to forget to place the Player Start because your Level will seem to work when it's really not set up correctly.

To place the Player Start Actor, drag it from the Class Browser in the Place Mode panel (press Shift+1), as shown in Figure 9.19. The blue arrow (the 3D arrow that is part of the Player Start Actor, not the yellow arrow) signifies what direction the Player will face when spawned.

Figure 9.19 Placing the Player Start Actor and rotating it to face the scene

You should now be able to click the Play button and be spawned into the game as your customized Character Pawn. Right away, you should notice that you are locked to the ground using physics and cannot pass through the walls.

When you are done walking around and want to return to the Editor, you can simply press Esc on your keyboard to exit the session.

Be sure to save any progress you have made.

Summary

Congratulations. You've created a custom UE4 GameMode complete with a Player Controller and Pawn and custom Input Mappings and have set up the project to use your new Classes as the project default.

These Classes will act as the base for adding new functionality and further customizing UE4 to fit your project's needs.

CHAPTER 10

PACKAGING AND DISTRIBUTION

Now that you have a Level and the associated Pawn, Player Controller, and Game Modes to walk around it with, it's time to prepare it to run as a standalone application. This is referred to broadly as **packaging**. After it is packaged, you will be able to share your application like any other installable application. This chapter walks you through the process of packaging the application.

Packaged Versus Editor Builds

When you run your application using the Play In Editor button, you're actually just running another window in the Editor, not a standalone application. The Editor uses the Assets and maps from your Content folder and what's been loaded into RAM already to populate the world, and the Editor code runs the simulation. This makes it very fast to launch, test, and iterate, but it requires the entire UE4 Editor to be installed.

This is obviously not how you want to hand an application over to your clients or the public.

To create a standalone application for the platform you are developing for that can be distributed easily, your content must be **packaged**. Packaging processes your content and creates a standalone application that is easy to distribute like any other game or app.

You can also choose to test your application in Standalone Mode by selecting that option from the Play in Editor option menu in the toolbar. This will launch the currently loaded level in a separate process that is more similar to a packaged build but is not. It's important to build and test your applications—bugs and inconsistencies can appear between editor and packaged builds.

Project Packaging

In broad terms, packaging takes your content and game code, optimizes it, and creates an executable application for the platform you've selected.

Packaged builds attempt to load as little as possible into RAM. This is to ensure maximum performance and compatibility. However, it can introduce issues, especially with Level streaming and loading Assets at runtime. For simple projects this isn't an issue, but larger projects should test using a packaged build regularly to avoid this issue.

Content Cooking

Cooking also goes through the process of compiling all your shaders, compressing all your Texture maps, and fixing up any redirectors in the project. This avoids your Players' needing to wait for the application to load while it does this.

This can take some time and is very CPU and RAM intensive. Cook your project on a beefy machine. The more Assets, Materials, and Textures your project has, the longer this will take.

Cooking then takes all the Assets and Classes that have been processed and copies them to a **.pak** file. This **.pak** file is designed to be read very quickly by even the slowest of drives allowing your application to load quickly.

Deployment

Packaging takes the cooked content and pairs it with the binary Engine files and places them together into a single folder for distribution. This final step creates a standalone application that can be launched without the Editor being installed.

Packaging Options

UE4 can generate packaged projects for a ton of platforms and systems (iOS, Windows, Mac, and so on). With that flexibility comes some options.

Platforms

The target platform is the hardware/software combination you are trying to create a project executable for.

You can package your project for a myriad of platforms supported by UE4. From mobile devices to Windows and Mac and Linux to consoles, UE4 can package your project for nearly all the most popular devices and operating systems.

Each will have its own optimizations, input methods, and other limitations that you must consider. This book focuses only on desktop platforms (Mac and Windows).

Build Configuration

The other major decision you must make is the build configuration. The two main options are Shipping and Development.

The biggest difference between Shipping and Development builds is access to debugging tools, logging, and the command prompt. Development builds allow these whereas Shipping builds have these features stripped out.

I generally use Development unless I plan to distribute the package to the public as a wide release. The console commands, logging, and debug info are useful if I need to debug any issues.

Shipping builds are great when you want to distribute your application to the public and you do not want them to have access to the Console.

How to Package

You can package your project most easily through the Editor. Simply select Package Project from the File menu. This menu presents a few options and provides quick access to more detailed options in the Project Settings dialog (see Figure 10.1).

Figure 10.1 Packaging menu in UE4 Editor

Upon selecting your desired platform, you are prompted for a location to save your packaged project. Don't put the packaged project into your project folder—it can lead to confusion.

Packaging takes some time. A small notice appears letting you know that packaging is underway (see Figure 10.2). This process is fully threaded so you can continue to work on your project while it processes your content in the background.

Figure 10.2 Packaging notice UE4 Editor

Launching Your Application

After packaging completes, the Editor alerts you (see Figure 10.3).

Figure 10.3 Completed packaging notice in the Editor

Proceed to the directory you defined earlier and look for a folder called WindowsNoEditor (this might be different on another platform). You can rename this folder.

Inside the folder, you will find an executable file and some folders containing all your data and Classes along with a lightweight, binary version of the engine (see Figure 10.4).

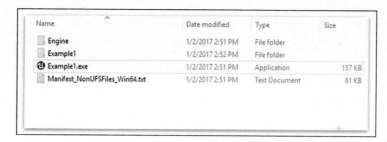

Figure 10.4 Packaged project in Windows Explorer

You can launch your application simply by double-clicking the executable file. Your application should launch, load the Level you built, and spawn the proper Player Controller and Pawn giving you mouse access.

Packaging Errors

Sometimes, packaging encounters an error. A simple Blueprint compiling error or running out of disk space can halt the entire Packaging process.

When this happens, you should turn to the **Output Log** window, which can offer helpful information in most cases.

To access the Output Log window, in the Editor, go to Window > Developer Tools > Output Log (see Figure 10.5). I generally dock this window with my Content Browser for easy access.

Figure 10.5 The Output log

Distributing the Project

You can now copy, zip, and send this folder to whomever you like. It's really that simple (mostly).

Of course, you still have platform issues and hardware compatibility, but that's par for the course for any application.

Some computers that try to run your application might be missing some system components that UE4 requires. These are referred to as **Prerequisites**. By default, these files are included in your packaged project. If your packaged UE4 project detects that they are not installed, it will prompt the user to install them when they try to run the executable.

Other than the prerequisites, a packaged UE4 application does not require any sort of formal installation process; it can be run from any location.

Using Installers

UE4 does not have any installer packager built in. Developing or using an installer for your application and for the platform you are developing for is up to you. However, because UE4 doesn't require a formal installation, providing the project files in a zip file with simple instructions is usually adequate.

Of course, if you want to set up desktop shortcuts, register for uninstalling, and all the other things a full installer does, you'll need to develop an installer.

Although these tasks are outside the scope of this text, they are fairly straightforward to accomplish using one of the many free and commercial installer authoring applications.

Summary

Now that you've built your first application from the ground up in UE4, you should feel accomplished. Congratulations!

The following chapters explore a more traditional-style visualization by looking at the data pipeline and some of the most important systems for visualizations: Lightmass, Sequencer, and Blueprints in specific.

ARCHITECTURAL VISUALIZATION PROJECT

CHAPTER 11

PROJECT SETUP

Now that you have a firm understanding of how to use UE4 to create a simple scene, you can dive into a real-life example. Interior visualizations are important to architects, marketing, designers, and potential buyers, and they are one of the most common types of visualizations being made in UE4. In this part of the book you will gain knowledge and explore using Lightmass to generate high-quality global illumination (GI) lighting, building and rendering a cinematic walkthrough using Sequencer. You then dive into learning how to use Blueprints to create dynamic interactions.

Project Scope and Requirements

In this example, imagine you have been provided a 3D model of an architectural interior (see Figure 11.1) and have agreed to produce an interactive visualization that allows the Player to freely explore the space from a first-person walking perspective. The Player should be able to modify specific materials using a simple, mouse-driven user interface. The client has also requested an architectural animation to be developed using Sequencer and recorded to video for offline playback and editing.

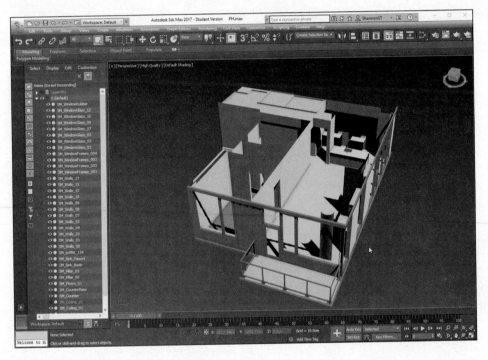

Figure 11.1 Provided 3D model in 3D Studio Max

The first step is to prepare the 3D model for import to UE4, including proper materials, UV coordinates, and Lightmap coordinates and focusing on making clean geometry that imports in-place and is easy to update and iterate on. I'll also show you how to harness UE4's automatic Lightmap coordinate generation to save time and improve the quality of your scenes.

After importing the model to UE4, it's time to begin the iterative process of applying Materials and placing lights, reflection probes, lighting portals, and post-process volumes to get great-looking results quickly.

After the scene is satisfactory, the next step is to create the animated walkthrough using Sequencer. You'll learn how to create compelling animations easily and how to get them to play and stop using Player input.

Next comes merging the Pawn developed in the Chapter 9 into the new project, and setting up the scene to allow the Player to walk through the scene by enabling collision and setting up the proper Actors and world settings.

The final step is to create Material and Geometry-switching systems that use Blueprints and UMG to add the final layer of polish and make the application ready to be packaged and delivered to the client.

> ### note
>
> Don't forget—you can download this project and all the associated source files from www.TomShannon3D.com/UnrealForViz and follow along.

Here are the requirements for this project:

- Develop an interior architectural visualization application using client-provided 3D models.
- Use Lightmass to create high-quality GI lighting and aim for photorealism.
- Create pre-defined architectural animation using Sequencer using multiple camera angles and transitions.
- Merge the Pawn from Chapter 9 and prepare the scene to allow the Player to move about the space.
- Develop a UMG- based UI that allows the Player to switch to different versions of the scene.
- Develop a mouse-driven, Material-switching Blueprint.
- Package the project for delivery.

Setting Up the Project

This section covers creating a blank project from the Epic Launcher and migrating the Player Controller, Game Mode, and Pawn to the new project along with the needed configuration files.

This migration lets you build upon the systems you built in Chapter 9 and focus on preparing your source 3D and 2D data for UE4.

Creating the Project

Using the **Epic Launcher**, start the version of the Engine you want to use and select the **New Project** tab when the **Project Browser** appears.

This time, you won't be including the Starter Content, so uncheck that option, but do leave the **Target Hardware** settings at Maximum Quality.

The project is named Example2. Put it next to the previous project, Example1.

> **note**
>
> The only way to open the Editor is by opening a project. You can also create a new project from within the Editor by choosing **File > New Project**.

Migrating from Another Project

You will often want to take the Assets, Blueprints, and other work you've done in previous projects and copy them over to new projects.

UE4 relies on the concept of Assets referencing other Assets. For example, Materials might reference several Textures. Each Material, in turn, will be referenced by Meshes it's applied to, and even Material Instances that are derived from it.

Because of this, you must be careful when manually copying content between projects so that they retain these references and the correct folder structure; otherwise, the references will not be maintained, potentially causing loading errors, bugs, or even crashes in your target project.

The most reliable way of copying content from one project to another is to use the Editor's **Content Migration** feature. Migration ensures that all Assets referenced by the Assets you want to copy are copied over into the target project.

To migrate your content from one project to another, open the source project (the project with the files you want to copy) in the Editor. In this case, that would be the Example1 project.

After it's open, select the Assets you want to copy in the Content Browser. You can select single Assets, Levels, or entire folders. In this case, select the **Pawn**, **PC**, and **Game Mode** Assets (see Figure 11.2). Right-click and select **Asset Actions > Migrate**.

A summary opens of the files that will be copied over to the new project. Review it and make sure you have everything you need—and nothing you're not expecting (see Figure 11.3).

Figure 11.2 Migrating Assets from the Example1 project

Figure 11.3 List of files to be migrated

Upon confirming the summary, a screen appears asking you for the new **Content** directory within the new project. Navigate to the new project's **Content** folder and click OK (see Figure 11.4).

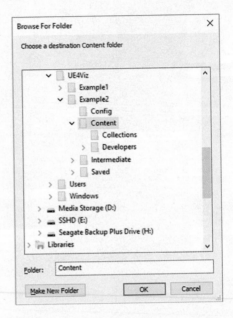

Figure 11.4 Targeting the Content directory in the new, Example2 project

UE4 copies the files over and reports on the success. You should immediately see the copied content in the Content directory of the new project.

Don't Forget the Input

A good deal of work went into the input settings of the first project, and getting those into a new project is easy to do. In fact, the PC and Pawn would fail to compile at this point because they reference the input bindings created for Example1.

These settings are stored in the Project's Config folder. These files are not governed by the Content Browser and are not copied over when you use the Content Migration tool, so you must move them manually.

To do so, locate the DefaultInput.ini file in the source project's Config directory (Example1 \Config\) and copy it to the target project's Config directory (Example2\Config\).

Copying, Renaming, and Moving Assets

Upon opening the Example2 project, notice an Example1 folder containing the Pawn, PC, and Game Mode.

You want to move these to a new folder that is project-independent and easy to find, and now is a good time to get rid of that Example1 folder in the Content Browser. You're on Example2 now!

Always perform moving, copying, renaming, or any other file operations within the Content folder using the Content Browser. This ensures that references to moved or renamed assets are maintained. If required, a **redirector** is created. These are small 1-2kb files that act as a pointer to the correct location of the asset.

Follow these steps:

1. Create a new folder in your Content directory called **UE4Viz** and within that folder another called **Blueprints**. I've chosen this folder to contain reusable code that I might bring from project to project without my needing to rename or copy anything.

2. Drag the Pawn, PC, and Game Mode Assets onto the Blueprints folder you just created. UE4 asks whether you want to move or copy the Assets. Select Move.

3. Right-Click on the Example1 folder and select **Fix Up Redirectors in Folder**.

4. Delete the old Content1 Folder by right-clicking on it from the Content Browser and selecting Delete.

5. Select **Save All** from the Content Browser's toolbar to ensure all your changes are saved to disk.

Applying Project Settings

A few rendering options can help optimize the Engine for use in architecture visualizations. These scenes are typically much less intense than a video game scene, which lets you pump up some of the settings and still maintain a stable frame rate.

Open the Project Settings dialog from the Edit menu and navigate to the Rendering button in the left column (see Figure 11.5). Modify the settings as shown in the figure and described in the following list.

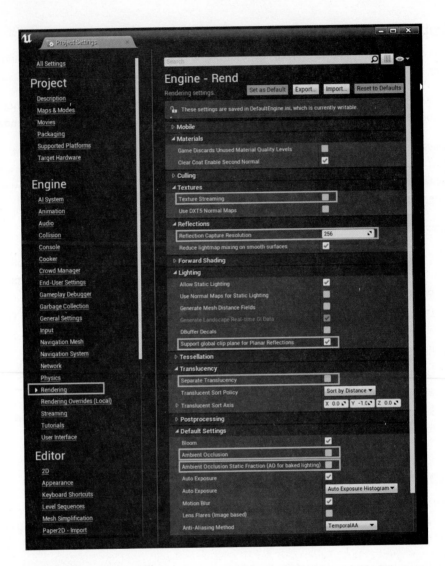

Figure 11.5 Project rendering settings

- **Disable Texture Streaming:** This setting is designed to enable large game worlds in constrained memory on consoles and older PC hardware. It can cause lightmapping errors when you use Architectural Meshes and high-resolution Lightmaps. Disabling Texture Streaming forces all the textures used in the Level to be loaded into RAM at once. Use this setting with some level of caution. Texture streaming is an important optimization for complex scenes, and disabling it can cause performance issues.

- **Set Reflection Capture Resolution:** To get the highest quality reflections, you can increase the resolution of the Reflection Capture Actors you place in your scenes.

Be careful turning this up too far: It can eat up a lot of memory if you have a lot of high-resolution reflection captures. I don't recommend going past 512 for this setting unless you have only one or two reflection captures in each of your Levels.

- **Turn on Support Global Clip Plane for Planar Reflections:** Mirrors and reflections are a staple of visualizations, and UE4 has support for mirror-style Planar Reflections. This is a *very* expensive setting, and you should enable it only if you absolutely need it. Even when reflections aren't being rendered on-screen, they have a significant impact on rendering performance project-wide.

  You can mitigate this impact using the Details Panel to disable a lot of heavier features like some of the Post-process settings such as Screen-space Ambient Occlusion and Reflections. You can even limit the Actors that are visible or the distance the reflected scene will render.

- **Turn off Separate Translucency:** Separate Translucency is a performance enhancement for games with lots of Alpha transparency effects such as sparks and explosions. These effects can be very expensive to apply effects like Depth of Field to, so these effects are rendered separately and ignored by the post-process pipeline. You don't want or need that because you want your translucent surfaces to behave as realistically as possible.

  This setting has no effect on Masked-type materials so things like vegetation will not typically be affected.

- **Turn off Ambient Occlusion and Ambient Occlusion Static Fraction:** These options refer to the Screen-space Ambient Occlusion (SSAO) post-process effect. SSAO is a great way to add detail to dynamically lit scenes and objects. Because your scene is almost entirely static and you are using high-quality Lightmass settings, you can disable this setting for a significant performance boost, especially at higher resolutions.

  These settings only affect the SSAO effect and does not affect AO calculated by Lightmass. Static Fraction controls how much the SSAO effect blends with baked Lightmaps and also has a performance overhead that can be alleviated by turning off the effect.

Project settings are written automatically to the project's DefaultEngine.ini file and there's no need to save before closing the Preferences window. However, because we changed settings such as Planar Reflections, you will need to restart the Editor so that these settings can be initialized. Upon reopening the Editor, you might experience a recompile of the shaders that can take a while, but should happen only once.

Summary

Your project is now ready to roll. Enabling some of UE4's advanced rendering features and turning off some unneeded ones improves image quality and avoids issues with Texture streaming, SSAO, and translucent materials.

You've also learned how to use UE4's Content Migration feature to move your work from one project to another, ensuring you don't have to reinvent the wheel for each project. Input settings have also been copied over using .ini files.

You're now ready to start learning how to light your world, apply Materials, and use Blueprints and Unreal Motion Graphics (UMG) to allow the Player to make interactive changes.

CHAPTER 12

DATA PIPELINE

Getting accurate architectural data into UE4 can
seem challenging and at odds with your workflows
at first glance. But with a couple of strategies,
workflows and under-the-hood understanding,
you'll be able to get any type of data into UE4 easily.
You'll be importing massive datasets into UE4
without breaking a sweat in no time.

Organizing the Scene

For this project, you will be spending a good deal of time outside UE4, inside your DCC applications creating 3D models and Textures to be imported into UE4.

The scenario: The data provided by your client is of good quality. It can be used almost "out-of-the-box," but you still want to take the time to prepare the content so it comes into UE4 as effortlessly and reliably as possible.

Begin by organizing the scene in your 3D application. CAD and engineering apps often don't generate the most elegantly named or organized scenes. Often, specific logic is used to name Objects, which are difficult to read or not compatible with UE4 or the FBX pipeline. Names that are long or contain complex characters can cause issues with the FBX exporter and UE4.

Determining the best organization for your particular content and adapting your tools and processes to the needs of the FBX pipeline is up to you.

In this case, you can use a simple renaming script to simplify the names of the Objects in the scene, and conform them to the accepted UE4 naming scheme of putting an SM_ prefix before Static Meshes (see Figure 12.1).

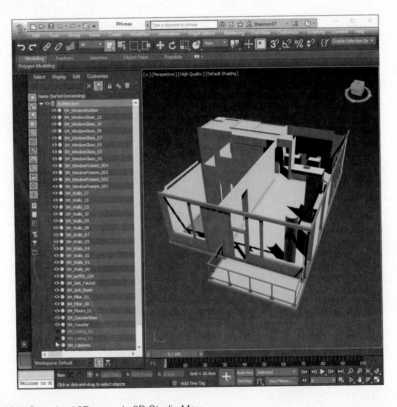

Figure 12.1 Organized 3D scene in 3D Studio Max

Doing this now is fast and easy compared to trying to rename everything once exported; or in UE4 where renaming is much more involved.

You may also want to sort your scene into layers based on the type of model, the most common types being Props and Architecture. This makes it easy to select layers for export or to control Object visibility in the scene.

Materials

Although UE4 doesn't support full Material import/export from 3D applications, it does support importing basic Material features such as color and simple Texture Maps. Importing even basic Materials saves a lot of time initially setting up your scene.

UE4 also supports assigning your Material's attributes to specific Parameters in a specified parent Material. Instead of creating a Material Asset for each Material imported, a Material Instance Asset is created and its parameters are set up. This is a great workflow for advanced users, and I encourage you to return to it as you look to increase efficiency in your workflows.

Note that UE4 only supports application-standard Materials. Materials from custom renderers, like V-Ray, might not come in at all or might come in poorly.

In this case, the source model used Autodesk Architectural Materials, which do not adhere to the texture formats and inputs supported by UE4. I used a simple script that replaced each one with a standard 3D Studio Max Material of the same name, discarding all other parameters and assigning simple bitmaps to the Diffuse inputs when possible.

Multi-subobject (MSO) Materials are also supported by UE4, but the Mesh needs both the Material ID assigned to the faces and an MSO Material with a unique Material assigned to each ID. For example, a Mesh with four Material IDs with only a single Material assigned in Max would import as a Mesh with only a single Material ID.

You should also take the time to rename your Materials and Textures to conform to your naming convention. Again, this is far easier in your 3D application than it is in UE4.

Architecture and Fixtures

First you want to get the main Architectural Meshes—the walls, floors, ceilings, fixtures, and appliances—imported into UE4 and placed into our scene. These Meshes are unique and do not need to move. It's also important that they are placed in the exact same location as the source data.

Ensuring Clean Geometry

Clean lighting requires clean, good-fitting geometry. Flickers, blotches, and lighting errors can be frustrating to fix after a long lighting build, as you will need to rebuild lighting after your geometry is reimported.

The two biggest culprits are bad face normals (flipped faces) and coincident or stacked faces. Both cause flickering and bad lighting. Lightmass cannot correctly calculate bounced light from these faces and often returns black.

To look for flipped normals, turn off backface culling or double-sided Materials in your 3D application. Some applications also offer visualization tools to help you find flipped faces easier.

Finding coincident faces can be harder. For performance reasons, UE4 uses a 16-bit depth buffer that is more prone to flickering when faces are stacked too closely than you might be used to with a raytraced renderer. This model had many overlapping faces that needed significant cleanup. Many of the errors were not apparent until importing them into UE4 and seeing them flicker there. Be patient; you'll get them all. Ensuring you have a good iterative workflow set up makes fixing issues like this much less painful.

You also want to avoid single-sided Meshes. Light will pass through the back side and cause light leaks and other rendering errors. In this scene, I had to create the exterior walls as well as ceiling and floor volumes to ensure good lighting.

Using Good UV Coordinates

Having good UV coordinates is essential in UE4. Bad UV coordinates not only make applying Materials difficult and look poor, but can also adversely affect the rendering quality of Objects.

Base Channel (Channel 0)

Channel 0, the base UV channel, is the default channel for applying Textures to Meshes.

The model provided contains Meshes with good UV coordinates, but they are far too tiled, repeating every 1 cm (CAD data often will be mapped with real-world units like this). Although you can scale your Textures in your UE4 Materials to compensate, I prefer not to because it makes the preview Mesh difficult to read—the Texture becomes stretched at the large scale needed to compensate.

I prefer to scale my UV Coordinates to around 1 m. I do this either by applying a box UV modifier (see Figure 12.2) or, if there are already real-world scaled coordinates like the ones in this model, I use a UV map scaler modifier to scale the coordinates to a more UE4-friendly scale.

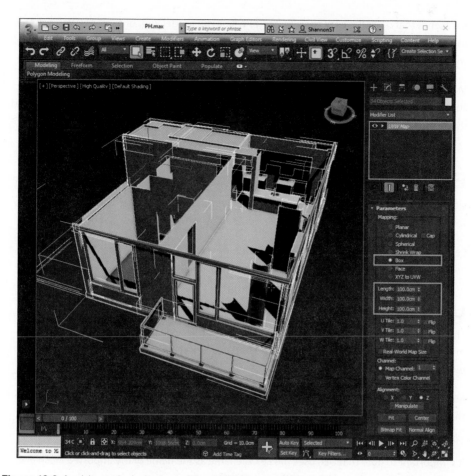

Figure 12.2 Applying a single, instanced Box UVW map modifier to all the walls, floors, and ceilings

Lightmass (Channel 1)

Lightmass requires clean, undistorted UV coordinates to be effective. You can either re-pack your coordinates in your 3D application, or rely on UE4's repacking system.

I typically lean on UE4's Automatic Lightmap Coordinate Packing system, ensuring my models have good base channel UV coordinates before export. More complex Meshes might require manually editing these coordinates more for the best results, but most Meshes work very well.

This system does not split edges, apply, or modify your UV charts in any way. It simply takes the Channel 0 UV data and repacks it.

The model provided for this chapter's example was built in Autodesk Revit and already has high-quality, tiling UV coordinates. This is fortunate and will make for an easy import, because the coordinates are compatible with the Automatic UV generator.

For scenes that don't have UV coordinates, or when you model your own scenes, you can still use the auto-packing in UE4, but you'll have to make sure your base UV coordinates are clean, without UV distortion, and have well-placed seams.

Most walls, floors, and ceilings can be mapped with a box-style mapping. Of course, non-square faces might need extra attention, but if your base Texture Maps look good, UE4 should be able to make a good Lightmap coordinate set for you.

Exporting the Scene

Now that your Meshes are prepared, it's time to get them into UE4. To do so, first you need to save them to a file format UE4 can import. For Static Meshes, the file format of choice is FBX.

Several methods are available for getting your model exported to FBX. Each has advantages and drawbacks and each might work better for your situation or scene.

Using Multiple FBX Files

The option I prefer is to export Objects in the scene to individual FBX files. Doing so allows me the most control over my data and I can update, export, and reimport my data easily and reliably.

Most 3D applications do not support batch exporting FBX files, forcing you to tediously export them one by one. Because of this, I developed a Max script that allows me to quickly do so (see Figure 12.3). You can grab this script at www.TomShannon3D.com/UnrealForViz.

It's important to note that UE4 uses the FBX filename as the name of the imported Mesh and ignores the name assigned in your 3D application.

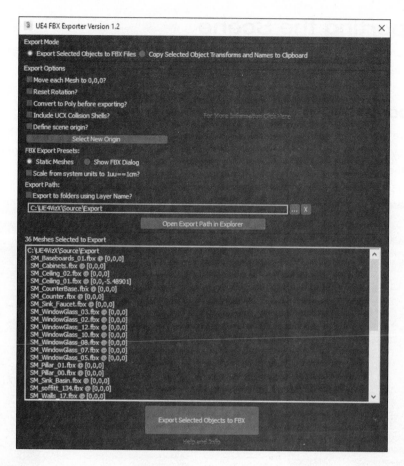

Figure 12.3 Max script used to batch export FBX files for UE4; for more info go to www.TomShannon3D.com/UnrealForViz

Using a Single FBX File

You can also choose to export all your geometry in a single FBX file. UE4 can import single FBX files with multiple Objects in them in several ways. Options range from as a single, monolithic Static Mesh to importing each Object as a Static Mesh in the file individually using the Content Browser. UE4 also offers an **Import to Level** feature in the File menu that can automate importing complex, hierarchical models complete with cameras, lights, and animation.

These options are very easy to use and a great way to quickly get large datasets into UE4.

The biggest drawback I've encountered with these methods is difficulty with updating specific Meshes or sets of Meshes from within the FBX file. UE4 expects the structure of the FBX file to remain the same between reimports, so it's easy for reimporting Static Meshes to cause errors unless you are very careful with your exports and maintain a strict set of exported Objects for each FBX file.

Importing the Scene

Based on how you exported your data and how you want to manage it in your own scene, you have a few options when you import your content into UE4.

Importing into the Content Browser

If you've exported your content as individual FBX files, you can import them one by one, or in a batch by either dragging and dropping your FBX files from your system's file (see Figure 12.4) or using the **Import** button in the Content Browser.

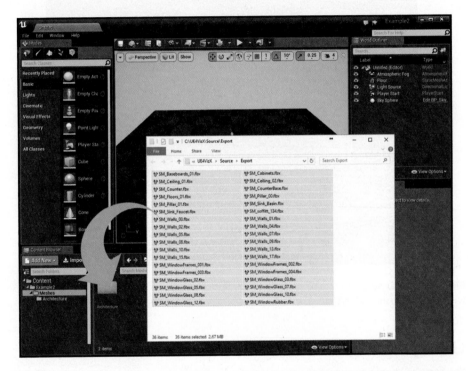

Figure 12.4 Importing multiple FBX files by dragging and dropping from Windows Explorer into the Content Browser

If you've exported your content as a single FBX file with many Mesh files, you can import these files into the Content Browser as a single, combined Static Mesh Asset, or as individual Meshes by selecting **Combine Meshes** in the FBX Import Options dialog that appears when you import FBX files (see Figure 12.5).

As you can see in Figure 12.5, this dialog offers many options, most of which you can leave at their default settings, with a few notable exceptions.

Auto Generate Collision

The Auto Generate Collision option creates a very simplified collision box around your Mesh and isn't typically suitable for visualization data. Because this scene is simple, you can rely on per-polygon collision. This is more expensive than using a low-polygon collision primitive, and can cause performance issues in more complex scenes. For this project, you should set this to **false**.

Generate Lightmap UVs

You have ensured your Meshes have good, clean UV coordinates, so the Automatic Lightmap Generation system should produce good results. Set Generate Lightmap UVs to **true**.

Transform Vertex to Absolute

Transform Vertex to Absolute allows you to decide whether UE4 is using the pivot point as authored in your 3D application or if it will be set to 0,0,0. For your Architecture Meshes set this option to **true**.

Import Materials and Import Textures

Set these to **true** to import the applied Materials and Textures along with your model.

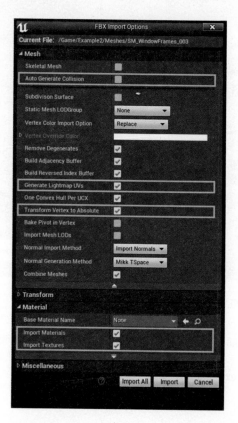

Figure 12.5 The FBX Import Options dialog. Auto Generate Collision is disabled while Generate Lightmap UVs is enabled as is the Material and Texture import options

Importing into the Level

Another option is the new **Import into Level** feature. This allows you to import the contents of an FBX file, including the linked hierarchies, animation, and lights and cameras.

In UE4 go to **File > Import into Level** and select your FBX file (see Figure 12.6). Select a folder to import to (see Figure 12.7).

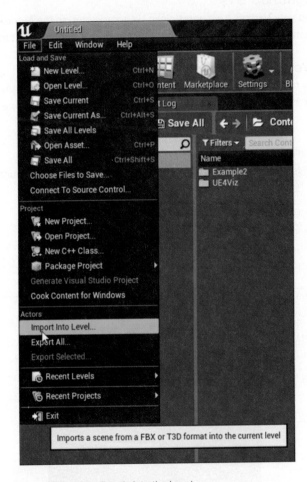

Figure 12.6 Importing an FBX scene directly into the Level

The import/reimport dialog appears (see Figure 12.8), letting you preview the Meshes and Materials that will be imported. This is a good time to take a quick look and make sure you're importing what you're expecting.

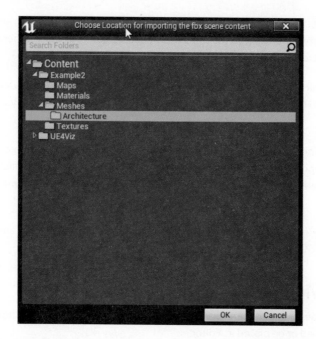

Figure 12.7 Selecting a target folder

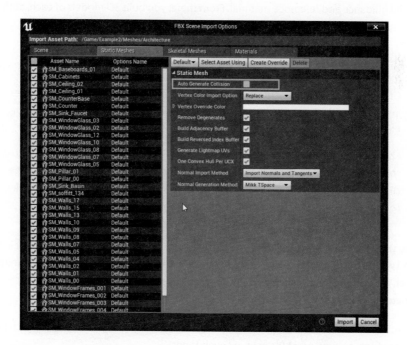

Figure 12.8 FBX Scene Import Options dialog

Be sure to turn off **Auto Generate Collision** because it's not compatible with architecture visualization—style Meshes. You will use per-poly collision on your walls, rather than relying on proxy collision Objects.

The importer will import each Mesh as a single **.uasset** file along with any Materials and Textures applied to those Materials. You can also define a different folder for your Materials to import to.

A single Blueprint Actor is created and placed into the loaded scene with references to each Mesh. This Blueprint works in conjunction with an FBX Import Data Asset to allow you to reimport the FBX file, and it will add, delete, and modify Meshes and Materials to match the FBX file on reimport.

After importing, remember to save your work because the imported Meshes are not saved to disk until you explicitly save them.

Prop Meshes

The chairs, glasses, and plates are all what I consider **props**: Meshes that are duplicated and/or need to be moved or be placed in-Editor.

The model provided by the client in this chapter's example lacked any furniture, but you were provided guidance and reference material. From there, you built 3D models of each, authored for UE4 specifically or found Meshes in your content library that you could import.

> ### note
>
> Often, you are given datasets with Props in specific locations. These can number in the hundreds. An example might be streetlights in a masterplan or vegetation Meshes in a landscape plan.
>
> This scenario is common for visualization that does not have an obvious workflow solution in UE4. I have written a 3DS Max Script that copies Mesh locations to the clipboard for copying and pasting into UE4. You can download it from this book's companion website at www.TomShannon3D.com/UnrealForViz.

Placing your Props in UE4, rather than your 3D application, is best. FBX doesn't respect instancing and will treat each plate, glass, and chair as a unique Object, importing each as a unique **.uAsset**, each taking up memory, disk space, and processing power. It also means that you have to update every instance of the Object if there's anything you need to modify.

When you have a lot of repeating Objects in the scene, having a single **.uAsset** file with many references to that single Asset file in your Levels is best.

Also, as discussed next, by authoring good pivot points, you can make modifying, moving, and even animating your Meshes much easier than placing them explicitly.

Setting Pivot Points

You must author Props differently than Architecture Meshes, with the biggest difference being the pivot point. Although Architecture Meshes are exported and imported in-place, with their pivot points all set to 0,0,0 upon import, Prop Meshes need to be imported with a well-authored pivot point.

Pivot points cannot be edited in UE4 directly, so setting up your pivot points in your 3D application is essential.

Place your pivot point where you want your Mesh to attach to the world. Getting this right can save a huge amount of effort when it comes to placing, moving, and even animating your Meshes in UE4.

Having a pivot point in the center of an Object is typically not the best place. The pivot is where the Actor will scale, rotate, and move from in UE4. It's also where it will snap to other Actors' surfaces as you place it into the Level. For chairs and other furniture, this means you should place the pivot at the height where the furniture hits the ground. You should set a framed picture back where it would attach to the wall.

UE4 refers to rotations as a combination of Roll, Pitch, and Yaw axes. Roll is left and right rotation around the X axis and Pitch is up and down around the Y axis; Yaw rotates the Actor around in Z (see Figure 12.9).

This means you should model Actors in your 3D application facing toward positive X, just like they appear in UE4. UE4 will manage the translation of the Y axis.

Figure 12.9 Object pivot point in UE4, where red is Roll or X, green is Pitch or Y, and blue is Yaw or Z rotation

Using Mindful Geometry

The Props provided by the client are great starting points, but for visualization, most of them don't look good enough to be used for a high-end visualization.

I have used the models provided along with guidance from the client as reference and remodeled most of the furniture. You can see that most of the models are very simply modeled. Although modern video games utilize a very labor-intensive artist workflow for meshes, characters and environments, visualization projects typically don't have the time, budget, or need for that level of attention to be spent on each Asset.

I have focused on making the geometry clean, well UV mapped, and fairly low polygon. UE4 and modern hardware can push millions of triangles per second, and most visualization scenes are relatively sparse when compared with video game environments. This lets you use more polygons to define your Meshes, but being mindful and optimizing as much as possible is still important.

Exporting

Although you can export a single **.FBX** with all of your Props in a single file, I don't recommend it. It's inefficient and it can make your workflow more difficult, as you need to re-export *all* the exact same Meshes to the FBX file if you need to make changes to a single Mesh.

Use the following settings or similar settings in your 3D application's exporter (see Figure 12.10):

- Ensure you are exporting the Smoothing Groups, Tangents, and Binormals and that Triangulate and Preserve Edge Orientation are true.

- If you are working in a scene that is not scaled to centimeters, you can also scale your data using the exporter's unit scaling system. To do so, set the **Automatic** switch to **false** and set the **Scene unites converted to** option to **Centimeters**.

You should export each Prop as a single FBX file, naming each FBX file what you want the imported Static Mesh Asset to be named. UE4 uses the filename to set the Mesh name.

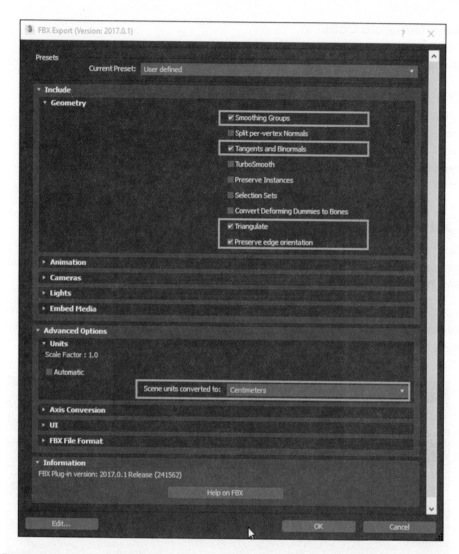

Figure 12.10 3D Studio Max FBX Export dialog showing the settings that will ensure your model can be imported into UE4 with all the smoothing groups, UV coordinates, and proper edge orientation to ensure your Assets appear in UE4 exactly like they did in your 3D application

Importing

Just like with your Architecture Meshes, import your props using the **Import** button in the Content Browser or by dragging and dropping your files into the Content Browser. You can import all your files at once or one by one.

As before, the UE4 Import Dialog for Static Meshes appears. Use the settings shown earlier in Figure 12.5 with the following considerations.

Auto Generate Collision

I don't recommend using auto-generated collision. I typically don't use collision on my Prop Meshes for architectural visualizations because it often limits the Player's movement too much.

Transform Vertex to Absolute

Setting Transform Vertex to Absolute to **false** lets UE4 use the authored pivot point in your model rather than using the scene's 0,0,0 and baking the rotation and other transforms into the Mesh's vertexes. If you have not moved your props to 0,0,0 in your 3D application before exporting, you will want to set this to **false**.

Summary

Getting data and content into UE4 can seem intimidating at first, but preparing and organizing your content and ensuring the right import and export settings for it make the process smooth and predictable.

You should now have a good understanding of the differences between Prop and Architecture Objects and how to get them into UE4 reliably (see Figure 12.11). You are now ready to place these Assets and begin building an interactive world.

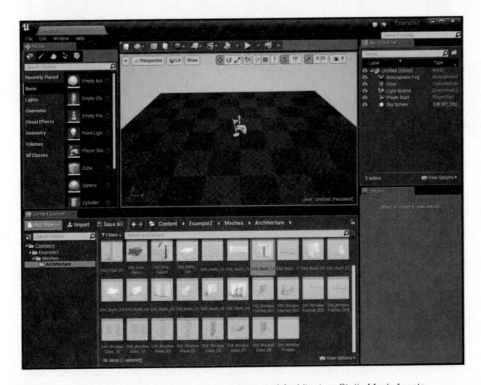

Figure 12.11 The Content Browser showing your imported Architecture Static Mesh Assets

CHAPTER 13

POPULATING THE SCENE

Populating scenes in UE4 can be a challenge for visualizations. Designers are often tasked with representing data or designs that require precision and accuracy. In this chapter, I show you how to get your Prop and Architecture Static Mesh Assets into your scene exactly where you want.

Scene Building for Visualization

UE4 offers a powerful suite of tools for Level Designers (LDs) and artists to build fantastic games and visualizations quickly. Artists can drag assets, lights, and other assets into the world using the Content Browser; move, scale, and rotate them easily using the transform gizmos; and modify properties easily using the Details Panel.

Scene building for visualization can be a challenge as you often need to represent your data very accurately, prioritizing precision over creative license.

For Architectural Visualizations, you often must balance the need for precision with the artistic freedom to create beautiful, compelling spaces.

You must exactly place your Architecture Meshes within your Level. There is no artistic license to be had here because it's the data you've been given to visualize.

However, your Props must be hand placed into the Level, moved, rotated, and scaled freely, populating it with life and interest.

In this chapter, I demonstrate how I set up my Levels and how I populate them with my Architecture and Props. I show the Viewport tools and shortcuts I use the most and to end up with a scene ready to apply Lighting and Materials to.

Setting Up the Level

Before you build a Level, you need a Level to build in. By default, UE4 provides a simple Level with clouds, lights, and a Player Start atop a simple Box Static Mesh Actor.

I prefer to start fresh with a brand-new Level, avoiding any issues that might arise from using a preset.

Creating a New Level

To start with a blank slate for a new project choose **File > New Level** in the Editor (see Figure 13.1).

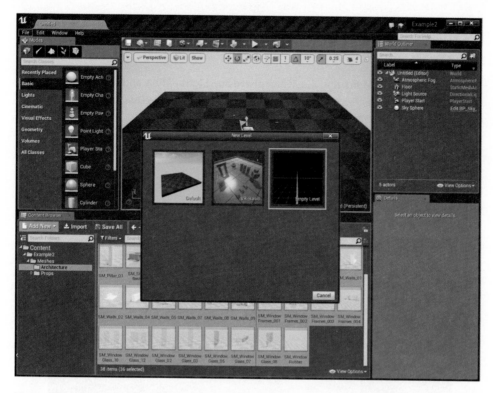

Figure 13.1 Creating a new, empty Level; the default Level is visible in the Viewport

This creates a new, completely blank Level. Save your Level by choosing **File > Save Current As.**

Adding Basic Lighting

Like in the first project, the first task is to put in some simple lights before placing any Meshes. Without lights, UE4 either renders the scene black or renders it in its Unlit View Mode, making it difficult to see what you're doing. Getting some basic lights in first makes things much easier to see and work with.

Atmospheric Fog

From the **Modes** panel, select **Visual Effects** and drag an **Atmospheric Fog** into the Viewport. This provides a horizon, atmospheric scattering (blue sky) and a sun disc that makes for a good, simple sky.

Directional Light

Select **Lights** from the **Modes** panel and drag a **Directional Light** into the Viewport. This will act as your sun.

Select the **Directional Light**, find the **Atmosphere Sun Light** option, and set it to **true** (you might have to look under the Advanced Options rollout). This lets the Directional Light control the Atmospheric Fog Actor's colors and sun disk position.

Sky Light

Drag a Sky Light into the scene. This samples the environment around it and uses that information to provide indirect lighting to the scene. You should now have a basic lighting setup (see Figure 13.2).

Figure 13.2 Basic lighting setup showing the **Directional Light** selected and **Atmosphere Sun Light** set to **true** in the Details Panel, allowing it to set the position of the sun in the sky

Placing Architecture Static Meshes

By preparing your Architecture Assets to use the origin of the FBX scene as the pivot point (0,0,0), placing them into your Level in the exact location you exported them is easy.

Dragging and Dropping Meshes

Drag and drop your Meshes into the Viewport from the Content Browser. You can select one or many Static Mesh Assets using common keyboard shortcuts (Shift-click, Ctrl/Cmd-click, and so on) and drag them anywhere into the Viewport (see Figure 13.3).

Figure 13.3 The results of the drag-and-drop operation, and then setting the Location property of the placed meshes to 0,0,0

Setting the Location to Zero

When you drag these Meshes into the Level, the Static Mesh Actors created are selected in the Level and World Outliner. If you look in the Details Panel, you will see that you can edit the properties of all the Meshes at the same time. This lets you easily set the Location to 0,0,0 (refer to Figure 13.3).

Now all your Architecture Meshes are placed exactly where they were in your 3D application.

Placing Prop Meshes

Now that the walls, floors, and other Architecture are placed, it's time to place Props.

As with most content, simply drag-and-drop Props to place them from the Content Browser into the Map to place them into your Level.

In this example, I've been given license to populate the scene with a combination of furniture and props selected by the client with some generic props from my library of models.

Surface Snapping

When you first drag and drop a Mesh into the Level, notice that it is projected into the scene and "sticks" to whatever it lands on. This is great for getting your Props into the Level, but what about after they are in there?

Enabling Surface Snapping in the Viewport toolbar locks the Actor you are moving around to the surface as you move it about (see Figure 13.4).

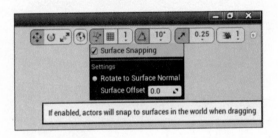

Figure 13.4 Surface Snapping dropdown

You can also turn on **Rotate to Surface Normal** so the Mesh being placed will reorient to the polygon surface on which you're placing it. This is great for placing Actors on walls because they will rotate as you drag them from wall to wall.

Cloning and Copying

Be sure to use the cloning tools such as copy-paste and the Alt-Drag method of creating copies. These methods make populating the scene very fast to do.

Shift+Dragging

If you hold down the Shift key while you move an Actor using the Transform gizmo, the view will follow that Actor. You can use this technique in combination with the Alt-Drag method—it is a great way of moving Actors around larger levels using the Perspective Viewport.

Scene Organization

Adding Meshes, lights, and other Actors to a scene soon results in hundreds of Actors in it. Organizing them is essential to a fast workflow, and UE4 offers tools to help manage your scene.

World Outliner

As you add Actors to your Level, they become listed in the **World Outliner**. This list can quickly grow unwieldly and difficult to navigate. Thankfully, you have a few options for cleaning it up.

You can easily create folders using the New Folder button (located in the upper-right corner of the World Outliner next to the search bar), but I prefer to use the right-click method. Select the Assets you want to put into a folder in the World Outliner and right-click on one of them, which opens the context menu (see Figure 13.5).

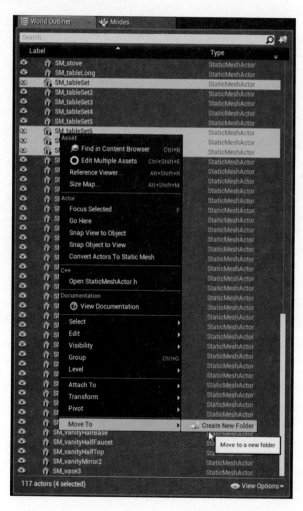

Figure 13.5 Adding Actors to a new folder in the World Outliner using the right-click menu

Here, you can add them to a new folder or to an existing one without having to search for it in the World Outliner.

Layers

A less obvious organizational method, but one likely comfortable to visualization artists, is UE4's Layer system. Like most 3D applications, UE4 features a full-fledged layer system in which you can hide, unhide, and select Actors via layer easily.

The Layers interface is not exposed by default, but you can get to it through the Window menu (see Figure 13.6).

Figure 13.6 Enabling the Layers tab; notice the Layers tab to the right with Props placed in

You can also use both the World Outliner and layers systems or neither, because they have no effect on runtime performance or features; they are simply there to help you organize your scene.

I find the Layers system to be difficult to use and easy to mess up. I much prefer to use the World Outliner's folder system to keep my scene organized.

Grouping

Grouping is a great way of making reusable or easily selectable sets of Actors in your Level.

Select the Actors you want to group, right-click, and select **Group** (see Figure 13.7). A Group Actor is created and the selected Actors are bound to it. Selecting any of the Actors or the Group Actor selects them all.

Figure 13.7 Grouping Meshes together to be duplicated around the scene

Groups are great for building reusable sets of geometry in your scenes.

After the Actors are grouped, you can **Ungroup** or **Unlock** the group for editing by using the context menu as well. You cannot name or modify the Group Actor that's created.

Actor Blueprints

You can take a set of Actors (including lights, particles, sounds, and so on) and create Blueprint Asset from them. This has several advantages over Groups.

To make an Actor Blueprint Asset from Actors in your Level, select the Assets you want to convert and select **Convert Selected Components to Blueprint Class** (see Figure 13.8).

Figure 13.8 Convert Selected Components to Blueprint Class

You then must choose where to save the new Blueprint Asset in the Content Browser. This Blueprint contains Components that reference the Static Meshes and other classes you had selected. It does not create a copy or merge them into a new Mesh Asset.

You can now modify the one Blueprint Asset, and all Level Actors based on it will update. An Actor Blueprint is great for creating things like light fixtures or other complex sets of Actors or even just groups of Actors that you want to reuse.

Summary

Getting your content placed in UE4 is both fun and challenging. You should now have a better understanding of how to get your Architecture Meshes into your scenes at the exact position they were in your 3D application and how to organize and maintain your scene as you add more and more content.

With the scene populated (see Figure 13.9), it's time to start populating it with lighting, Materials, and post-process effects to achieve your goal of creating a photo-real scene.

Figure 13.9 Populated scene with preview lighting

CHAPTER 14

ARCHITECTURAL LIGHTING

Developing clean, accurate, realistic lighting is essential for creating visualizations. The interplay of lights, shadows, reflections, and materials brings worlds to life, creating depth and telling stories. In this chapter, you learn how to set up great-looking Global Illumination (GI) lighting using Lightmass.

Getting the Most from UE4's Lighting

UE4's Lighting and Materials systems are tightly intertwined. You must work between them to achieve your final result. This chapter demonstrates how to light an interior scene using UE4.

Unreal's high dynamic range rendering pipeline combines with effects like auto-exposure and bloom to create a realistic, warm, and dynamic lighting environment. Getting your lighting right using these techniques can be tricky, but using some baseline settings you should be able to get great results quickly.

In this chapter you learn how to adjust Level and Static Mesh properties and settings to achieve great lighting with reasonable lighting build times.

The chapter also shows how to use post-processing effects like vignette, color grading, and depth of field to create a more photorealistic image (see Figure 14.1).

Figure 14.1 Final lighting preview

Finally, you learn how to place Reflection Capture Actors into the Level to improve lighting and help mirrors look more accurate.

Materials and Lighting

Like all Global Illumination (GI) rendering, lighting in UE4 is affected directly by Materials and vice versa. Materials tint and attenuate bounced light, and light reflects off surfaces informing us about its surface properties.

Because of this, you cannot separate the two completely. This chapter and the next are intended to cover both topics individually; however, to get the best results you'll use the techniques from both chapters in parallel.

Static Lighting with Lightmass

UE4 has made a big splash in architectural visualization industry, thanks to its impressive visuals. One of the ways UE4 manages to render such incredibly well-lit scenes so quickly is by precomputing the lighting using a GI renderer called *Lightmass*.

Lightmass calculates the light hitting the surface of each Static Mesh in your scene using a photon-based, Global Illumination solver like Mental Ray. It then records this data to several Textures, called Lightmaps and Shadowmaps. This process is referred to as *building* your *Static Lighting*. Upon completing the lighting render, the Textures are automatically imported and applied.

As the name suggests, you cannot move or modify objects lit with Static Lighting or the lights used after you build them. If you add, remove, move, or otherwise modify the Static Lights or Static Meshes in your scene, you will *break* the lighting and must rebuild it.

Note that you can *add* lights to an already-built lighting scene. Although you will need to build your lighting again to see the GI contribution of these newly placed lights, the existing static lighting will remain. This can be helpful as you add more and more lights to your scene.

Lightmaps and Shadowmaps are stored in a special **BuildData** UMAP Level file (the custom file format UE4 stores Levels as) alongside your saved Level. This file and your project will grow significantly as you add more Assets because each one increases the memory overhead of the Lighting Textures.

Adjusting the Sun and Sky Lights

In the previous chapter, you placed a Directional Light Actor, a Sky Light Actor, and an Atmospheric Fog Actor. These three Actors provide the base for building a lighting solution, but they need some adjustments to work with Static Lighting.

Sun Light

The Directional Light will act as your sun light, providing intense, direct light that contributes greatly to the GI solution.

The three main light types or classes in UE4 are Point, Spot, and Directional. Point and Spot lights radiate from a single point in space. They are great to use for nearby lights like lamps, fixtures, and spot lights. They are not great for the sun, which from our perspective here on Earth radiates light in parallel. For this, you need a light that simulates the light coming from a single direction instead. Enter the Directional Light Actor class.

Like most Actors, you can easily place lights into your scene by dragging and dropping them from the Class Browser into the Viewport.

You can place the light anywhere in your scene because it does not radiate from that point; only the rotation is important. I put mine where I can easily find it again.

Find a pleasing or realistic rotation for your light. The dynamic shadows act as a preview and give you a good idea where the static shadows will land (see Figure 14.2). Take a look around as you do this. UE4's dynamic shadows provide a good approximation where the baked shadows will land in your scene.

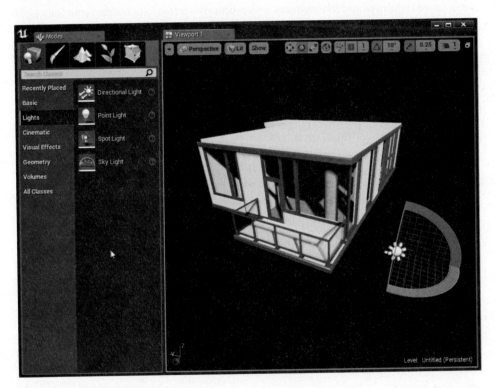

Figure 14.2 Directional Light placement

The Details Panel shows the various options available for the selected light (see Figure 14.3). You need to adjust several settings to get the best quality and performance from this Light Actor.

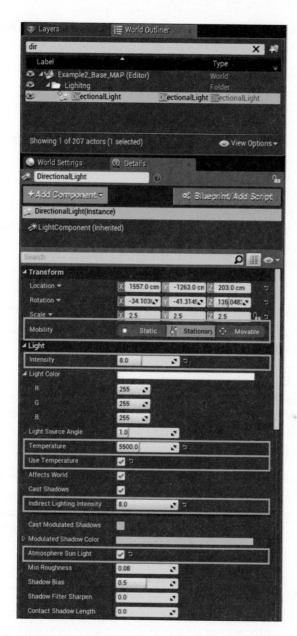

Figure 14.3 Directional Light properties in the Details Panel

Mobility

The first and most important setting to modify is the **Mobility**. For this light, you need to use a
Stationary Light. This is like a Static Light (it cannot move), but doesn't record its direct lighting

in a Texture; rather, it calculates the direct lighting dynamically. That means you can change the brightness and color after building the lighting.

Note that changing the Intensity does not affect the GI lighting because that is baked into Static Textures.

Intensity

To get a bright sunlight effect, use an **Intensity** value of 8–10. This ensures the sun is the brightest light in your scene.

Indirect Lighting Intensity

Because the intensity of Stationary Lights can be changed, you need to tell Lightmass how bright you want it to calculate this light as. For this you can use the **Indirect Lighting Intensity** setting to adjust how bright the GI from this light is. Set this somewhere between 1.0 and the Intensity you set for your light.

Temperature

Check the **Use Temperature** checkbox and set a **Temperature** of around 5000–5500. This provides a slightly yellow sun that's still significantly "whiter" than a typical incandescent light that has a value of 2700–3500.

Atmosphere Sun Light

Ensure the **Atmosphere Sun Light** option is selected to let it work in conjunction with the Atmosphere Fog Actor to generate a physically correct lit sky that will provide the environment color for the scene. If you don't see it at first, this setting can be hidden in the light's Advanced Options.

UE4 features an atmospheric light scattering fog system that simulates earth's atmosphere. This is driven using an Atmospheric Fog Actor and the Directional Light Actor. Just drop an Environmental Fog Actor into your scene. If your Directional Light Actor has Atmosphere Fog Light enabled, it will orient a sun disk and set the sky colors based on the sun's position, creating a simple but effective skybox.

Sky Light

To simulate the ambient light from the atmosphere, UE4 uses a Sky Light Actor. This special light can either capture the existing scene as a Cubemap to use for indirect lighting, or you can provide it an HDR Texture.

In this example, let's just capture the scene.

Place this light somewhere in your scene where you can find it easily. You will also want to ensure it is not enclosed within any geometry so it can capture the unoccluded sky. The Sky Light Actor has some settings to tweak to get optimal results (see Figure 14.4).

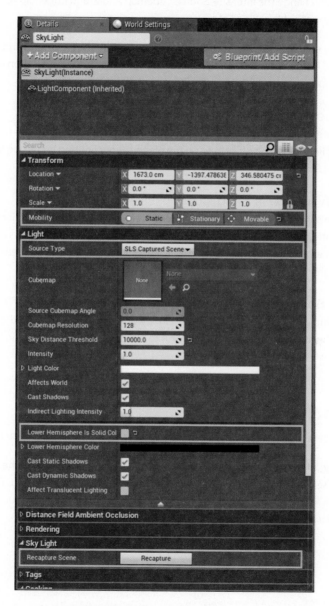

Figure 14.4 Sky Light placement

Mobility

The Sky Light is set to Static for this scene. You can also choose to use Stationary for this scene but you will trade a certain level of quality and detail in your indirect sky lighting with the ability to dynamically change the Intensity, Source Cubemap Angle, and Cubemap Texture properties dynamically without breaking lighting.

Setting Mobility to Static bakes all the indirect sky lighting into the Lightmaps and Shadowmaps generated by Lightmass, avoiding some of the inaccuracies that the stationary pipeline can introduce, such as light leaking or inaccurate lighting.

Source Type

You can select between an imported HDR Cubemap or a Cubemap of the scene taken by the Sky Light Actor in the Editor. In this case, use the scene as your lighting by setting Source Type to SLS Captured Scene.

Lower Hemisphere Is Solid Color

The Lower Hemisphere Is a Solid Color setting is a bit of a personal preference. Setting it to true replaces the bottom half of the captured Cubemap with a single, solid color. This can limit the amount of light entering a space, so I prefer to leave it set to false for interior scenes where getting as much light into the scene as possible is important.

Recapture Scene

If you make lighting or scene changes, the Sky Light won't dynamically update the Cubemap it's using to light the scene. You must manually tell it to recapture its Cubemap using the Recapture Scene button.

Building Lighting

Now that the scene has some rudimentary lighting, you can build the lighting for the first time.

To build lighting, click the Build button in the Editor's toolbar. You can click on the arrow next to it to see the settings. The most important is the Lighting Build Quality setting. This lets you quickly go from a fast preview build to a great looking but slow-to-render production quality build (see Figure 14.5).

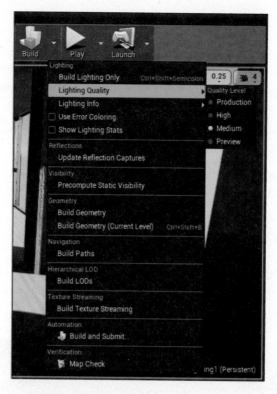

Figure 14.5 Setting the Lighting Quality from the Lighting Build dropdown

Lightmass offers several presets for lighting quality from preview up to production. Production lighting builds can take orders of magnitude more time than preview builds, but lower quality builds can introduce artifacts and inconsistencies that can be hard to distinguish from actual issues with geometry or lighting.

> **note**
>
> To improve build times when lighting your scenes, you can hide Actors, leaving only the Architecture and Fixtures. This decreases the time needed to build the lighting significantly, letting you iterate faster. To do so, select the Actors you don't want to light and set the Visibility property in the Details Panel to false.
>
> To unhide them again, you must find the Actors listed in the World Outliner because they won't be visible in the Viewport anymore.
>
> Alternatively, you can select the Static Meshes you want to avoid calculating lighting for and set their Mobility to Moveable.
>
> Either way, you should use groups, layers, or folders to organize your scene to make toggling these properties easier.

Figure 14.6 shows a comparison between preview and production lighting builds. You can see that accuracy is greatly reduced with the preview build, but the lighting time was significantly reduced.

Production Quality   79.8 seconds   Preview Quality   2.8 seconds

Figure 14.6 First lighting build in production quality and preview quality

As you can see, even using production quality, the lighting still isn't very good. Shadows are undefined, blocky, and low-res, and errors exist on the baseboards and in dark areas. By making a few adjustments, you can have this scene looking a lot better in short order.

Lightmass Settings for Architecture Visualizations

The first stop for getting things looking better is to pump up the Lightmass settings. Architecture Visualizations prioritize image quality over render time, and in UE4 this is no different. You increase lighting build times, but end up with a much better-looking scene.

The settings for Lightmass are stored on a per-Level basis and can be modified in the World properties options. The Lightmass panel offers a lot of settings (see Figure 14.7). Thankfully, UE4's defaults are very good for most circumstances. Each setting has a dramatic effect on build times, so always starting small and working your way up is a good idea.

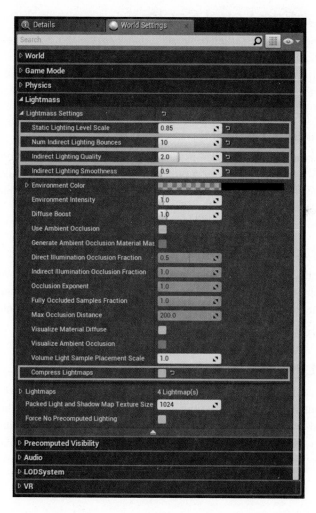

Figure 14.7 Lightmass World Settings

> **note**
>
> If you have researched Lightmass online, there's a good chance you've seen some complex **.ini** file adjustments and other tweaks to get Lightmass to produce clean lighting solutions for architecture visualizations.
>
> These adjustments have largely become unnecessary in later versions of the Engine (and, possibly detrimental to your image quality and certainly your build times). Epic Games has done extensive work to improve Lightmass for visualization and you should only need to adjust the settings exposed in the World Settings.

Static Lighting Level Scale

The Static Lighting Level Scale setting controls the density of the photons in the scene. Smaller numbers mean tighter photons with more detail. This can increase build times significantly. You can leave this setting at the default of 1.0 or reduce it slightly. Any lower than 0.8 increases build times, and noise can become visible.

Num Indirect Lighting Bounces

The Num Indirect Lighting Bounces clamps the number of times a photon can bounce off surfaces in the scene before extinguishing. A setting of 10 provides very good results, allowing the photons to get into the darkest areas of your scene. Increase this setting if you have splotches in your darker areas.

Indirect Lighting Quality

The Indirect Lighting Quality setting has the largest effect on build times and overall quality. It increases the amount of sampling done to smooth out the GI solution. Very high settings produce very smooth GI. Leaving this setting in the 1–4 range is a good idea; only go higher if you are experiencing noisy GI.

Indirect Lighting Smoothness

Use the Indirect Lighting Smoothness setting to control how soft or sharp your indirect GI lighting is. Lower numbers make for sharper, but noisier indirect shadows, whereas higher numbers make for softer shadows. Lower this setting slightly if you want that sharpness, but don't go too much lower than .75 or you will have to increase the overall quality of your solution to remove the noisy artifacts.

Compress Lightmaps

The most important setting for architecture visualizations is Compress Lightmaps, which disables Texture compression on the Lightmass Textures. As you can see in Figure 14.8, the compression can introduce banding and blocking artifacts. This is acceptable in many games that don't rely on clean lighting, but not for architecture visualizations, where the lighting and surface fidelity are the highest priority.

You should not adjust any other settings until you have disabled this setting. The noise it introduces will make your lighting unsuitable for architecture visualizations and no amount of tweaking can eliminate it.

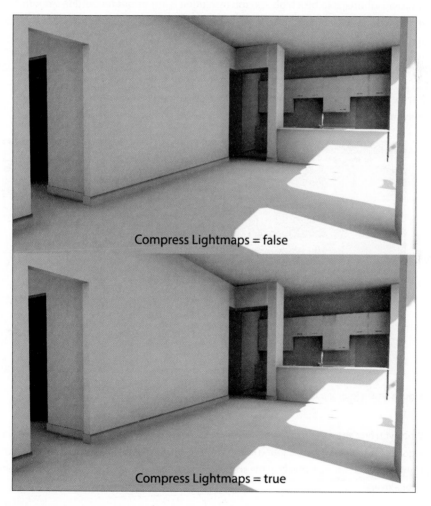

Figure 14.8 Compress Lightmaps comparison (with increased contrast to enhance artifacts) showing artifacts on the cabinets, door frames, and on smooth surfaces like the wall on the left

Using uncompressed Lightmaps comes at the cost of memory. Uncompressed Lightmaps take up significantly more disk space than compressed Lightmaps. They also use more video memory when running in-game.

If your Level is very large (a stadium or an entire building) or you are targeting lower-end hardware (laptops, mobile devices, and so on), you might want to use the Compressed Lightmaps setting to allow these Levels to load into RAM.

Lightmap UV Density Adjustments

Getting your Lightmaps to be a high enough resolution is important for getting smooth, detailed lighting. However, too high a resolution can cripple your scene with long build times and massive memory footprints.

Finding the balance can be challenging, but here's one way to set Lightmap resolution in UE4:

1. Enable the Lightmap Density visualization by choosing **View Mode > Optimization Viewmodes > Lightmap Density** (see Figure 14.9).

Figure 14.9 Lightmap Density visualization view mode toggle

When you first enter this mode, you will see something like Figure 14.10—lots of grids of varying sizes and colors with no lighting information. What you're looking at is a visualization of the Lightmap pixels on each object in the scene. This helps you adjust the resolution quickly and interactively.

Blue indicates that the Lightmap resolution is too low and red indicates that it's set too high. You should aim for green to orange on all your surfaces for the best quality with reasonable build times.

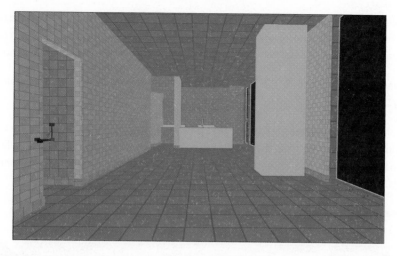

Figure 14.10 Lightmap Density visualization showing far too low-resolution that doesn't allow for very detailed shadows and lighting

2. To adjust individual Mesh Actors in the Level, select each Mesh in the scene one by one and adjust the Overridden Light Map Res setting in the Details Panel.

After they're adjusted, the Lightmaps should be much more even in density and higher resolution, as shown in Figure 14.11.

You do not need to set the resolution to a power of two (64, 128, and so on), but you should not go too big. Resolutions more than 1024 are supported but should be used sparingly. The higher the resolution, the longer the build time, the larger the Level on disk, and the more memory it takes up. Keeping it as low as you can without unacceptable artifacts is best.

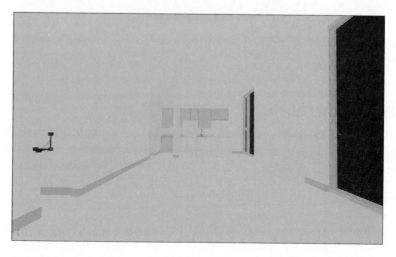

Figure 14.11 Lightmap Density visualization view mode with better settings

Adjusting the Lightmap resolution on Props is different, so you adjust them at the Asset Level. This ensures that each one in your Level will have the proper resolution because the changes you make to the source Asset will be reflected by any scene Objects that reference those Assets.

Be aware that any changes to the Static Lighting settings for the Mesh Asset will break lighting in any Level that has the Asset referenced.

You can also adjust the density of Props on a per-Object basis in your Level using the Overridden Light Map Res property in the Details Panel. I sometimes give my Props (especially if they have a lot of detail or organic shapes) a higher relative density than Architecture Meshes, as shown in Figure 14.12, which makes them appear to be rather reddish in color.

Be careful; repeated Props can quickly generate a lot of high-resolution Texture data.

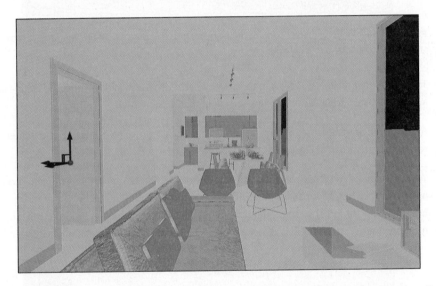

Figure 14.12 Final Lightmap density showing higher density on the more organic Props such as the sofa and the chairs

Rebuild and Save

Now is a great time to rebuild your lighting. You'll notice right away that with the increased density of your Lightmaps, your build times have gone up significantly. Your overall quality should have also gone up significantly with more detailed shadows and indirect light.

This is also a good time to save your work.

Placing Interior Lighting

Now that you have the sun and sky lighting in the scene, you can start placing some lights inside to help brighten up some of the dark corners.

Spot Lights

Point and Spot Lights share many of the same settings as lights in ray-traced renderers, and you should feel right at home (see Figure 14.13.) There are only a few differences to keep in mind.

Figure 14.13 Placing Spot Light Actors

Mobility

I recommend using Static Lights almost exclusively for interior lighting. Although Stationary and Dynamic Lights offer some advantages, they add complexity and significant performance cost to your scenes.

Intensity

Try to remember that your interior lights should be much less bright than your sun light. Even the brightest interior light doesn't seem to cast much light in a sunlit room.

Getting the lighting brightness right is an art. It is affected by the number of lights in an area, the brightness of the sunlight, and even the color of the materials it's reflecting off of. Brightness has a dramatic effect on the final look of your lights.

You need to iterate and adjust your lights to find a suitable balance for your scene and tastes.

Temperature

In this example, I used the temperature setting for my lights. This gives them realistic color based on the brightness of the light. I used a warmer tone for the interior lights, which lets them contrast with the sun and sky.

Attenuation

Limiting the distance a light's direct lighting can travel is used for both performance and artistic reasons. Limiting the attenuation of a light limits the number of Meshes it affects in the world. This is critical for performance—especially for dynamically shadowed lights. In Lightmass, a limited attenuation radius will affect fewer Meshes, making the lighting build faster; but as the light and shadow data is baked into textures, there's no real-time benefit.

IES Files

UE4 supports IES (Illuminating Engineering Society) Light Profiles for Spot and Point Lights. You can import IES files and apply them to lights to achieve interesting lighting patterns (as seen in Figure 14.13). You can find IES profiles around the Internet from real-world lighting manufacturers and vendors, or even from the Unreal marketplace.

Auto Exposure

Turning off Auto Exposure temporarily can be a big help when setting up the lighting in your scene. The default Auto Exposure is very aggressive and can get very bright or very dark easily.

Locking the exposure using the View Mode menu in the Viewport ensures the lighting brightness does not adjust as you move from light to dark areas, and more easily allows you to balance your lighting.

Placing Light Portals

Light Portals are special Actors that help Lightmass focus photons toward openings that have a lot of light coming in. This improves build times and lighting quality.

Place these Actors on your windows and other openings and loosely adjust the box to fit. You don't need to be terribly exacting; it's just a helper for the photons and doesn't need to be precise.

Using Reflection Probes

Reflections are integral to PBR. UE4 uses Reflection Capture Actors to capture Static Cubemaps of the scene and automatically applies them to the Materials within their influence.

Although you can get away without placing these around your Level, you do achieve much higher quality with them.

The two types of Reflection probes are Sphere and Cube. Simply put, for square-shaped areas, use the Box Reflection Capture Actor. For all other areas, use the Sphere. As you can see from Figure 14.14, a mixture of both kinds is useful to fine-tune the reflections in the scene.

Figure 14.14 Reflection Probes

Size

Sphere Reflection Actors use a radius of influence to determine what pixels they will affect. Typically, smaller radius Reflection Actors have priority over larger ones. This lets you "nest" smaller reflection Actors within larger ones, letting you add detailed reflections to areas that might need it.

Box Reflection Capture Actors expose a 3D Scale value. You should adjust the Scale of the box until the corners of the box shown in the Viewport fits as closely to the corners of your room as possible.

Performance

In addition to the memory overhead of the captured Cubemaps, Reflection Capture Actors automatically apply their reflections to any pixels that are rendered within them. For this reason, overlapping reflection captures can cause a performance impact. You should avoid having too many overlapping.

It's also worth noting that Box Reflection Capture Actors have a higher performance impact than the Sphere Reflection Capture Actors.

Post-Process Volume

The final piece to the lighting puzzle is to apply post-processing effects such as vignette, bloom, motion blur, and depth of field to the image to give it a filmic, realistic look.

When you create a new Level in UE4, default post processing settings are applied to the scene automatically. These settings are a good start, but you'll almost always want to adjust them in each of your scenes to match its unique lighting and to achieve the look and feel you are after.

To access these settings, you need to add a special class of Actor to your scene: the Post-Process Volume.

Volume Actors

A Volume is a special type of Actor class in UE4 that can tell if other Actors are within its bounds. Post-Process Volumes use this ability to blend between different post-process setups as the player's camera enters and leaves each volume.

You can adjust Volumes by setting their Brush settings. You can define the shape of the volume, as well as the size. You can also scale, rotate, and move them like any other Actor.

Placing the Post-Process Volume

You'll find a list of the different types of Volume classes available in the Modes Panel under Volumes (see Figure 14.15). Simply drag and drop the Post-Process Volume into the Viewport. You can place it anywhere in the scene—just be sure it's easily selectable.

Figure 14.15 Placing the Post-Process Volume in the Level

Post-Process Volume Setup

The Post-Process Volume has a lot of settings and allows you to refine your image to a significant degree. While many settings—such as color adjustments and effects like bloom—are almost entirely up to your personal tastes and styles, others have a direct impact on performance and image quality.

To access the settings, simply select the Post-Process Volume in the Level and look in the Details Panel.

The following are the settings you will be adjusting most often, and the ones adjusted for this example.

Unbound

You can set up your Post-Process Volume to skip the bounds check and apply its settings level-wide by enabling the Unbound option. This is much easier than setting the volume to encompass the entire Level.

Priority

You can have Post-Process Volumes that overlap each other. To determine which one's settings will be used, use the Priority option. Volumes with a higher Priority will override volumes of lower priority.

It's important to note that only properties that have been manually overridden (by selecting the checkbox to the left of the property in the Details Panel for the overlapping volume) will be applied. This is a great way to adjust only a single property without having to ensure all the other settings match.

Blend Radius

This is a world-space radius around the Volume that interpolates between two volume's settings. As the player's camera moves in and out of the volume, the settings will smoothly blend from one to another. Volumes set to Unbound have this option grayed out.

White Balance

There are a lot of settings for Color Correction in UE4, but you should probably start with the White Balance. This defaults to 6500, which is a very pure, blue white that's not terribly common in the real world. This can give your scenes an overly cool tone and make it difficult to get the right balance between warm light and cool shadows. You can set this somewhere between 5000 and 6000 for a warmer tone in your scene and higher for a cooler look.

Saturation and Contrast

The **Saturation**, **Contrast**, **Crush Highlights**, and **Crush Shadow** settings work together to help control the image balance. You are probably familiar with Contrast and Saturation, but maybe not the Crush settings. These simply clip the black and white points, giving a greater apparent contrast.

The default settings are often too contrasted, making shadowed areas very dark. This is a very filmic look, but it can be too dark for arch-viz where it might be preferable to have very dark areas.

These settings are very sensitive, so small adjustments go a long way.

Vignette, Noise, and Fringe

Use these effects to simulate camera lens effects.

Vignette adds a dark gradient to the edges of your image, which can allow you to increase the overall brightness of the image—the only fully bright pixels are in the very center of the screen.

Fringe simulates the chromatic aberration effect of light passing through a camera's lens, separating the colors closer to the edges of the image.

Grain adds animated noise to the image. Grain Intensity controls the Noise Texture overlay's opacity while Grain Jitter controls how much the grain displaces the image. Use these sparingly as they can become overbearing quickly.

Color Grading (LUT)

The Color Grading system in UE4 uses a special texture called a Color Lookup Table (LUT) to modify the scene's color. The LUT is generated by applying color grading to a baseline image in your compositing or image editing application.

UE4 reads the difference between the baseline image and the modified LUT and applies that delta to the scene. This is a great way to bring your existing color correction pipeline into UE4. You can find more information about LUTs and some LUT files for download on the companion website for this book at www.TomShannon3D.com/UnrealForViz

Bloom and Lens Flares

Some of the most common post-process effects in both games and traditionally rendered content, Bloom and Lens flares help to simulate over-bright areas by simulating camera lenses and the human eye.

The default Bloom and Lens Flare settings in UE4 are a little aggressive and can decrease the contrast and clarity of scenes if used too much. Decreasing the Intensity or increasing the Threshold are good ways of reducing the overall amount of Bloom and Lens Flare in the scene.

You can also adjust the size of the effects. Larger sizes will have a more significant impact on performance.

I will often disable Lens Flares in scenes completely or turn them down so far as to only occur with extremely bright pixels.

Auto Exposure

Because UE4 renders scenes using an HDR lighting environment, you can have very different lighting brightness levels from one area of your map to the next. For this reason, UE4 has a sophisticated auto-exposure system.

This system can help create dynamic, engaging lighting interactions as your player moves from one area to another and sees the exposure adjust in response, much like the human eye or a camera with auto-exposure. It can also make setting up your lighting quite challenging.

I recommend setting up your lighting with Auto-Exposure disabled, then enabling it as-needed for your scene. You can disable this effect either through the Exposure Settings in the View Mode dropdown in the Viewport, or by setting the Min and Max Brightness parameters in the Post-Process Volume to 1.0. You can then use the Exposure Bias to manually set the exposure of the camera.

After your lighting is set up, begin to play with Min and Max Brightness to allow the camera's exposure to adjust. To allow the camera to overexpose, brightening dark areas, set the Min Brightness to a value below 1.0. To allow the camera's exposure to be reduced when in bright areas, increase the Max Brightness above 1.0.

Ambient Occlusion

Although we are not using Screen Space Ambient Occlusion (SSAO) in the example, it's a very important effect and used widely in all sorts of visualizations and games. If you are generating scenes with dynamic lighting or a lot of Dynamic Actors, you will likely want to enable this because it dramatically increases the scene's depth and lighting quality.

Global Illumination

This controls the intensity and color of the Lightmaps generated by Lightmass. You can use this to quickly modify your baked lighting. This does not control any kind of real-time GI in UE4.

Depth of Field (DOF)

UE4 exposes several methods for creating Depth of Field effects. For visualization, the **Circle DOF** is easily the best. This is a physically accurate effect that simulates actual lens aperture blurring characteristics and creates a very subtle, realistic effect. It's also fairly performant compared to other effects. Like many post-processing effects, however, it can be come expensive at higher resolutions. I don't recommend it at all for VR.

To increase the blurring effect, reduce the **Aperture F-Stop** parameter's value. Lower settings will produce more blurring (see Figure 14.16). It's important to note that this is a realistic effect, so you might not notice the effect until you get very close to an object.

For an interior scene, you will want to ensure your **Focal Distance** is set to around 300–500 (3 to 5 meters) and the **Aperture F-Stop** is fairly large at 4–8.

Figure 14.16 Circle Depth of Field F-Stop comparison

Motion Blur

UE4 employs a high-quality motion blur system that generates a velocity map each frame and uses it to blur the scene accordingly. The default settings are typically very good for most scenes; however, if you're running at higher frame rates or want a cleaner presentation, you might consider turning this off or down by reducing the **Max** parameter.

Screen Space Reflections

Screen Space Reflections provide you with detailed, dynamic reflections based on the rendered image. These are essential for achieving the highest quality, but you'll want to increase the Quality and Max Roughness settings. Set the Quality to 100 and the Max Roughness between .6 and 1.0. Higher values are more expensive to render, but can look more accurate. Go as low as you can while still maintaining the look of your scene.

Anti-Aliasing

UE4 offers several Anti-Aliasing (AA) methods. For most visualization, the Temporal AA (TAA) system in UE4 produces superior results and has very little performance overhead.

The following example scene shows the result of enabling the Ambient Occlusion, Vignette, Grain, and Depth of Field settings. Each improves the look of the image, adding the imperfections and other effects one expects to see from a photograph.

As you can see, the settings in the post-process volume have a dramatic effect on the look of the scene. Even the subtle settings used here significantly changes the look and feel of the scene (see Figures 14.17 and 14.18).

Figure 14.17 Scene with default post-process settings

Figure 14.18 Scene with post-process adjustments showing the noticeable change in Contrast, White Balance, and Saturation

Summary

Lighting in UE4 has many components that all work together to make a whole. Although these concepts were presented in the order you might encounter them, as you learn and iterate on your scene, you will move among their settings because adjusting one influences another.

This interaction between light, color, and Materials is familiar to visualization artists and is where technology diverges into artistry. Through practice you will learn to understand your instrument and begin to craft warm lighting effortlessly in UE4.

CHAPTER 15

ARCHITECTURAL MATERIALS

UE4's Material system is like a good video game: simple to learn but takes a lifetime to master. Making great UE4 Materials for production isn't only about artistic quality, but about creating reusable Materials, getting the best-performance possible, and learning new techniques that aren't used in raytracing renders such as Parallax Occlusion Mapping.

Materials and lighting work hand-in-hand to create a rich, realistic environment for your Player. You can achieve amazing results using simple Materials. Now that your lighting is started, you can begin getting some Materials into your scene and making it come to life with color, reflection, and surface detail and variation.

Getting great-looking Materials in UE4 is straightforward because using PBR (physically based rendering) is straightforward. By defining the Base Color, Roughness, Metallic, and Normal parameters, the Engine does the hard work and creates a Material that follows the rules of physics to create amazingly rich surfaces to populate your scenes.

Be sure to review Chapter 5, "Materials" for coverage of the basics of Material creation in UE4, especially the creation of Material Instances. You will rely heavily on them to quickly make a large library of Materials and apply them to your scene.

What Is a Master Material?

As discussed in Chapter 5, you could create a unique Material for each surface as you might in a traditional 3D renderer. This could be very time consuming, especially when you start adding more functionality into your Materials.

Instead, you will use **Material Parameters** to create a single **Material** and then several **Material Instances** of that Material, assigning Textures and overriding properties to create almost every Material used in your scene.

This single Material is often referred to as a Master Material. A Master Material isn't a specific Asset type in Unreal Engine. Rather, it is a concept. Any Material can be a Master Material if you author it with Material Parameters. Material Parameters expose variables to Material Instances that can be changed on the fly both in the Editor and at runtime using Blueprints.

Thanks to the simplicity of physically based rendering, your Material network does not need to be excessively complex. Using only Color, Normal, Metallic, and Roughness Textures along with the occasional height map, you can define almost any surface.

You can even create typically difficult-to-achieve surfaces like metal, glass, and architectural wall coverings with minimal effort and without resorting to authoring complex custom Materials. You can follow along, building your own Material, or you can download the complete project files at www.TomShannon3D.com/UnrealForViz.

Material Network Overview

Figure 15.1 shows a Master Material. At first glance, it might look complicated, but it's really straightforward.

Materials are like Blueprints and use a node-based graph to help you visualize what are essentially programming concepts. Nodes are connected to other nodes and data flows from left to right, finally terminating in one of the Material's various **attributes** such as **Base Color** or **Roughness**.

You'll take the concepts covered in Chapter 5 and expand upon them, adding some new node types that allow greater flexibility in the Material instances or that provide advanced rendering features such as Parallax Occlusion Mapping.

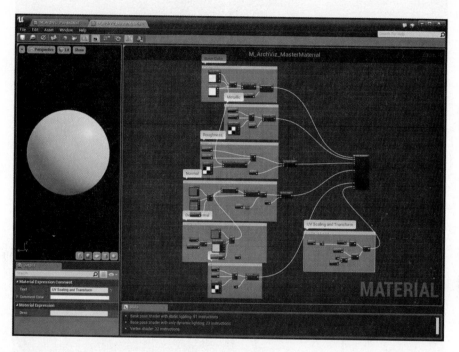

Figure 15.1 Complete M_ArchViz_MasterMaterial shader graph showing a single Material that can be used for almost every Material in the scene via the use of Material Instances

Parameter Nodes

There are special kinds of Material Expression Nodes you can place in your Material Graph, called Parameters. These nodes let you expose certain aspects of your Material that can be dynamically modified using Material Instance assets or at runtime with Blueprints.

Parameters authored in a Material are exposed as editable Properties in Material Instances that derive from that Material. In the Material Instance Editor (see Figure 15.2), you must click the checkbox to the left of the property you want to override before modifying the value. To return the value to default, click the small yellow arrow next to a modified property. You can also turn off the checkbox to cancel the override.

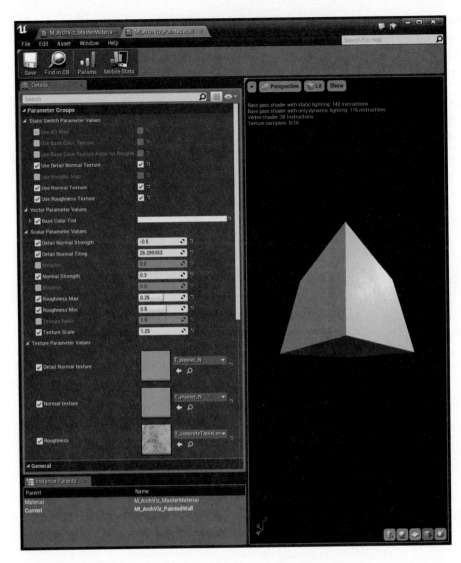

Figure 15.2 Painted Wall Material Instance based on M_ArchViz_MasterMaterial

Creating the Master Material

As shown in Figure 15.1, there's a lot that needs to be set up to create a good Master Material. Each Material input (Base Color, Metallic, Roughness, and Normal) has a series of nodes connected to it that enable you to create endless variations to your Materials with Material Instances.

Let's go through each input and see how it's set up. You can follow along, making your own Master Material, or refer to the files at www.TomShannon3D.com/UnrealForViz.

Base Color

Figure 15.3 shows a **Texture Parameter 2D** called **Base Color Texture** that is multiplied by a **Vector Parameter** called **Base Color Tint**. Remember that Materials are Math and that Colors are treated as RGB Vectors. This means you can perform all manner of vector math operations to the colors in textures, allowing you to perform adjustments on the fly.

Adding Parameters

To place a **Texture Parameter** node, simply use the palette or the right-click menu and select Texture Parameter from the list. You then want to name the Parameter something meaningful. Parameters can have spaces and punctuation in their names making them easier to read, but it might make those variables more difficult to access through code.

Parameter nodes can be renamed and modified using the Details panel. Using the Details panel, you also need to define the default Texture asset to be used for this node. You can either click on the thumbnail to bring up a browser, or drag and drop a Texture from the Content Browser onto the node's properties[1].

Place a **Vector Parameter** in the same manner, again giving it a meaningful name. A Vector Parameter can be edited by either modifying the RGBA values in the Details panel, or by double-clicking on the color swatch in the node. This brings up a color picker, which is a lot easier to use.

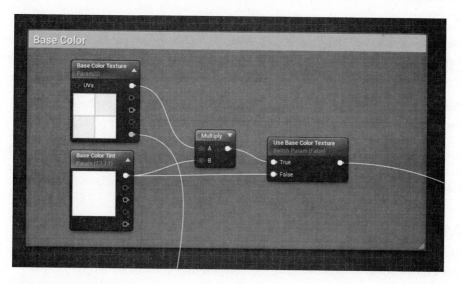

Figure 15.3 Base Color node graph

---

1. You can also create Texture 2D node in your graph by dragging a Texture from the Content Browser into the Material Graph. This will not be a Parameter node, but can easily be converted into one by right-clicking the Texture 2D node and selecting Convert to Parameter from the context menu.

Multiplying Colors

Add a **Multiply** node using the Palette, or the right-click menu and connect the Base Color Texture output to the A input and the Base Color Tint output to the B input.

The Multiply node multiplies each channel of input A with input B, and returns the result. Multiplying a vector (the base Color Texture's RGB output node) with another vector (BaseColor Tint's RGB output node) means each of the individual RGB channels are multiplied by one another (RedA x RedB, BlueA x BlueB, GreenA x GreenB). You can also multiply one data type by another, such as a Vector and a Scalar (float)—in this case, it would multiply each channel of the Vector by the value of the Scalar.

Using a Multiply node for colors is the same as a Multiply blend mode you might be familiar with in many applications. Black (0,0,0) completely colors your Base Color black, because anything multiplied by 0 is 0. Pure white (1,1,1) does not modify the incoming value at all. Of course, you can choose a color instead, tinting the pixels. You can also go past 1 (or below 0) in your Vector Parameter, acting as a brightness adjustment for the Texture. This can sometimes cause non-physically accurate results, so take care when overdriving your inputs this way.

Static Switch Parameters

The **Static Switch Parameter** node displays a Boolean checkbox in Material Instances. If the parameter is set to *true* (either in the Material or Material Instances that derive from it), the Material will evaluate the code path connected to the True input; and if *false*, to the False pin.

Changing the value of the Static Switch may also update the Material Instance's interface. Parameters that are not being called, such as Base Color Texture, will not be shown the Material Instance Editor, resulting in less clutter and avoiding presenting the user with options that don't do anything.

Connect result of the Multiply node to the True input and the Output of the Base Color Tint Parameter to the False input of the Static Switch Parameter.

In this case, if **Use Base Color Texture** is *false*, the Material will use Base Color Tint to define the Base Color, bypassing the Texture and Multiply nodes. This saves on Texture reads and Shader calculations, making for a more performant Material.

Metallic

The **Metallic** input channel is one of the least used attributes and can usually just be set to 0 or 1 via the **Metallic** Scalar Parameter (see Figure 15.4).

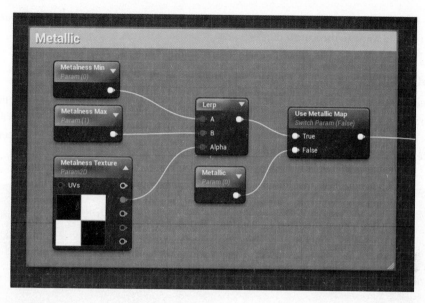

Figure 15.4 Metallic Input node graph

However, sometimes you might want to use a Texture as a mask to define areas of a model that are metallic and those that are not; for example, a wood texture with nails or screws visible, or a material representing chipped paint, revealing a metallic surface underneath.

To allow for this, create a **Texture Parameter 2D** node called **Metalness Texture**.

Place a **Linear Interpolate** (or **Lerp**, as it is more widely known as) node to allow you remap values to other values using simple Min and Max Parameters for each. The Alpha input acts as a percentage weight between the A and B inputs, 0.0 being fully the value of the A input and 1.0 being fully the value of the B input. By modulating these values, you can easily adjust the surfaces of your scene interactively and predictably.

Create two Scalar Parameters called **Metalness Min** and **Metalness Max**, and connect them to the A and B inputs of the Lerp node. Set the Default Value of Metalness Max to *1.0* using the details panel. Adjusting the **Metalness Min** and **Metalness Max** settings lets you tweak the mask values easily without having to modify the Texture (see Chapter 5 for more information).

To allow the Texture to be turned off completely, place another Static Switch Parameter on the Graph and name it. If this Parameter is set to *true*, the Red channel of the **Metalness Texture** is sampled and then modified using the Lerp node. Because the Metallic input only requires a gray-scale or scalar input (0-1), only the Red channel of the texture is used as the alpha of the Lerp node[2].

---

2. Using only a single channel from a Texture allows advanced users to utilize each channel of an RGB texture to store a different grayscale image.

If the **Use Metallic Map** Parameter is set to false, it will use a **Metallic Scalar** Parameter that is set to 0.0 and wired to the False input.

Roughness

The Roughness channel is probably the most important channel besides Base Color (sometimes more so as discussed in Chapter 5). However, as you can see in Figure 15.5, it's set up much like other channels, with the **Use Roughness Texture** Static Switch Parameter toggling between the Texture-based roughness and the **Roughness Scalar** Parameter.

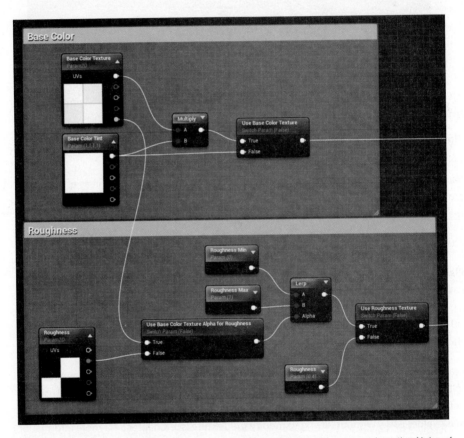

Figure 15.5 Roughness node graph also showing the Base Color so you can see how the Alpha of the Base Color Texture can be used as your Roughness map

Build your Material Graph as shown in Figure 15.5. Pay attention to the default values of each Parameter node as you prepare building your network.

The **Use Base Color Texture Alpha for Roughness** Static Switch Parameter allows either the Alpha channel of the **Base Color Texture** to be used as the Roughness mask or the Red channel of a **Roughness Texture** Parameter. Using the Alpha of the Base Color Texture is a common workflow, and many Assets available in the Marketplace and freely in the community are authored to use this method for defining the Roughness in Materials.

Another Static Switch Parameter called **Use Roughness Texture** allows you to switch between a single Roughness scalar value connected to the False input and the Texture-based pathway that flows from the True input. If Use Roughness Texture is set to *true*, the texture data returned by the Use Base Color Texture Alpha for Roughness Parameter is modulated using a Lerp node and the **Roughness Min** and **Roughness Max** Scalar Parameters.

Normal

The **Normal** channel is likely the least familiar to most visualization artists. Most 3D applications rely on bump and height maps to define surface microvariation. Real-time applications, UE4 included, use normal maps instead, because they are faster to calculate than a bump map, and they can define surface curvature, making them higher quality than bump maps.

You create Normal Texture Parameter nodes much like any other Texture Parameter. However, you must set the **Sampler Type** to *Normal* in the node's Details panel. This is done automatically if you assign a normal map texture to the node's Texture property.

To control the normal map's intensity, Lerp between the Normal Texture's value connected to the A input and a Constant Vector value of 0,0,1 (the value for an unmodified normal) connected to the B input (see Figure 15.6).

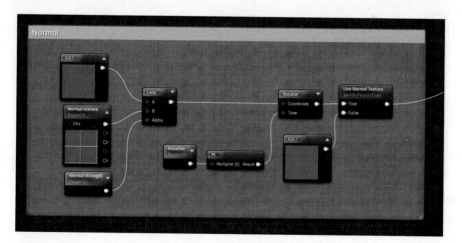

Figure 15.6 Normal node graph

To account for rotation, normal maps need to be modified to maintain the correct vector math. Use a **Rotator** node to rotate the data returned by the Lerp. A Scalar Parameter called **Rotation** is multiplied by Pi and used as the Time input on the Rotator node tied to the UV and Texture

Transforms (explained later). To be clear, you are rotating the *value* of the normal map, rather than the Texture.

Vector math like this is the lifeblood of 3D applications. Everything from movement in 3D space to the colors of Materials are vectors. Learning vector math is one of the best things you can do as an artist looking to increase your capabilities and skills in every part of UE4.

Ambient Occlusion

The optional Ambient Occlusion (AO) map is for manually defining the microsurface ambient occlusion of a Material (see Figure 15.7). If this input is not defined, UE4 will generate this data dynamically using the normal map, but sometimes this isn't entirely accurate or what the artist intends. The AO channel is most often used when Texture sets have been baked using a program like Substance designer or XNormal and can be left off in most cases.

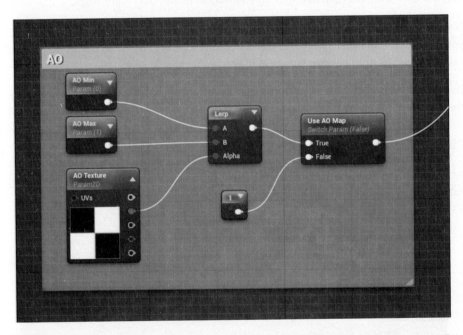

Figure 15.7 Ambient Occlusion node graph, typically only used in special circumstances when UE4's Materials need some help

Set up your graph as shown in Figure 15.7. Like the roughness and Metallic inputs, AO only requires a scalar or grayscale input; therefore, only the Red channel of the **AO Texture** Parameter is used.

The **Use AO Map** Static Switch Parameter allows Material Instances to skip using the AO map altogether. Unlike some of the other Switch Parameters where the False input is fed a

Scalar Parameter, here we will simply assign a **Constant** node and set it to *1.0*. Unlike Scalar Parameters, Constant variables cannot be changed at runtime.

Texture Scaling and Transform

Adjusting the scale and positions of Textures is essential for getting the look of your Materials right. In UE4, rather than adjusting the scale of the Texture as you might in a 3D application, you modify the surface's UV coordinates in real time using the shader network (see Figure 15.8).

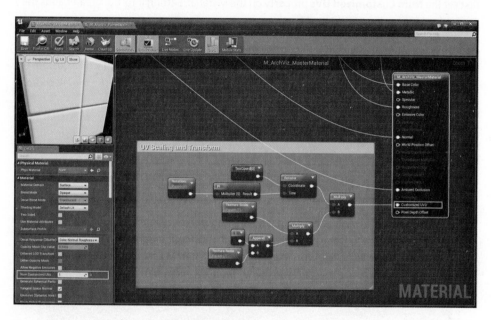

Figure 15.8 UV Scaling and Transform shader graph.

Start by adding a **Texture Coordinate** node (titled TexCoord[0] in Figure 15.8). This node returns the UV coordinates of a specific UV channel.

You then modify the UV coordinate it returns by first rotating it around the center of the Texture using the **Rotator**. This node is driven by wiring the **Rotation** Scalar Parameter into the Time input[3]. To make the Rotation Parameter easier to author in Material Instances, it is multiplied by pi, converting **Rotation** into a 0.0–1.0 range with 0.5 being 180 degrees.

To scale the coordinates, therefore scaling/tiling the Texture, they must be multiplied. The **Texture Scale** Parameter handles this task. Values over 1 cause the Texture to tile more, whereas values below 0 cause the Texture to appear larger, tiling less.

---

3. The Rotation Parameter is used multiple times in this shader. If parameters have the same parameter name, changes to the single value affects all nodes with that name.

The **Texture Ratio** Parameter allows the Texture to be non-uniformly scaled. The **Append** node creates a *Vector2* value (a value with two floats; in this case the U and V channels like 0,0 or 0.2,1.0) with a **Constant** of 1.0 as the first value and the Texture Ratio as the second. This returns a vector2D value like 1.0, 0.5, which is then multiplied by the Texture Scale Parameter, the result of that then being multiplied by the rotated coordinates.

The result of all this is a modified UV coordinate that you then wire into the **Customized UV0** attribute of the Material. This input is not exposed by default. To enable this option, you must first set the **Num Customized UVs** property on the Material. Setting it to 1 or greater adds the Customized UV input nodes to the Material.

Custom UVs allow you to avoid having to wire the transformed UV coordinates into each and every UV input on all the Texture nodes in your Material. Instead, the data fed to the Custom UV inputs modifies the UV channel's coordinates. Now, any Texture that's set to use the UV coordinate channel will be provided these modified UV values.

Creating Material Instances

Figure 15.9 shows many of the Material Instances used in the scene. Almost all of these Instances are based on the single Master Material detailed earlier. Each Material Instance has had new Textures applied and Parameters adjusted, creating the diverse Material Library available here.

Figure 15.9 Content Browser with Materials and Material Instances derived from the Master Material

Painted Walls

Many different colors of paint are required for this scene. For each is a Material Instance is created, each a different color defined by changing the Base Color Tint Parameter. However, as you can see from Figure 15.10, I also had to set a lot of Parameters to get the right look for this Material Instance: I had to assign Textures, toggle Static Switch Parameters, and modify scalar values, resulting in a rich-looking wall surface.

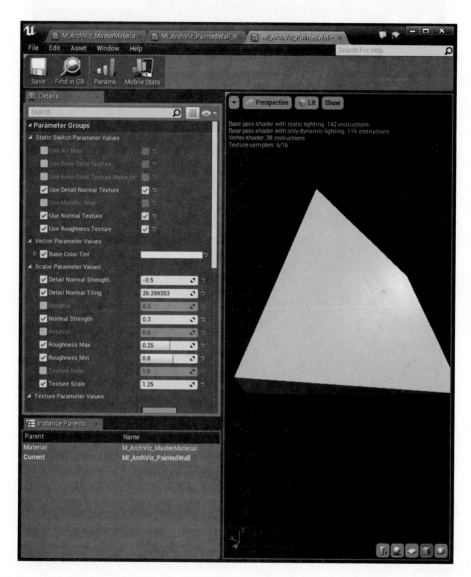

Figure 15.10 Painted Wall Material Instance with many Parameters modified to adjust the Material exactly to the desired look

All the different painted wall color variations derive from the same Master Material; however, they are parented to another Material Instance instead of directly to the Master Material (see Figure 15.11). This demonstrates one of the most powerful features of Material Instances: the ability to base Material Instances on other Material Instances.

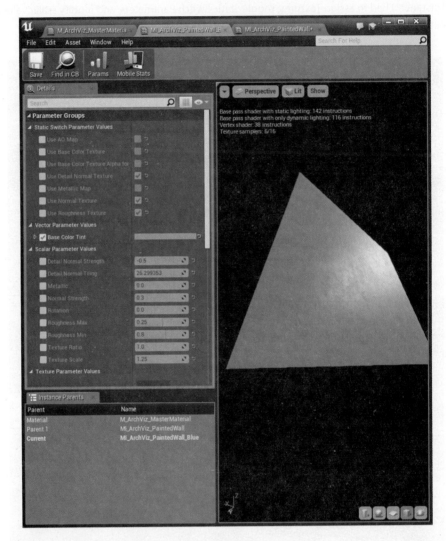

Figure 15.11 M_ArchViz_PaintedWall _Blue Material Instance derived from another Material Instance: M_ArchViz_PaintedWall

Creating Material Instances from other Material Instances enables you to set up a single Master Material Instance that when modified, the changes cascade down to all the Material Instances that inherit from it.

Figure 15.19 A single glass Material being used for the glasses, bowls, and the plate glass windows in the background

Several ways exist to create Glass Materials, each with advantages and drawbacks. Typically, the more accurate the Material is, the longer it takes to render. The Material demonstrated in Figure 15.19 is rather expensive to render, but it's worth it because of the increased quality of simple translucent Materials.

Because we will need to set the Material to Translucent, we cannot easily use the Master Material as our basis for Glass Materials. We need a new Material.

The first thing you need to do is to make the Material you are creating Translucent. This lets it render after the main scene and be blended on top afterward. In the Material's Detail panel with no nodes selected, set the Material's **Blend Mode** to **Translucent** and the **Lighting Mode** to **Surface Translucency Volume** (see Figure 15.20).

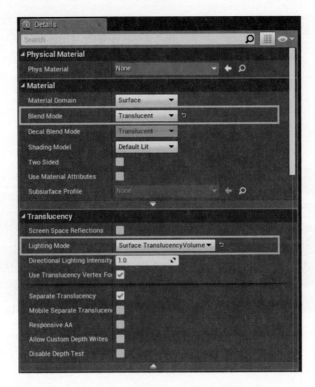

Figure 15.20 The glass Material's Detail Panel with the Material's Blend Mode set to translucent and the Lighting Mode set to Surface Translucency Volume

Most translucent Materials rely on the Opacity attribute to modulate the object's opacity, allowing the scene behind it to be rendered. In this case, you will bypass that (setting the Opacity to almost 1.0) and provide your own version of the scene behind the glass, this one tinted and distorted.

To do this, you need to sample the **Scene Texture** (see Figure 15.21).

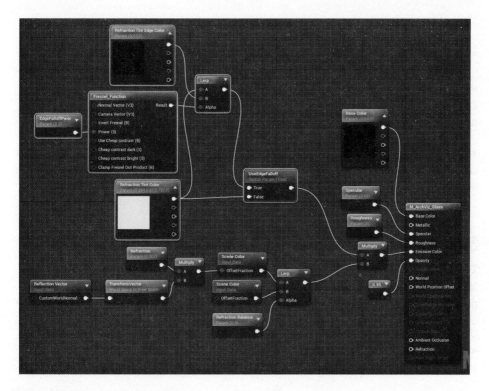

Figure 15.21 The ArchViz Glass Material network; bypassing the Opacity channel and building your own, modified scene Texture enables you to more effectively control the refraction and allow the surface reflections to stay bright

The **Scene Texture** is the rendered scene before the translucency is applied (translucent objects in UE4 are rendered after the rest of the scene then composited into the final frame). If you were to pipe the Scene Color directly to the Emissive attribute of the Material, it would make your glass look completely see through, aside from the surface reflections.

To distort the Scene Texture, you take the Reflection Vector (a Vector input provided by the Engine), transform it to your view (taking it from 3D worldspace to a 2D viewspace value) and then use that data to distort the Scene Color using the Offset Fraction. The offset fraction is a percentage (0.0–1.0) that lets you sample the Scene Color at a different pixel location on the screen.

This is a completely non-physically accurate refraction technique but it provides good-looking results.

You'll notice two Scene Color nodes in the Figure 15.21 graph being Lerped together by the **Reflection Balance** Parameter. One is the distorted Scene Color whereas the other is unmodified. This gives a double-pane look that's great for architectural visualization plate glass.

You can then easily tint the distorted and doubled-up Scene Color samples.

Assuming you have set **Use Edge Falloff** to true in your Material Instance based from this Material, the **Fresnel** Function provides a simple Fresnel falloff based on the surface normal relative to the camera. Using this falloff, the Tint is interpolated between the defined **Refraction Tint Color** Parameter to the **Refraction Tint Edge Color** Parameter. Otherwise, the Scene Color is tinted by the **Refraction Tint Color** Parameter.

You set the Material's **Roughness** and **Specular** attributes using simple Scalar Parameters. You could expand on this Material to use Textures to drive any of these Parameters as well; however, this makes the Material much more expensive to render and should be used with caution.

Summary

Thanks to the PBR system in UE4, the visual Material Editor and the power and convenience of Material Instances, building beautiful Materials is quick and easy. It can be so much fun that going back to authoring Materials in 3D applications might be difficult.

Using Material Parameters and Material Instances make reusing your Material networks a snap, and the interactive node-based Material Editor lets you experiment, learn, and expand your Materials as your abilities and project requirements grow.

CHAPTER 16

CREATING CINEMATICS WITH SEQUENCER

Interactivity and exploration are the hallmarks of interactive visualizations in UE4. However, UE4 is also extremely capable of creating pre-rendered, static animations that rival the quality of raytraced renderings. And it can do so in a fraction of the time. Using Sequencer, Unreal Engine 4's innovative animation tool, you can combine your interactive worlds with keyframed Camera and Actor animations to create stunning animations.

Getting Started with Sequencer

The **Sequencer Editor** is a cinematic editing tool within UE4 that allows you to edit **Sequences**.

Sequences are Assets you can place into Levels as Actors that contain keyframed animation **Tracks**. Sequencer takes a lot of inspiration from tools like After Effects, Final Cut, and other video editing and compositing applications. This helps make for an easy learning curve for many visualization artists who are already adept at video editing tools like these.

Sequencer replaces the previous cinematic editing tool in UE4, **Matinee**. Matinee still exists alongside Sequencer, but it's depreciated, and in comparison to Sequencer is a very limited tool.

Master Sequence

Unlike most Assets that you either import or create in the Content Browser, you create Sequences in the Level using the Cinematics dropdown menu (see Figure 16.1).

Figure 16.1 Creating a Master Sequence from the Cinematics dropdown menu in the Editor

You are given the option to create a **Master Sequence**, a single **Level Sequence**, or a legacy Matinee Sequence. A Master Sequence is basically a wizard that creates a Sequence with several sub-sequences (see Figure 16.2). The wizard also creates the various Sequence Assets and saves them to a specific location in your Content directory.

You can also start with a single Level Sequence if you only need to create something simple. You can include individual Sequences in other Sequences at any time as well.

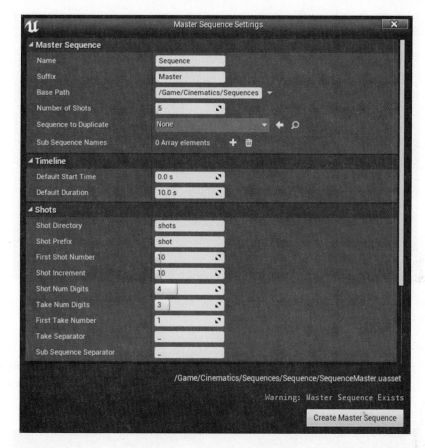

Figure 16.2 Master Sequence wizard settings showing that I have only modified the Default Duration and set it to 10 seconds from the default of 5

You can accept the standard settings for most projects unless you need to follow a naming scheme or other standard. The only setting I changed here is the Default Duration, which I set to 10 seconds.

When you create a Master Sequence, a Sequencer window appears showing all the track Sequences laid out in a row (see Figure 16.3).

For anybody familiar with non-linear editing applications, you will feel right at home. You can move **Shots** and add, remove, and easily change the duration of each track, making Shots Track Editor behave like Adobe Premiere: fast, streamlined, but lacking in fine control.

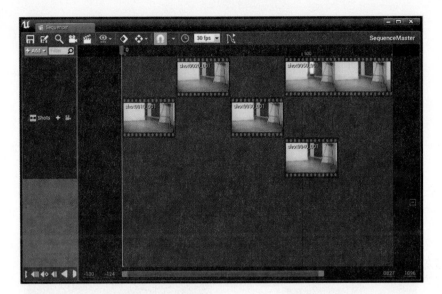

Figure 16.3 Master Sequence Editor, in which you can move and edit Shots as in a non-linear video editing program

To get that control, double-click any of the Sequences to open that shot in the Sequence Editor (see Figure 16.4). Although this is the same Sequencer Editor, it looks different and it serves a different purpose. By exposing the Camera Cuts and Camera Actor Tracks, this editor is much more akin to Adobe After Effects: It's a keyframe-driven animation and effects interface.

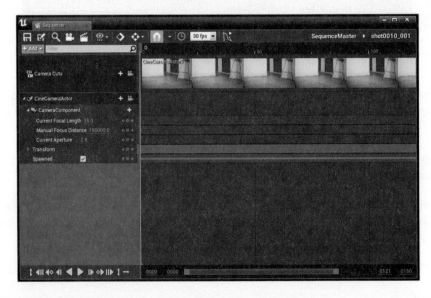

Figure 16.4 A single shot opened for editing in the Sequence Editor, showing how the editor changes to look more like a keyframed effects package like After Effects

Dynamic Cameras

In each of these shot Sequences, a **CineCameraActor** is spawned dynamically in the Sequence and destroyed when the Sequence is finished. This feature is really powerful, and it means you don't have to have a single Camera Actor placed in your Level because they are created and destroyed on the fly in Sequencer.

These cameras act like any other Camera Actor and displays the lens settings, depth of field, and focus settings as well as all the post-processing effects available, letting you configure each camera exactly as you need it (see Figure 16.5).

Notice the Details Panel and the Add Keyframe button that appears just to the left of each of the animation-related properties. Like with most windows in UE4, you can dock Sequencer in the UE4 window to help fight clutter.

Figure 16.5 Sequencer docked in the UE4 Editor

Animating the Camera

Getting your camera to move and change over time is the next obvious step, but getting that to happen easily might not be so obvious.

Setting Keyframes

You have a couple ways to set keyframes in Sequencer. You can turn on Auto-Key, creating a keyframe each time you modify a property or move, rotate, or scale an Actor. This can quickly get messy.

You can also manually set keyframes. You can do this in either the Sequencer interface or in the properties and Viewports directly. When the Sequencer is up, animation-related properties in Actors show an Add Keyframe button (refer to Figure 16.5), letting you easily add a keyframe when you need it.

A third way is a little of each of the preceding options. You can automatically set keyframes, but restrict them to only the properties to which you have already added keyframes to (see Figure 16.6). I typically use this option because it combines the ease of use of auto-keyframing without the worry of accidentally adding keyframes to tracks you don't intend to animate.

Figure 16.6 Setting the Auto-Keyframe settings to only add keyframes to already-animated tracks and properties

Piloting the Camera

Now that you can set some keyframes, let's get the camera into position.

To view through the camera, select the camera icon to the right of the camera you want to animate. This sets the Viewport to pilot the camera, letting you fly the Actor around the scene, attaching it to your view.

Camera icons appear in many areas of the Sequencer interface and it can be a bit confusing (refer to Figure 16.6). You'll notice that the Camera Cuts track also has a camera icon. Clicking it lets you see the view from the perspective of the Sequence, including any camera cuts you author.

You'll typically want to move between these views as you work, adjusting the Camera's keyframes, and seeing the result in-context with other cuts.

When piloting a camera, you see through the lens of the camera and move it about the scene using the standard Perspective Viewport controls. You can adjust the camera's keyframes in the Orthographic views or by adjusting the Camera Actor's properties in the Details panel.

Track and Camera Naming

You might notice that the name of the track in Sequencer differs from the label in the timeline's preview. This is a bit confusing, because these can be named independently (You may, for instance, use the same Camera Actor for several different tracks in several different Sequences). The name in the preview thumbnail is the name of the Actor in the world. You can rename your Cine Camera Actor using the Details panel to update the name in the timeline.

The name in the left panel is the track name. You can double-click this name to rename the track.

Transitions

The only **transition** UE4 offers is a **Fade** track. No cross-dissolve or other transition effects are available. This is mainly due to performance considerations. Doing a cross-dissolve requires the scene to be rendered twice and both scenes composited on top of each other during the dissolve. Although some scenes could manage this, most would struggle to render so much information.

Editing the Shots

To return to the Master Sequence, select the title in the upper-right of the Sequencer window (see Figure 16.7).

Figure 16.7 Completed shot with the SequenceMaster track highlighted in the upper-right of the Sequencer window

You will see that the preview of your shot has been updated with the view from your shot. You can use this as a guide to help when adjusting your in- and outpoints in the Sequence. To see better, zoom on the timeline using the range slider on the bottom of the Sequencer window.

Continue the editing steps for your remaining shots. Edit the shot, then return to the Master Sequence to see it in context, modify it, and iterate until you are happy with all the shots in the Sequence.

Saving

Remember to save regularly. Sequences are saved as UASSET files in your Project's Content directory.

You don't need to save the Level that the Sequence is in after you have placed the Sequence Actor for the first time. This Actor acts as a reference to your Master Sequence, lets the Sequence data initialize when the Level loads, and allows Blueprints to access it easily by referencing the Actor.

Collaborating

Because the shots are stored as individual UASSET packages, several team members can work on the same Sequence at the same time. Also, lighting, props, and other set dressing can continue while the animations are being developed in parallel. This saves time and lets you produce drafts earlier in the production pipeline.

Rendering to Video

After your Sequence is perfected, it's time to get it to disk. This is where the speed of UE4 is astounding. Entire animations can be delivered (not just rendered, but up on YouTube) in the time it takes for a single frame to render in a standard ray-traced renderer like Mental Ray or V-Ray.

With your Sequence open, click the Render to Video button (see Figure 16.8) in the Sequencer toolbar. The Render Movie Settings dialog opens (see Figure 16.9). Here, you can set a wide array of rendering and export options. From bumper frames to pre-roll to burn-ins, UE4 exposes professional-level tools for video editors and compositors.

Figure 16.8 Selecting the Render to Movie button in Sequencer

Render Movie Settings

As you can see, I have it set to render at 4K resolution at 60 frames per second (see Figure 16.9). This creates silky-smooth, razor-sharp animations that are truly eye catching. These files are huge at more than 100GB per minute of uncompressed footage.

Figure 16.9 Render Movie Settings dialog set to 4K (3840x2160) resolution at 60 frames per second

I am rendering directly to AVI (Video Sequence), but if your studio has a more extensive post-production pipeline that relies on linear color, you can also render out the HDR image buffers individually using the Custom outputs option.

You can also chose to compress your AVI to save space (not recommended) or export to individual frames in common formats like BMP and EXR.

Rendering Process

When UE4 begins rendering, it spawns a small rendering window and begins writing to disk (see Figure 16.10). The render window is located in the upper left of the window, and the Editor is in the background. Notice the Capturing video notice in the lower right. Also, note the high disk write usage—the faster, the better.

Figure 16.10 UE4 rendering the Sequence to disk

At this point, the rendering is being limited not by the visuals being generated but by the speed of the hard drive it is being written to. I can't stress that enough. The act of writing the frame to disk takes longer than rendering the frame.

Write to the disk that provides the fastest, most consistent performance. Be sure to test. I was surprised to learn that my SSHD is significantly faster in the long haul than my typically very fast SSD that I had assumed to be the better choice. Drives with better sustained write performance will pay huge benefits.

After your animation is complete, process it just like you would any other video file. It may go straight to the Web or be included in a larger video, just like your standard visualization videos.

Summary

The ability to adapt to the client's needs at a moment's notice is just one more reason so many visualization studios are turning to UE4, not just to generate interactive content, but to deliver stunning pre-rendered content as well.

This 90-second Sequence took about 10 minutes to render—at 4K resolution at 60 frames per second. It takes more time compressing, copying, and uploading most video files produced using UE4 than it takes to render them.

With the powerful features of Sequencer, the ability to see exactly what will be in your camera frame at all times, and the physically correct Cine Camera model, you can begin producing video content in UE4 that meets and sometimes exceeds the quality from traditional renderers.

CHAPTER 17

PREPARING THE LEVEL FOR INTERACTIVITY

Building upon your simple Pawn, Game Mode, and Player Controller from the first example project will allow you to easily add exploration to your Level. However, you must set up your Level with collision, a Player Start, and other settings before the Player will be able to successfully navigate the Level.

Setting Up Your Level

To set up your Level for Interactivity, you'll want to get your Level and Player Controller set up to use a mouse cursor and touch-style input. You'll also enable the mouse interaction events, which allows you to highlight and click Actors in the game world at runtime.

Of course, you'll want to open your Level before continuing. You might want to save out a new version of your Level as I have, so that you can return to an unmodified version of your Level easily.

Adding the Player Start Actor

As covered in Chapter 9, every UE4 Level needs a Player Start Actor. This simple Actor tells UE4 where to place the Player in the Level when the game begins.

Drag and drop a Player Start Actor from the Modes palette into the Level near where you want the Player to enter the world each time (see Figure 17.1).

You should also rotate the Player Start Actor to face the direction you would like the player to begin. The blue arrow in the middle of the Player Start Actor indicates the Player Start Actor's forward vector.

Figure 17.1 Placing the Player Start into the Level

Adding Collision

You can now test your application by clicking the Play in Editor button. There's a really good chance, however, that you will find yourself falling through the air below your Level when you do. This would likely be due to missing collision information.

Collision detection is serious business in interactive games and simulations. Knowing when one Actor collides with another Actor or has entered an area is essential for creating living worlds.

In UE4, you can use the **Player Collision** View Mode as shown in Figure 17.2 to preview what Actors have collision. In the Viewport, select the ViewMode button and select Player Collison from the dropdown list. To return to your regular view, set the Viewmode dropdown back to Lit.

As you can see (or, more accurately cannot see) in the figure, there are no floors or walls, but some of the prop and door Meshes have collision already. These are represented by the flat-shaded versions of their collision primitives.

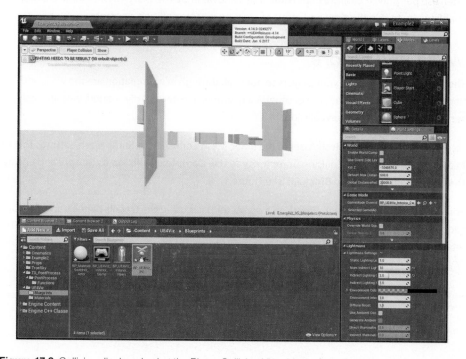

Figure 17.2 Collision displayed using the Player Collision View Mode

Collision in UE4 can be complicated and hard to understand at first glance. Fortunately, visualizations tend to be more simple, static affairs with few dynamic Actors (compared to a game with tens or hundreds of characters onscreen and in the game world at once), so you get to avoid some of the complexities that can make setting up collision so challenging.

Complex Versus Simple Collision

Games tend to rely on simplified version of models to perform collision calculations on. This is because these calculations are costly and get more and more costly the more polygons and information there is to process.

UE4 uses **collision primitives**—simple shapes like boxes, spheres, and capsule shapes—that can be authored in-Engine or by using low-polygon shapes made in a 3D application to use as **simple collision**. This allows orders of magnitude more polygons to be used graphically, whereas the physics engine uses an optimized version of the scene to do its calculations.

UE4 can also do **per-polygon collision** as needed. This is often used cosmetically in games to add precise effects graphically such as damage on walls or vehicles that happens in the exact spot of the apparent hit, while the actual physics collision uses the simplified Mesh for speed.

Because visualization scenes can be relatively simple with few interacting elements, you can often use per-poly or **complex collision** (as it's known in UE4) in place of the simple collision, enabling you to skip the time and effort of creating custom collision geometry.

Walls and Floors

The main things you want your players to not walk through in a simulation are the walls and floors. Because these Meshes are geometrically simple and awkwardly shaped, we can safely set these to use per-polygon collision.

To do so, open the Static Mesh Asset in the Static Mesh Editor. In the Static Mesh Settings rollout in the Details tab, set the Collision Complexity to **Use Complex Collision as Simple** and ensure the Collision Preset is set to **BlockAll** (see Figure 17.3).

You can override the Collision Preset on a per-Actor basis using the Details panel; however, you cannot change the Collision Complexity property. You can only do that in the Static Mesh Editor interface or in the property matrix.

Figure 17.3 Setting the Floor Mesh to use per-polygon collision

Bulk Editing with the Property Matrix

You must set up collision complexity for each Mesh you want your player to collide with. This could take a very long time if you had to open every Asset one by one.

Fortunately, UE4 has a Bulk Edit function.

Select all the Meshes you want to enable collision on in the Content Browser. Right-click one of the Asset icons to open the context menu. Under **Asset actions**, select **Bulk Edit via Property Matrix** (see Figure 17.4).

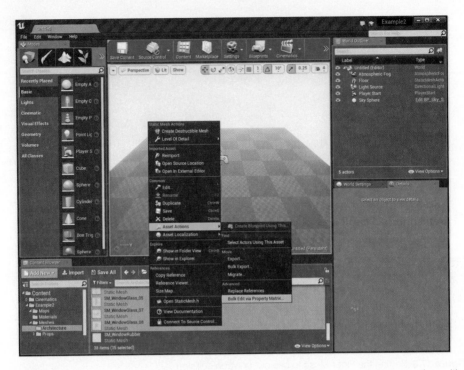

Figure 17.4 Selecting multiple Assets in the Content Browser and editing them at the same time with the property matrix

The property matrix shows all common properties in a modified Details Panel. From here, you can set the Collision Complexity for all of your Meshes in a single go (see Figure 17.5). You can also display properties as columns in the list on the left so you can visually compare Assets and modify individual Assets like a spreadsheet.

Sometimes, properties have differing names in different interfaces. The Collision Preset is one of those. To modify this property using the property matrix, look for the property named Collision Profile Name. Filtering the properties for **collision** helps to narrow down the list. To set the Collision Preset, type in **BlockAll** into the Collision Profile Name property text field.

When you are done editing your Assets, be sure to save so the changes are written to disk.

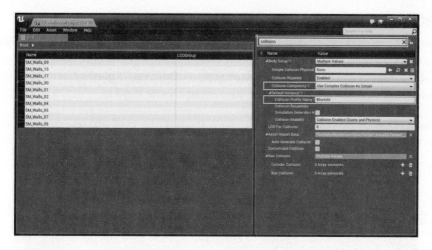

Figure 17.5 Using the property matrix to set the Collision Complexity of all the walls and floors at once

Visualizing Collision

After you set up your collision, check out your collision environment by setting the Perspective Viewport to the Player Collision View mode (see Figure 17.6). This lets you see the collision environment, which is the physics engine UE4 uses to calculate collisions.

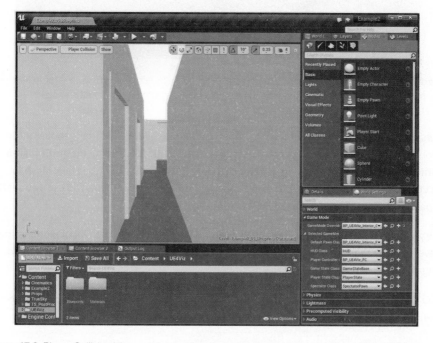

Figure 17.6 Player Collision View mode showing the per-polygon collision of the walls and floors being successfully turned on

Setting Prop Collision

Setting collision on Props is a little trickier. I personally prefer to turn off collision on most Props in my simulations, allowing the Player to freely move through and over most obstacles. I prefer to only have waist-high objects or taller stop my player. This allows a greater feeling of mobility in smaller spaces and makes navigation much easier for novice Players.

In Figure 17.7, you can see that most of the smaller Props still have collision on, potentially making it difficult for the Player to navigate this space.

Figure 17.7 The final Collision setup showing that only the walls, floors, windows, and large furniture have player collision enabled, allowing the Player more freedom to move around the space

To enable the Props to still have collision (important for interactions, including mouse interactions like clicking), change the **Collision Preset** in the Static Mesh Editor (or the **Collision Profile Name** in the property matrix) to **Ignore Only Pawn**. This allows the Static Mesh to react to all other physics events, but won't impede the Player's movement. You can also set this property on a per-actor basis via the Details Panel.

Now you should be able to click Play and walk around your Level without fear of plummeting forever through the void. Walls and floors should feel solid, and the Level should be easy to navigate.

If you find yourself getting stuck or falling, you'll need to look at the collision setup in your Level.

Enabling the Mouse Cursor

Because you want this to be a mouse-driven application, you want to see the cursor. Open the Player Controller and look for the **Mouse Interface** group of the class's default properties (see Figure 17.8). Enable **Show Mouse Cursor**, **Enable Click Events**, and **Enable Mouse Over Events**, which allow 3D Actors in the scene to interact with the mouse cursor.

If you test now, you'll notice that you can only rotate the camera when the mouse button is being held down. Releasing the button displays the cursor and releases rotation control.

You also might notice that the axis of rotation feels "off." The camera turns right when you expect it to turn left or up when you want to look down.

This is because of how Players expect to control the camera. When the Player doesn't need to hold down a button to rotate, it usually feels more natural for the horizontal axis to follow the direction of the mouse. Right turns right, left turns left.

However, when the user clicks and drags to turn, it feels more natural for this action to act more like a touchscreen, anchoring the cursor to the point in 3D space and rotating the camera as if the user were using a trackball. This means dragging right on the mouse should turn the view left while dragging down should pitch the camera up.

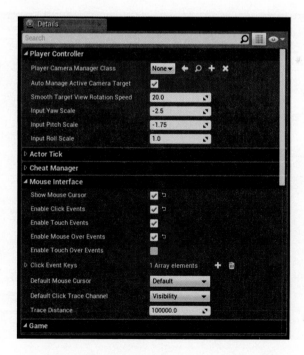

Figure 17.8 Setting up the Player Controller to use Mouse Cursor, Mouse Click, and Mouse Over events and adjusting Input Yaw and Pitch to compensate for the inverted turning feeling

You can adjust for this change in Player expectation via the Input Yaw and Input Pitch Scale values in the Player Controller (refer to Figure 17.8). The reason that the Yaw (Horizontal turning) is faster is due to human perception and what "feels" right. Having symmetrical axis speeds "feels" wrong.

It's worth mentioning that a camera's interactivity is all really up to personal preferences. Age, experience with different kinds of technologies, and even people's favorite game will inform them how an interactive camera should behave. Listening to your Players about this and adapting to their needs in each project is important.

Creating Post-Process Outlines

To make it clear what Actor is highlighted, I want to use an outline similar to what's used in the Editor. This effect is unavailable at runtime because it uses a completely different rendering system than the main Viewport.

Instead, you can use a post-process Material to draw outlines. I have (predictably) merged my own Marketplace content into this project, instanced the Material, and modified it to fit my needs (see Figure 17.9).

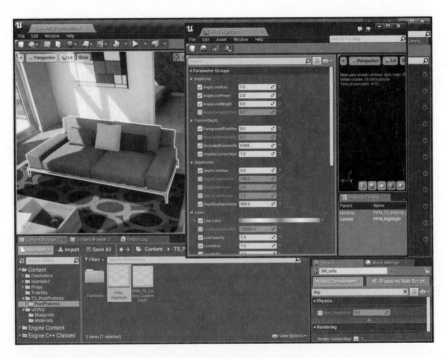

Figure 17.9 Testing the Post-Process Material by enabling the Render Custom Depth property on the couch Static Mesh Actor

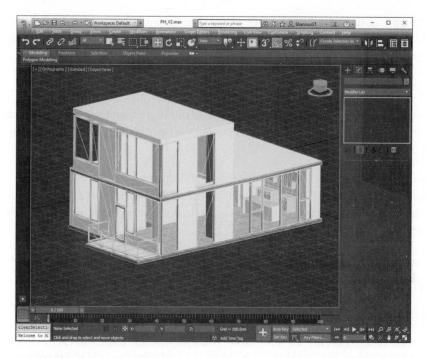

Figure 18.1 The updated data in 3DS Max

This change is significant and will affect the look, feel, and lighting of the Level so much your best bet is to create an entirely new Level, complete with its own lighting and geometry.

Luckily you don't have to do that from scratch. You can use your existing Level as a starting point. First, load up your Level in the Editor if it's not already. You can load Levels by going to **File > Open Level** or by finding the UMAP Asset in the Content Browser and double-clicking on it.

Making a Copy with Save As

Create a copy of the Level by choosing **File > Save Current As** and then name it something descriptive like **Example2_V2_MAP**.

This gives you two Levels in your project: **Example2_MAP** and **Example2_V2_MAP**.

At this point the Levels are exactly the same apart from the name.

Importing the New Architecture

Because your Levels share so much in common, including the prop placement, lighting, and other details, you will only need to replace the Architecture Meshes. You can also choose to replace only the Meshes that are changing, but for the sake of this example, let's create a fully unique Level with fully unique geometry.

As in Chapter 12, "Data Pipeline," prepare your content in your 3D application. Apply UVW mapping, check for poor geometry, and organize your content as you have before. You should come up with a new naming variation for these Meshes to avoid potential conflicts.

After it's prepared, export to FBX and import into UE4.

When you import your FBX files into UE4, you should put your content into a new folder apart from the previous Architecture Meshes; this ensures the two datasets are maintained separately, avoiding data conflicts.

As before, import your FBX files into the Content Browser using the suggested settings for Static Architecture Meshes—most importantly, ensuring **Auto Generate Collision** is set to false, **Generate Lightmap UVs** is set to true, and **Transform Vertex to Absolute** is set to true as well (refer to Figure 12.5 in Chapter 12).

After importing the FBX files, don't forget to save the Static Mesh Assets you just created before moving on.

Replacing the Architecture Meshes

In your *new* Level (Example2_V2_MAP), select all the Architecture Static Mesh Actors in your scene. Press the Del key or right-click on the Actors and select Delete to delete them, leaving only the Props, Lights, and other Actors.

To place your new Architecture Meshes, drag them into the Viewport, and then reset their position to 0,0,0 using the Location property in the Details Panel. You should now have updated Architecture.

While your recently placed Static Mesh Actors are still selected, it's a good time to also organize them into a folder in your **World Outliner** so you can easily select them in the future.

Setting Up Lightmap Density

Now that you've replaced the walls, floors, and ceilings, they have returned to their default Lightmap resolution. You must go through and modify your newly placed Meshes' **Overridden Light Map Res** property, using the Lightmap Density Optimization View Mode.

You should try to match the density you set up in the previous map as much as possible. This ensures the lighting builds look consistent between the two Levels.

Applying Materials

Your newly imported Meshes will undoubtedly be either lacking Materials or have the default, imported Materials applied. Take the time to apply the materials as applied in the first Level.

Enabling Collision

The last thing you need to do is ensure your Collision is set up correctly. Use the Player Collision View Mode to determine what Meshes need to have Collision enabled.

Decorating (Optional)

You can take this opportunity to make as many changes as you want to the Level—try some different Lighting, Materials, Props, you name it. In this example, the Props, Lighting, and Materials are left the same, leaving the only change to be the architecture. This allows the Player to focus on the differences being distracted by any other changes.

Building Lighting

Lighting is stored on a per-Level basis. So, you can have the same Assets in different Levels with vastly different lighting setups and Lightmaps. This allows you to bake lighting on a per-Level basis while using all the same Asset references.

An advantage of using the Save As method for creating a new Level is that it retains all the World Settings you applied earlier, including the Lightmass settings. This makes building lighting very easy indeed; you should simply be able to set your Lighting Build Quality to the Level you want and click the Build button.

After building the lighting, you should have a new variation of your Level with awesome vaulted ceilings and the lighting changes that provides (see Figure 18.2).

Save your Level. The Light and Shadow maps will be written to the Level (or as of version 4.15, to a separate Build Data file alongside the Level that is only visible in the Content Browser or File Explorer).

Figure 18.2 Completed production lighting build for the new data

Level Streaming

UE4 can load and unload entire Levels on the fly. This is called **Level Streaming** and the system can be used to easily swap large datasets in and out using simple Blueprint commands.

The way Level Streaming works is fairly simple. A single Level, called the **Persistent Level**, is first loaded. This Level is often very simple or even almost completely blank.

This Level, or an Object or Actor within it (a Blueprint or the Player Controller, for example) can load another Level or Levels into or out of it. You can also toggle the visibility of the loaded Levels both in the Editor and at runtime, making for a convenient way to switch datasets quickly.

To set up your Level Streaming, you first make a Persistent Level, then add your two versions as Streaming Levels using the **Levels** interface (see Figure 18.3).

Making a New Level

Let's first make a new, blank Level for your Persistent Level. Choose **File > New Level** and select **Empty Level** from the options available.

When your new, blank Level is open, save it and name it (for example, Example2_Persistent_
MAP). This map contains only some Blueprint code in the Level Blueprint to handle the toggling
of your streaming Levels.

Accessing the Levels Interface

The Editor exposes the Level Streaming system through the Levels list. You can access it by
choosing **Window > Level**. This opens the Levels window (see Figure 18.3).

Figure 18.3 The Levels window

You will see the currently loaded Level listed as the *Persistent Level*.

Adding Streaming Levels

Click the Levels button in the upper-left corner of the Levels window and select **Add Existing**
from the dropdown menu. Select the original Level (Example2 _MAP) you made (see
Figure 18.4). You can also create a new, blank streaming map, or create a new map with the
selected Actors.

Figure 18.4 Adding a streaming Level from an existing map

The map loads into the Viewport and you see it listed in the Levels window.

Do this again to add the new version (Example2 _V2_MAP) into the Levels window.

You should now see both Levels in the Levels window as well as in the Viewport.

You can hide and unhide Levels using the Eye icon on each Level. You can also save Levels, open their Level Blueprints, and toggle an editing lock to prevent changes. Even if your project isn't using Level Streaming at runtime, using them can be a great way to split up a big scene into smaller files or to organize things (see Figure 18.5). Note in the figure that Example2_MAP is hidden using the Eye icon that now displays as a closed Eye icon.

Figure 18.5 Both versions of the Level loaded into the Levels window

Remember that the view toggles set for each Level in the Levels window are Editor-only and that Level visibility at runtime is handled through Blueprint logic.

You now need to save your Persistent Level because you have modified it by adding the Streaming Levels using the Levels interface.

Using Blueprints Versus Always Loaded Levels

Notice the small blue dot next to your two new Levels in the Levels window. This means that the Levels are loaded using Blueprints, and that they will not load until you tell them to using Blueprints. You can also unload and hide and unhide these Levels at runtime.[1]

Alternatively, you can set Levels to be Always Loaded. As the name implies, these Levels are always loaded and cannot be hidden or unloaded at runtime.

Levels that need to always be loaded can be set this way by right-clicking on the Level in the Levels window and choosing **Change Streaming Method > Always Loaded**. These Levels will load as if they were part of the Persistent Level when the game is played.

---

1. Unloading and loading Levels removes them from memory and can take some time to happen at runtime. Hiding and unhiding keeps the Level loaded but simply toggles rendering of that Level's content. This happens instantly.

Keep your Levels' Streaming Method as Blueprints because you want to be able to hide and unhide them at runtime using Blueprints.

Defining a Player Start Actor

Even though your two Streaming Levels have Player Start Actors already in them, you need to define one for your new Persistent Level. This can sometimes be a little confusing because you can clearly see the Player Start Actors and select them in the Editor Viewport, but they will not be there when the Level initially loads. This is because the Player Controller is spawned before the Streaming Level has a chance to load.

You can easily copy and paste one of your Player Start Actors from one of your Streaming Levels into the Persistent Level Select the Player Start from the Content Browser or the Viewport and then go to **Edit > Copy** or choose Edit > Copy from the right-click menu.

Pasting requires a little more care. When you have multiple Levels loaded in the Editor, you need to define what Level is your *active* Level before pasting the Player Start.

You want this Player Start to be placed in the Persistent Level, so double-click on the Persistent Level in the Levels window to make it active. You can tell it's the active layer because the name will turn blue.

Paste the Player Start Actor into the Persistent Level using the Edit menu, the right-click menu, or simply using Crtl/Cmd+V.

You could also just place a Player Start using the Class Browser as you did before, but you would still need to ensure the right Level is active.

Now you have a Player Start placed in your Persistent Level. However, if you click Play now, you'll still just load into a black, empty world. You need to set up the Level Blueprint to load streaming Levels.

Setting Up the Level Blueprint

Now that your streaming Levels are set up in the Editor, you can write the Blueprint logic to get them to switch using the **Level Blueprint**.

Opening the Level Blueprint

Each Level has its own Blueprint Event Graph called the **Level Blueprint**. This Blueprint is a great way to do Level-specific actions; things that would only happen in a single Level based on specific Actors or Events in that Level. An example might be the Player triggering a door to open or setting specific music to play when a Level opens.

Any functionality that needs to be common from Level to Level (player movement, for example) should be handled by a regular Blueprint Class, because you wouldn't want to have to duplicate and maintain that code for each Level you make.[2]

To access the Level Blueprint you can either click on the Gamepad icon in the Levels window that corresponds to the Level you want to edit or click the Blueprints button from the Editor toolbar and select **Open Level Blueprint** (see Figure 18.6).

You can also access the Level Blueprints of the loaded Levels and get quick access to your Game Mode's Classes.

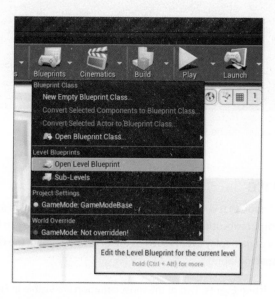

Figure 18.6 Opening the Persistent Level Blueprint

note

Streaming Levels can have their own Level Blueprints. This is because a Level Blueprint can only reference the Actors that are in its own Level.

The Level Blueprint opens in the Blueprint Editor window (see Figure 18.7). This Editor is a little different than the Blueprint Editors you have used so far. This one notably lacks the Viewport, Components, and Construction Script tabs Level Blueprints only have the Event Graph because they cannot have Components and do not undergo construction like Actor Classes do.

---

2. At runtime, all your Levels are loaded into a single world and everything can access everything else. However, in the Editor, Actors and Levels can only access other Actors with the same Level.

Figure 18.7 Level Blueprint opened in the Blueprint Editor

Using Events

An **Event** is a special node that is called from gameplay code. When called it fires the node graph wired to its output execution pin (the white arrow). These Events can be called in response to a variety of gameplay Events such as the game beginning, the Level being reset, or a player pressing a specific input.

UE4 has many pre-existing Events. Two of the most common are visible in Figure 18.7 above: **BeginPlay** and **Tick**. Also remember that you used **InputAxis** Events previously to set up input in your Player Controller.

BeginPlay

The **BeginPlay** Event is called automatically by the game one time when the Level is first loaded after all the Actors and world objects have been loaded and initialized.

This is where you set up your initial Level Streaming code. As mentioned, your Persistent Level is empty and needs to have the Levels streamed in.

To do so, you use the **Load Stream Level** function. You can see in Figure 18.8 that I have placed two of these nodes. Like with most nodes, right-click in the Event Graph and search for the Load Stream Level node.

Figure 18.8 Load Stream Level nodes connected to the BeginPlay Event node.

After placing both nodes, you need to fill in the settings on each to match Figure 18.8. Example2_MAP is loaded first using the Load Stream Level node with **Should Block on Load** and **Make Visible After Load** is set to **True**. Example2_V2_MAP is then loaded but is set to be hidden initially by setting the Make Visible After Load parameter to *False*.

You must set the Level Name property to the exact name of the Level in your Levels window. Also, you must have the Level loaded as a Streaming Level in the Levels window to be available to stream through Blueprints.

Should Block on Load forces UE4 to wait for the first Level to load before continuing to run any game code (this is what a "block" is—it *blocks* the game from continuing). Blocking prevents your Pawn from falling through the empty void of your Persistent Level before the Streaming Level and its associated collision are loaded.

> ### note
> Loading multiple streaming Levels at the same time can be extremely memory intensive. If you are running into crashes or poor performance, try to reduce your memory overhead, especially your video card VRAM. Start by reducing the resolution of your Reflection Capture Actors and/or reduce the resolution of your Lightmaps.

Latent Functions

Notice the **Clock** icon on the **Load Stream Level** functions. This indicates that this node is a **Latent** function. Latent functions take time to complete and only continue the flow of the event graph when their task is completed.

Loading Levels can take several seconds. Larger Levels and slower hard drives can increase this time. This can cause a hitch in your application while they're loading. This is why we've chosen to load them once at the same time, at the initial load of the Persistent Level, and toggle their visibility. By keeping them both in memory and simply changing their visibility, we can avoid this hitch and switching is almost instantaneous.

Testing Time

If you click Play now, your application should load the map almost exactly as before. However, it probably took a little longer than when you've tested with PIE before.

This is because you are waiting for the Levels to stream in; even the V2 map that isn't being shown yet takes time to load.

After the Levels load, however, you should be able to move about the space like you did in the previous chapter, but this time, you're doing it with fancy Level Streaming.

Programming the Switching

Now that you have the maps loading, let's get them toggling. With only a few nodes in your Level Blueprint, you can accomplish this. You will also see how to create an easy keyboard shortcut to test your Level switching before you tackle developing the UMG interface.

Creating Custom Events

You can create your own **Custom Event** nodes that can be called at any point in your Blueprint from other Blueprints in your world, providing a way for you to organize your Event Graphs and allow Blueprints to communicate with each other.

You need a few Custom Events that can toggle the visibility of the Levels. You'll use these Events to test the Level switching and then use the same Events later when you develop the UMG interface.

In the Persistent Level Blueprint, you create a Custom Event node by right-clicking on the Event Graph background and choosing **Add Custom Event** from the context menu (see Figure 18.9).

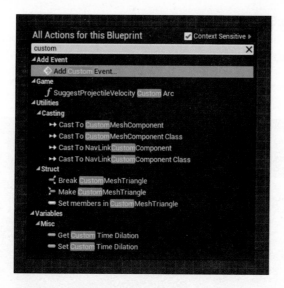

Figure 18.9 Adding a Custom Event to the Level Blueprint

When you create an Event, give it a unique Name and press Enter to confirm.

You need three Events for your switching system to work, so place three Custom Event nodes, naming the first *ShowVersion1,* the second *ShowVersion2,* and the third *ToggleVersions*. Your Event Graph should look like Figure 18.10.

Figure 18.10 The three custom Event nodes added to the Event Graph

Setting up the Show Versions Events

The Show Version 1 and Show Version 2 functions simply set the visibility of your Streaming Levels, allowing you to toggle between them.

Set up your Event Graph as shown in Figure 18.11.

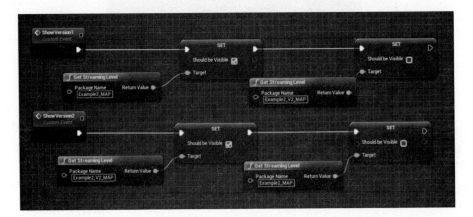

Figure 18.11 ShowVersion1 and ShowVersion2 custom Events and their execution graphs

These two, almost mirror image execution graphs hide one Level while showing another. The **Get Streaming Level** function returns a reference to the Level defined in the Package Name property. You must manually enter this name and it must be the exact name of your streaming Levels.

To access the **Set Should be Visible** property of the Level, drag a wire from the blue Return Value pin of the Get Streaming Level function node into the Event Graph and release to access the contextual menu for Streaming Levels and search for **Set Visible**.

Set it up so you are first unhiding a Level then hiding the other. You can see the Level's name being declared in the Package Name of the Get Streaming Level nodes.

Toggle Versions Event

The Toggle Versions Event toggles between the two variations each time it's called (see Figure 18.12). The **Flip Flop** node is specifically designed for this *and* it's fun to say.

The first time the Flip Flop is called, it only fires the A out execution pin. The next time, it only fires the B execution pin, then A, and so on, alternating between calling the two Custom Events you created previously.

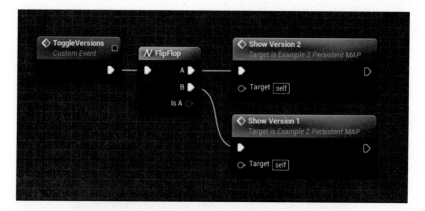

Figure 18.12 ToggleVersions and its Flip Flop node for toggling between the two Custom Events

To create a call to a Custom Event, right-click in the Event Graph and search for the name you gave your Custom Event when you created it. To ensure your Custom Events listed, you should Compile and Save your Blueprint.

Testing Time

Now that you have all this set up, take time to test before tackling the UMG interface. Without the UMG interface, how can you test your work so far? An easy way is to simply create a keyboard shortcut in the Level Blueprint.

Creating the Keyboard Shortcut

Level Blueprints can intercept Player input Events, just like the Player Controller can. You can use this to easily set up a keyboard shortcut to call out Toggle Versions Event.

From the right-click context menu, search for "Input L" (see Figure 18.13) and select L from the Keyboard Events list.

Figure 18.13 Creating an Input Event for the L key

Then, simply wire a call to the **ToggleVersions** Event from the **Pressed** execution pin on the **L Keyboard Input** Event, as shown in Figure 18.14.

Figure 18.14 The absurdly complex keyboard shortcut code

Compiling and Saving

You should now compile your Level Blueprint, ensuring there are no errors or warnings, then save the Persistent Level to save the code you've written.

Clicking Play

Now when you click Play, you should be able to press the L key on your keyboard and your Level will instantly toggle between your two versions.

You will notice what a dramatic change the additional windows make in the entire scene, even in hallways far away from the main modifications. This ability to switch options in-content like this is extremely powerful and gives the Player a personal experience. No two players will look in the same place and toggle the differences at the same time.

However, you can't expect everybody to know that they can press L to make this change happen. You need to present a user interface to the Player that gives him clear options. For this you use Unreal's built-in user interface system, UMG.

Unreal Motion Graphics (UMG)

Unreal Motion Graphics UI Designer (UMG) is a visual UI authoring tool that you can use to create in-game UI elements such as menus, titles, and buttons. UMG is hardware-accelerated, modern, and platform agnostic, meaning that it runs fast, looks great, and can be used on any platform UE4 supports. You can author a single interface for use on everything from PC and Mac to the Nintendo Switch and everything in between.

Using Widgets

UMG relies on **Widgets**, pre-made elements that you can use to construct your interface. Pre-built Widgets are available for most common UI elements including buttons, sliders, dropdown boxes, and text labels, along with Widgets to help organize and arrange other Widgets in the UI.

Widgets are assembled in a **Widget Blueprint**, a specialized Blueprint Class with a customized Editor.

You create Widget Blueprints like most UE4 Classes, in the Content Browser. In the Add New menu, navigate to **User Interface > Widget Blueprint** (see Figure 18.15). Name your new Widget **UI_Example2_HUD**. HUD means Heads up Display and is commonly referred to as the interface that is always showing when the game is being played. Other common UI setup examples would be a main menu or a pause menu.

Figure 18.15 Creating a Widget Blueprint

Now, double-click your newly created Widget Blueprint to open it for editing (see Figure 18.16).

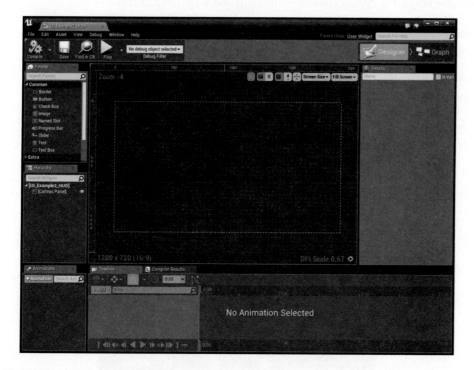

Figure 18.16 Widget Blueprint Editor window

This Editor is arranged in two main sections: the Designer tab that allows you to visually set up the elements of the UI, and the Graph tab where you can add functionality to your UIs. In the upper right, you can see the **Designer** and **Graph** tabs. Click these to switch between the two interface modes. In the center is the **Stage** and on the left is a **Palette** with all the Widgets available to build your UI. Below that is the **Hierarchy** that shows placed Widgets in a nested list. On the bottom are the **Animation** List and the **Timeline**. You can use these to develop key-framed animations for your UI elements. Finally, on the right is the **Details** Panel. Like all other Details Panels in UE4, it's contextual and displays the details of the currently selected Widget.

Horizontal Box

For this UI, you want two buttons to enable toggling between your variations. You want these buttons to be neatly arranged along the bottom of the screen with even spacing for a clean, professional look.

UE4 ships with a Widget that helps with this: the **Horizontal Box** Widget. This Widget can have multiple child Widgets nested within it, evenly spacing each of those Widgets horizontally.

Find the **Horizontal Box** Widget listed in the **Palette** window under the Panel group. Drag it into the **Stage**. The Widget appears on the Stage and in the Hierarchy list.

Your Widget likely didn't land in quite the right spot, so you need to move it to the bottom of the screen where you want it. You could simply drag it, but that's not the best practice.

UMG supports arbitrary resolutions and scaling so that it can be used on pretty much any device with any kind of screen.

One of the ways it does this is by using Anchors for Widgets. An Anchor ensures that a Widget is always stuck to a relative part of the screen: the side, the corner, or the center.

In this case stick it to the bottom center by clicking on the Anchors dropdown in the Details Panel (see Figure 18.17).

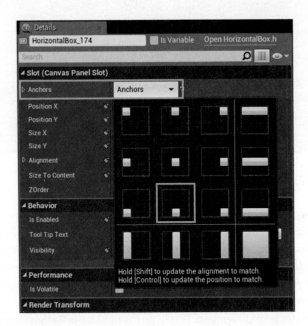

Figure 18.17 Setting the Widget's Anchor

When you do this, you won't see much change in the Viewport because UE4 tries to adjust all the layout properties so the Widget stays in the same location. You must modify those properties to get the Horizontal Box Widget where you want it and the size you want it (see Figure 18.18):

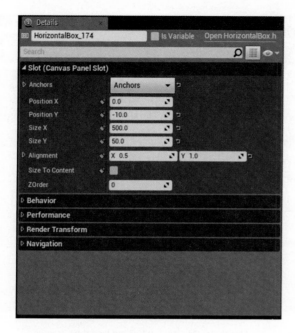

Figure 18.18 Setting the Horizontal Box Widget's Slot properties.

1. Set the **Position X** to 0 and the **Position Y** to –10. This centers the Widget, but leaves 10 pixels from the bottom of the screen.

2. Set the **Size X** to 500 and the **Size Y** to 50 to define the size of the box.

3. Set the **Alignment**. This is basically a pivot point offset. If you set it to 0,0, the Widget will transform from the upper-left corner and at 1,1 it transforms from the lower-right corner. An alignment of 0.5, 1.0 will cause the Widget pivot from the center bottom.

You should now have a box ready to organize some content, so let's give it some content!

Buttons

Simply drag two Button Widgets from the Palette *into* the Horizontal Box Widget. You can do this either to the Stage *or* the Hierarchy window (see Figure 18.19). Dragging to the Hierarchy window can be a big help when your UI Widget becomes complicated.

You need to do some styling and setup of your buttons to get them to look and behave right.

Select the buttons one by one and set them up as follows (see Figure 18.20):

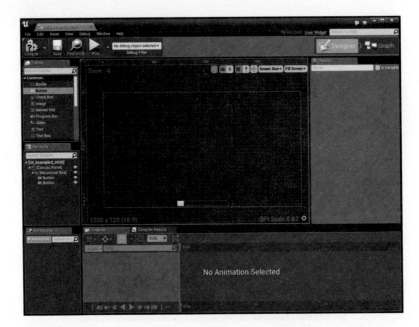

Figure 18.19 Buttons in the Horizontal Box Widget looking less than ideal

Figure 18.20 Setting the Button Widget's Slot properties

1. Most importantly, you need to provide each of your buttons a unique name. If you do not, trying to access these Widgets from Blueprints will be a challenge.

2. Set the **Padding** to have **10** pixels on the left and right. You might need to expand the Padding option by clicking the arrow next to it to reveal the individual padding options.

3. Set the **Size** to **Fill** and **1.0**. This makes the buttons fill up whatever area available, rather than trying to be as small as possible (Auto).

Labels

You need some labels for your buttons. Fortunately, the Button Widget Class can have a single child Class—perfect for a Text Widget to go in to act as a Label.

Find the Text Widget in the Palette and drag one into each of your buttons. Set up the Label's Text property to read Version 1 and Version 2. You might also want to add a slight drop-shadow to the text to make it slightly more legible (see Figure 18.21).

Figure 18.21 Adding the Labels

It's a great time to save your work if you already haven't. Your interface is complete and you won't need to add any code directly to the graph of this Widget Blueprint because you will handle all that in the Level Blueprint.

Back to the Level Blueprint

You have all the pieces you need to make this system work; now you just need to assemble them. You do all the final assembly back in the Level Blueprint.

Open the Level Blueprint—click on the **Blueprints** button in the **Toolbar** and select **Open Level Blueprint**.

The most obvious question at this point is: How do I get my UI that I just made and make it display? To do so in UE4, you attach your Widget Blueprint to the Player's Viewport using Blueprints as shown in Figure 18.22.[3]

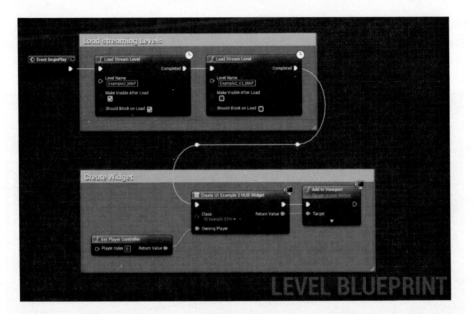

Figure 18.22 Creating an instance of your Widget Blueprint and adding it to the Viewport

The best place to do this is the **Begin Play Event** because you want the HUD to display when the Level loads. You'll add this code after your Level loading completes so you aren't presenting the Player with the UI before he can click on it. (That's rude!)

The following sections walk you through wiring all your components together.

---

3. Notice the Redirect nodes in the white execution graph. These allow the programmer to make their node graphs more readable by defining the shape of the execution lines. To add one, double-click on a wire.

Creating the Widget

The first step is to create the Widget object, which loads the widget class from disk and creates an instance of it in memory (you could, of course, create more than one of any given Widget, all instantiated from the one Widget Blueprint Class).

As usual, right-click in the Event Graph and search for **Create Widget** to create this node.

After placing the Create Widget node, you need to do two things:

1. Assign the Class you want to spawn; in this Case UI_Example2_HUD, by selecting the Class dropdown.

2. Provide this function with a reference to your Player Controller. Simply right-click on the Viewport, find Get Player Controller from the list, and then wire it to the Owning Player pin.

You need to do this because a multiplayer environment can have more than one Player Controller and you need to know who the HUD belongs to. In this case you only have one so you can simply just reference the first Player Controller available.

Adding the Widget to the Viewport

To get the Widget to attach to the Viewport and be seen and intractable, you need to add it to the Viewport.

To access the Add to Viewport node, drag a wire from the Return Value of the Create Widget node (that should now read "Create UI Example 2 HUD Widget") and release into the Graph Editor, which opens the context menu for your Widget Class. Search for the **Add to Viewport** node and add it to the graph. The blue wire will automatically connect to the Target pin of the newly created Add to Viewport function.

Now is a good time to click the Compile button and if there are no errors, save your Level Blueprint.

If you run the game now, you'll see your two buttons displayed at the bottom of the screen. If you click on them nothing happens. Luckily you've already set up the switching functions; you just need to get the buttons to call those functions when pressed.

Event Binding

A powerful feature of UE4 is the ability for one Blueprint to bind to an Event in another. This lets a single Blueprint handle multiple interactions or Events with a single, unified code path.

To detect Events, you must first get a reference to the buttons you made (see Figure 18.23). You can do this easily because the Create Widget method returns a reference to the Object it creates. So, drag a wire from the Return Value into the graph to access the context menu for your Widget Class.

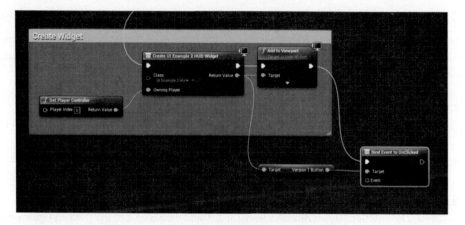

Figure 18.23 Getting a reference to the button you created in your HUD Widget

Search for **Get Version** and select **Get Version 1 Button**. From this Get node, again drag out a blue wire and search for **Bind**. You can bind to quite a few Events and you can also unbind Events as well. Choose **Bind Event to OnClicked** for your button. Wire it to the Add To Viewport function because it must get called for the Bind that you will set up to take effect.

You now need to define what Event will be called when the bound OnClicked Event is fired. You do this with the red/orange Event reference pin.

Drag from this pin to the similar pin on the ShowVersion1 Custom Event. You might need to move your nodes around so that doing this is easier (see Figure 18.24).

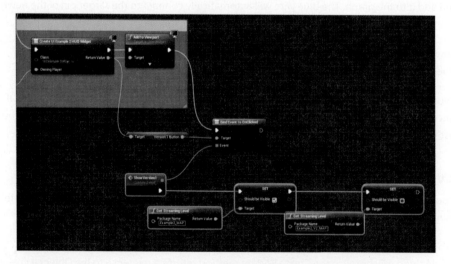

Figure 18.24 Binding your previously created **ShowVersion1** Event to the **OnClicked** Event of the **Version1Button** Widget

Now, of course, repeat for the other button by getting a reference from the Create Widget node and assigning your other Custom Event to that button's OnClicked Event (see Figure 18.25).

Now clicking the buttons causes the Events to fire, switching the Levels.

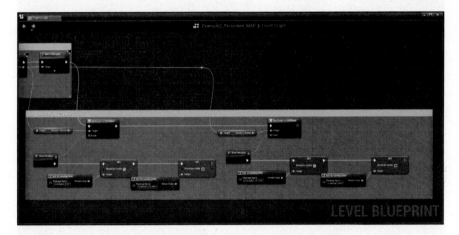

Figure 18.25 Both buttons bound to the switching Events in the Persistent Level Blueprint

Compiling and Saving

Be sure to compile your Level Blueprint and if there are no errors, save your work.

Playing the Game

You can now click Play on your Level and experience a fully fledged, mouse-driven user interface. You should be able to navigate about using the keyboard and mouse, toggling between the two versions effortlessly with the UI (see Figure 18.26).

Figure 18.26 Running the game in PIE, with fully functional buttons and instant switching

Summary

You've come a long way and tackled a lot of new ground in this chapter.

You've learned about the Level Streaming system in UE4 and used it to easily toggle entire Levels instantly at runtime. This is a great way to swap out datasets in visualization applications and is easy to set up and maintain.

You also looked at how Blueprints can communicate with each other using Event binding and used that ability to build a simple but effective user interface with UMG.

UMG is a great resource and one of the best user interface tools available. Combined with UE4's flexibility and power, you can create pretty much any application you can imagine.

Although this game is only a simple example, UMG has been used successfully on projects as complex as a full-blown AAA, blockbuster video game to a simple A/B comparison tool like this. Its performance, flexibility, and ease of use has made it one of the reasons UE4 is becoming such a dominant force in nearly every visual industry.

CHAPTER 19

ADVANCED BLUEPRINTS: MATERIAL SWITCHER

Building production-ready Blueprints is essential for your success with UE4. Good Blueprint systems create new functionality in your application and are built as a tool that is easy to use by yourself or others on your team. In this chapter you learn how to create a single Actor Blueprint that allows the Player to click on any Mesh in the scene and switch to the next defined Material in a list. By dissecting this Blueprint, you can see how Blueprints can communicate with one another and change properties on the fly.

Now that you've seen how to produce an interactive visualization application, create a Player Controller and Pawn, switch Levels, and develop a user interface in UMG, it's time to take the next step—okay, maybe a short flight of stairs.

This chapter is intended for individuals who have some experience with programming in UE4 in general or those who want to see how an advanced system is built. Either way, you should have a firm grasp of all of the topics covered previously in this book before attempting to re-create or follow along in this chapter.

This chapter demonstrates the overall most important part of this system and gives guidance on how to accomplish some common programmatic patterns in UE4 and Blueprints.

Of course, you can download the project files for this chapter at www.TomShannon3D.com/ UnrealForViz so you can dissect, follow along, or copy and paste into your own projects. (I don't mind, really.)

Setting the Goal

The goal is to create a Blueprint Actor Class that will:

- Allow the Level Designer (LD) to place the Blueprint into the Level using the Editor.
- Define a list of scene Static Mesh Actors that change Materials when clicked.
- Allow the LD to define a list of Materials that cycle through when the Player clicks on one of the Meshes.
- Highlight the listed Actors when the Player's cursor hovers over the Actor, demonstrating that it is modifiable.

I can think of probably five ways to make a system like this work. Programming rarely has a perfect solution. Each programmer approaches a problem a different way.

For this project, we will create a single Actor Blueprint to contain several Variables to store the lists of Meshes and Materials. This Blueprint will clearly show the LD what is being set via visual cues, making setup easy and reliable and making debugging issues easier (see Figure 19.1).

We'll also Migrate some Marketplace content into our project and modify it to produce object outlines using a Post-process Domain Material that will be toggled using the Blueprint.

Figure 19.1 Material switcher Blueprint placed in the Level showing LD-friendly design

Building the Actor Blueprint

You can use a single Blueprint to add all the functionality you need to create an easy-to-use system for both the Player and the designer tasked with setting up the Level (**the Level Designer or LD**).

An Actor Blueprint is one you can place into the Level, and it has a 3D transform that you can modify. You can attach Components to Blueprint Actors to extend their capabilities. Components include Meshes, Particle Effects, Sound Cues, and more.

Actor Blueprints can also do something special. They can reference other Actors in the Level. This is essential because you need this Blueprint to communicate to the various Static Meshes in your Level to modify them.

Create the Blueprint from the Content Browser. When the option appears to choose the Class on which to base your new Blueprint, select the Actor Class (see Figure 19.2).

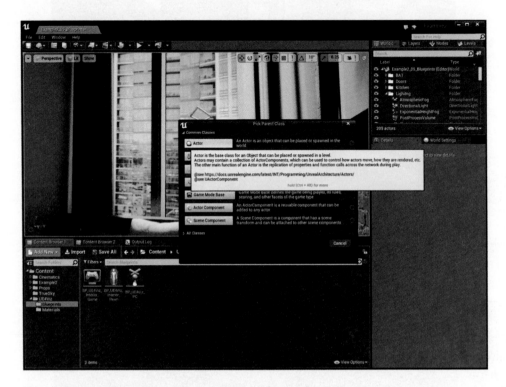

Figure 19.2 Creating a new Actor Blueprint from the Content Browser

I named my Blueprint BP_MaterialSwitcher_Actor and saved it alongside my PC, Game Mode, and Pawn in my "Blueprints" folder.

Creating Variables

You need to store some information or data in this Blueprint Class. To store data in a Blueprint, use a Variable. Variables come in many different Classes, including simple types you might be familiar with, such as booleans and floats, as well as any Classes you have included in your project.

This ability to use Classes and Actors as Variables allows you to reference the Static Mesh Actors you want to modify. You can also reference Assets stored in the Content Browser. This allows you to define the different Materials to be applied to the Static Meshes. The Switcher Blueprint only needs a few Variables to work (see Figure 19.3).

Figure 19.3 Material Switcher Blueprint Variables and Functions

You create Variables in the Blueprint Editor using the Add New button in the My Blueprint panel or by clicking the + icon next to the Variables section in this panel (refer to Figure 19.3).

When you create a Variable, you need to name it and assign a type to it. You can rename and assign the type either in the My Blueprint panel or in the Variable's Details panel.

Not only can you define the **type** (float, string, vector, and so on) of a Variable, you can also define it as an **array**. An array Variable becomes a list of whatever type it's set to. You can edit and modify this list in the Actor's Details if the Variable's **Allow Editing** parameter has been set to true.

Each time you create a new Variable, it will default to the type and array setting you chose for the last Variable.

Meshes To Modify Array

The **Meshes To Modify** Variable is an array of Static Mesh Actors (Static Meshes that have been placed in the Level, rather than Static Mesh Asset references from the Content Browser) that should change Material as a group when clicked on. This lets the LD define several pieces of furniture (such as all the dining room chairs) in the array and when one is clicked on, all of them will change Materials together.

An array type Variable can hold a list of Level Actors that can be accessed by the Event Graph nodes (see Figure 19.4).

After you create, name, and assign the type to the Variable, click the Grid icon next to it to convert it to an array. Notice that when you click on a Variable, the Details Panel populates with that Variable's properties.

Setting a Variable to **Editable** displays it in the Details Panel of Level Actors of that Class. This lets each instance of it in the Level have a different set of Meshes assigned to the array. You can see in Figure 19.4 that the Meshes To Modify property is displayed in the Details Panel.

Expose on Spawn is a special setting that allows you to easily set a Variable if you are programmatically spawning this Actor at runtime. You will not, so none of your Variables need to have this set.

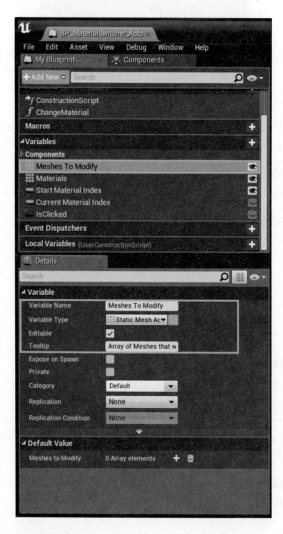

Figure 19.4 Meshes To Modify Variable properties

Materials Array

The **Materials** Variable is an array of **Material Interface** references. The Material Interface Variable type allows both regular Materials as well as Material Instances to be used.

Unlike the Meshes to Modify Variable, which references Static Mesh Actors in the level, the Materials array Variable references Assets in the Content Browser. This lets the system read from the library of Materials in your project, even if the Materials haven't been assigned to anything in the scene.

Set this Variable to Editable, allowing the LD to change these values on a per-Actor basis within each Level.

Start Material Index Variable

The **Start Material In**dex Variable is an **Integer** type. Integers are whole numbers like 1, –2, and 8675309. They cannot have decimals but can be negative. In this case, you are using it to define which Material from the Materials array to choose.

An **index** is a term that refers to the numeric position of an entry in an array. In UE4, the index begins counting at 0, so an index of 0 is the first item in an array and an index of 3 is the fourth. This is a bit confusing and has tripped me up more than I care to admit.

In this case, you will use it to define what Material to apply to your **Meshes to Modify** Actors from the **Materials** array.

You'll also set this to **Editable** (see Figure 19.5) so you can decide as you are authoring your Level what index to start at and therefore what Material to apply as a default.

Figure 19.5 Start Material Index Variable properties, set to Integer (whole numbers) and Editable

Current Material Index Variable

You set up **Current Material Index**, another Integer, exactly like you did the Start Material Index, but disable the Editable property because Current Material Index is a used only by the Blueprint code at runtime and won't ever be directly set by the user. You'll use this Variable to track the user's click, incrementing it by one each time the user clicks.

IsClicked Variable

The **IsClicked** Variable is a Boolean type Variable. A Boolean can only have two possible values: true or false. Like the Current Material Index, this is not an Editable Variable because the code uses it at runtime to determine if the Player's click on the Actor is on purpose or is a stray click.

Adding Components

Components are like sub-Actors for your Blueprints. They are C++ and Blueprint Classes that can contain anything another Blueprint Class can, including code, effects, and input.

The two ways to create Components in Blueprints are programmatically at runtime or manually using the Components and Viewport tabs in the Blueprint Editor (see Figure 19.6).

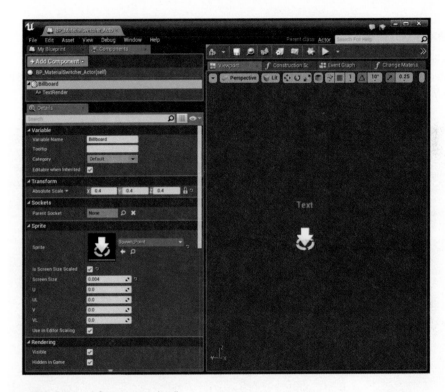

Figure 19.6 Billboard Component details

Billboard Component

The **Billboard Component** acts as the base of your Actor. The Billboard Class displays a Texture that always faces the player. You might use this for things like lens flares, or special effects. In this case, it's so you have something that the LD can see and select in the Level.

To create Components, use the Add Component dropdown and select the kind you want—in this case a Billboard Component.

To replace the DefaultSceneRoot Component that is set as a default, drag the newly created Billboard Component onto the DefaultSceneRoot Component, replacing it.

You can also define a custom **Sprite** Texture to display as seen in Figure 19.6. The Spawn_Point one shown is from the Engine content shipped with UE4[1]. You could also create and import your own Texture to use here, too.

Setting **Is Screen Size Scaled** to true ensures that the Sprite won't ever go over a certain size onscreen. This is helpful to avoid the screen's filling with giant sprites as the Viewport camera gets close to them.

TextRender Component

The TextRender Component is handy—it displays a 2D text string in 3D space that can be edited on the fly (see Figure 19.7). I'm using it to display the name of the first Mesh selected in the Meshes To Modify array. This is purely to help the LD when authoring the Level.

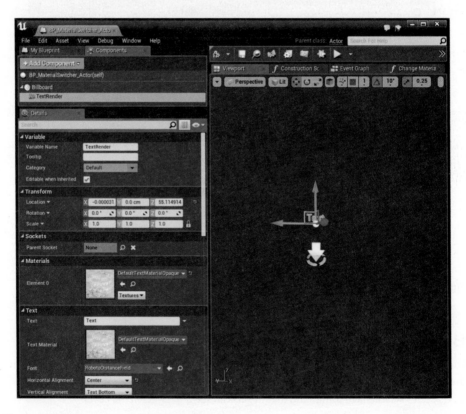

Figure 19.7 TextRender Component details

---

1. You can access the content that is included with the Engine by selecting the Eye icon in the Content Browser and selecting Show Engine Content. Be careful not to modify anything in your Engine content as it can cause issues with stability and sharing content between team members.

Creating the Change Material Function

The **Change Material** function (see Figure 19.8) is really the core of this entire Blueprint. It handles the work of assigning the Material to the assigned Static Meshes. It also has some logic to avoid errors and ensure Materials are always assigned.

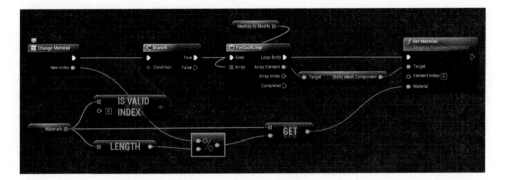

Figure 19.8 Change Material Function

Functions are used to encapsulate specific functionality, specifically when you want them to be reused. In this case, you want to change the Material during the Construction Script, after the Begin Play Event in the Event Graph and at runtime when the Player clicks on a listed Mesh.

You create Functions similarly to how you create Variables using the My Blueprint panel.

Click on the Add New button and select Function from the dropdown menu. Name it Change Material.

Upon creating the Function, it will open immediately for editing in a blank Event Graph. To open already created functions, double-click its entry in the My Blueprints panel.

New Index Input

A Function can have inputs and outputs that allow it to process and return data. The input and output can even be different data types. A simple Function that does this is an array **Get** Function. You provide it an index integer and it will return whatever the array has been defined as, such as a Static Mesh or a Material.

To add inputs, click on the Function's node in the Graph Editor; this displays the properties for the Function, including an area for adding inputs and outputs.

Click on the + button in the Details Panel next to Inputs to add a new input. Name it New Index and set its type to Integer.

This input will define what index of the Materials array to use. This allows the Function to become multifunctional. Rather than writing a new Function for each Material number, you can simply use this Variable to define the index you want.

Is Valid Index

An Is Valid Index check is performed on the Materials array before continuing to ensure your array is valid and that you aren't accessing an empty array entry.

For Each Loop

If the Is Valid check passes, the function then loops through each Mesh in the **Meshes To Modify** array and calls the Set Material function on it.

To determine what Material to apply, you must Get a reference to it from the Materials array using the provided New Index value.

A Modulo (%) node is used to ensure that whatever integer is provided will be within the available range of Materials. It does this by returning the remainder after dividing A by B—for example, 1 mod 4 = 1, 4 mod 4 = 0, 5 mod 4 = 1, and 55 mod 4 = 3.

Understanding the Construction Script

The two times when Blueprint code runs are during the Actor's construction, the **Construction Script**, and during runtime, the **Event Graph**.

The Construction Script only runs when the class is first spawned into the world. This can be either when you place or modify the Actor in the Editor or if an Actor or Object is spawned at runtime. The Construction Script is where you can program the Blueprint do things before the game runs. This includes spawning Components, modifying other Actors, and so on.

Actors that are placed in a Level (as opposed to being spawned there at runtime) only run their Construction Script in the Editor, and the results are saved to file when you save the Level. The Construction Script will not run again, even if the Level is reloaded.

The Construction Script in our Class does three main things: sets the text label, draws lines from the Actor to the Meshes it will modify, and sets the Mesh's Materials to match the Start Index Variable (see Figure 19.9).

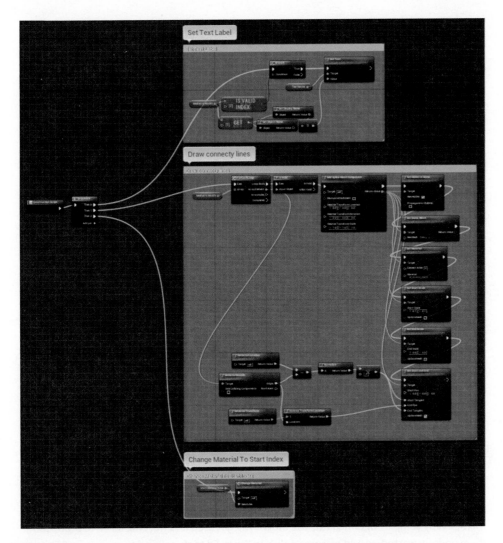

Figure 19.9 The final Construction Script with the three main Functions the Construction script handles

Set Text Label

The Construction Script first attempts to set the TextRender's Text property based on selected Meshes (see Figure 19.10). If no Meshes are selected, it will read "None," helping the LD to understand whether his systems are set up right.

To do this, the Construction Script gets a reference to the first item of the Meshes To Modify array, gets the name using Get Display Name, and wires that to the Set Text Function of the text Render Component.

Like with many Blueprint nodes that reference a specific Class, you need to first get a reference to your Text Render Component and then drag a wire from it into the Editor to see the contextual list of nodes available for that Class.

The Branch is there to ensure you aren't calling **Get** on an empty array (that's bad and can cause crashes) so it will only continue its code path if the first entry of the Meshes To Modify array (Index 0) is valid.

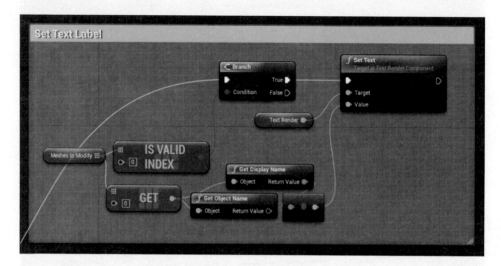

Figure 19.10 TextRender Component details

Draw Connecty Lines

When designing Blueprints for use in production, you have to not only consider how the Player interacts with the Blueprints, but also how the person setting up the Level has to interact with them. Overly complex or difficult-to-use tools don't get used and the time taken to produce them ends up wasted, so adding some polish to the in-Editor functionality can ensure it's easy for anybody to use.

To offer the LD a way to visualize what Static Mesh Actors are being referenced by each Material Switcher Actor they place a box extruded down a spline is added for each Mesh listed in the Meshes to Modify array (see Figure 19.11).

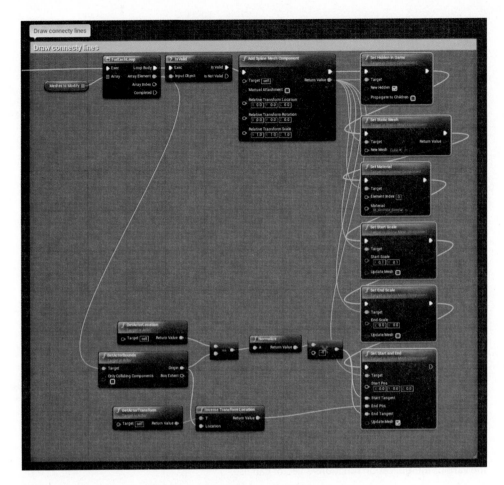

Figure 19.11 Drawing 3D lines to help visualize the assigned Meshes

Because you want to draw a line for each Mesh in your Meshes To Modify array, you need to loop through the array using a For Each Loop.

Each loop first checks if the **Array Element** the loop function is returning is valid (you could possibly have empty entries in your array). If it's valid, it then uses the **Add Spline Mesh Component** node to add a new Spline Mesh Component to your Blueprint.

Each line is then styled so that it points from the Switcher Blueprint to each referenced Mesh.

Set Hidden in Game allows the Component to be visible in the Editor, but when you enter Game Mode (by simulating, clicking Play, or pressing G to preview the Game Mode) it will be hidden. Many Editor-only Actors use this setting, such as the icons and arrows in Light Actors.

Then, the Cube Mesh Static Mesh Asset is assigned to the Spline Mesh Component along with a Material using the **Set Static Mesh** and **Set Material** Functions.

The start and end scale are set, creating an arrow-like shape using **Set Start Scale** and **Set End Scale**.

Finally, use the **Set Start and End** Function to set the position of the start and end verts of the spline relative to the Blueprint Actor's world position. Because these locations are relative to the Blueprint's position in the world, a value of 0,0,0 represents the location of the pivot point of your Blueprint.

The world-space position of the Static Mesh Actor is then queried using the Get Actor Bounds function. This is then converted to local-space using the Inverse Transform Positon node and piped into the End property of the Set Start and End node.

The spline at this point will look very strange because first you must define the tangent direction of each point on the spline. Because you want the tangents to simply face down the spline's direction, you calculate the tangent between them by subtracting their positions and then normalizing the result to get a Unit vector that you can then wire to both the Start and End tangent properties.

Using the Context Sensitive Checkbox

Remember that to access these Functions, you'll need to drag a wire from the **Return Value** of the **Add Spline Component** to access the Class-specific methods available. You can also uncheck the Context Sensitive checkbox in the pop-up as well. That will list all the available methods you can place in a Blueprint; however, you might get confused because you will be offered many more options than if you used the contextually sorted list.

The wire-dragging technique is useful for all kinds of nodes. For instance, to easily find the Vector * vector math node, you can drag a yellow vector wire from a pin and type * for a list of all the various multiplication functions a vector can use.

Change Material to Start Index

To allow the Material Switcher to work in the Editor, you can call the Change Material Function you created from the Construction Script (see Figure 19.12). Now, when the LD sets the Start Material Index Variable, he will see the Material change accordingly in the Editor.

Adding the Change Material function to the Construction Script is also a convenient way of testing your Function because you can manually provide the Index and see if it does, indeed, change the Materials as expected.

Figure 19.12 Calling the Change Material function in the Construction Script

Understanding the Event Graph

The Event Graph is the part of the Blueprint that runs when the game is running. In here you have Functions, Events, and nodes that respond to various game events such as Tick and Input Events. In this Blueprint, the Event Graph handles highlighting Actors and changing Materials on them if the Player clicks on the Actor (see Figure 19.13).

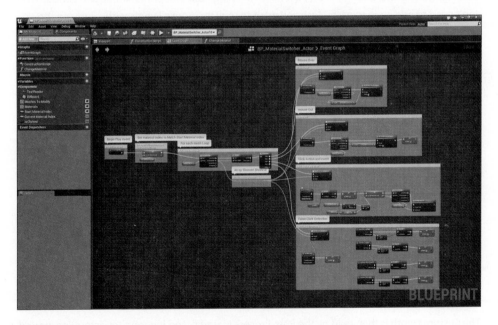

Figure 19.13 Overview of the Event Graph showing the major Functions

Before going forward, make sure you are working in the Event Graph tab of your Blueprint Editor.

The primary purpose of the Event Graph in the Material Switcher Blueprint class is to set up all the Meshes To Modify Actors to receive mouse input Events. To do this the code loops through each Mesh in the Meshes To Modify array and uses Event Binding to tell those Meshes how to behave when they are clicked on by the Player.

Begin Play

The Event Graph code in this Blueprint starts with the Begin Play event. This event is called only one time when an Actor or Object is first spawned into a game at runtime.

The first part of the Graph from the Event Begin Play node is likely familiar by now. For each Static Mesh Actor in the Meshes To Modify, the code loops through each mesh in the array, performing a validity check to avoid accessing a null pointer. If valid, it then assigns functionality to the various mouse interaction events available.

Event Binding

As you learned in the previous chapter, Blueprints can bind to Events that happen in other Classes in your game, and this is very useful for keeping your Blueprints simple and concise. You don't need to add code to each Mesh you want to register mouse Events with—just use the Bind to Event functionality.

As before, you must drag a wire from the Bind To Function's red/orange delegate box into the Graph Editor, releasing and selecting **Add Custom Event**. This creates a new Custom Event that has the Inputs and other settings properly configured for this Event. In this case, you can see the Custom Event returns a Touched Actor reference that's been added automatically.

Mouse Over and Mouse Out

Like many applications that have mouse-driven interfaces, UE4 offers Events for when the mouse cursor begins and ends hovering over the Actor.

In this case, an Event is used to set the Custom Depth on each Mesh in the Meshes To Modify array to allow a post-process Material to detect the Meshes. As you can see from the images (see Figures 19.14 and 19.15), as the Player hovers over Actors, the code simply loops through the Meshes To Modify array and sets the Custom Depth property of each Mesh to true, returning it to false when the cursor leaves.

The Custom Depth is then read by the Post-Process Material, and it generates an outline around the hovered actor.

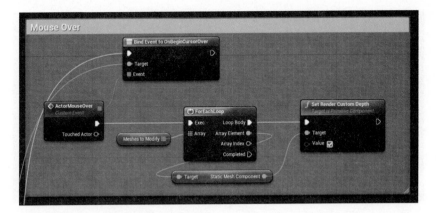

Figure 19.14 Mouse Over Event Graph

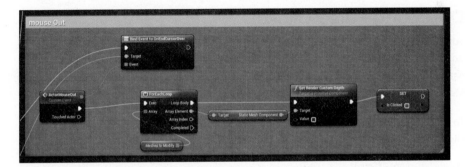

Figure 19.15 Mouse Out Event Graph

A node sets the **Is Clicked** Variable to false. This ensures that if the Player's cursor ever leaves the Actor's perimeter, even with the button being held down, it won't trigger the Material change when the Player releases the mouse button.

This sort of polish makes the difference between a frustrating system and one that behaves like the Player expects. This variable was added after testing revealed the Player could accidentally change the Materials of Meshes when they released the mouse button after dragging the view.

Click Action

When the Player clicks on a Mesh in the Meshes To Modify array, you want it to change Materials. This is done by incrementing the Current Material Index Variable, again using a modulo (%) operator (see Figure 19.16) to ensure its value stays within the range available; basically looping the integer at a specified number.

The result of the modulo is then sent to the Change Material Function, which in turn modifies all the Meshes in the Meshes To Modify array.

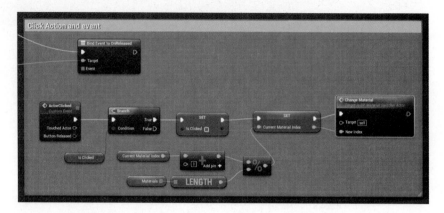

Figure 19.16 Click Action and Event

Detecting False Clicks

Sometimes, the Player will want to rotate the camera using the mouse and won't want to click on the interactive Meshes placed about the Level. If you are allowing walls and floors to be changed, few places might exist where the Player can click without accidentally triggering the Material switching.

To solve this, the Blueprint detects inputs that might indicate the Player isn't just clicking, but clicking and dragging, presumably to rotate the view (see Figure 19.17).

This is where the IsClicked Variable comes into play. Setting this Variable to true only when the Player directly clicks on a Mesh and then setting it to false for any other mouse inputs avoids calling the **Change Material** Function.

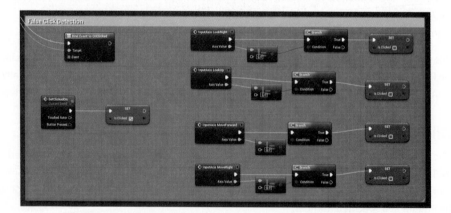

Figure 19.17 False click detection

Populating the Level

Like all Assets that you want to take from the Content Browser to the Level, your best bet is to simply drag and drop them from the Content Browser into the Viewport.

Begin by placing one of your Material Switcher Blueprints near the Meshes you want to modify (see Figure 19.18). Notice the Details Panel on the right that the Variables that were marked as Editable are visible and ready for the LD to modify them.

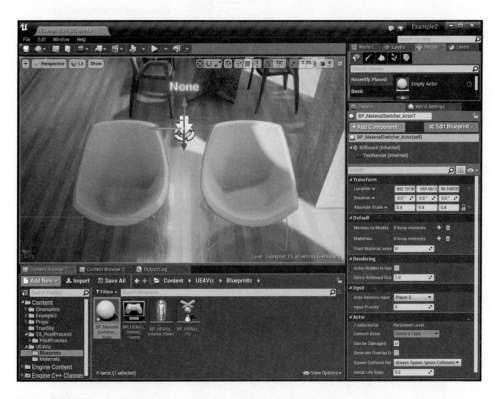

Figure 19.18 Material Switcher added to the Level near a couple chairs

Adding Meshes

Now define the Meshes you want the Blueprint to affect. In the Details Panel, find the Meshes To Modify array and click the + button to add a new item to the array. A dropdown list appears showing every Static Mesh in your Level. This can be a difficult way of selecting Meshes; instead, consider using the eyedropper tool (see Figure 19.19).

As you add Meshes to the list, the Construction Script will run and you should see a line drawn between the Blueprint and each Mesh in the list (see Figure 19.20).

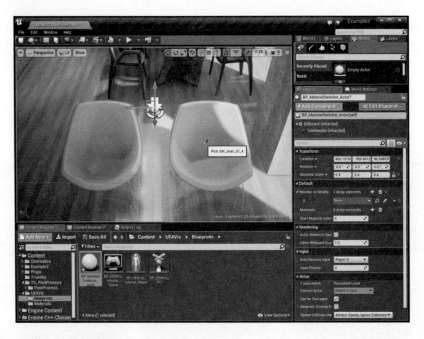

Figure 19.19 Using the Eyedropper tool to select Meshes

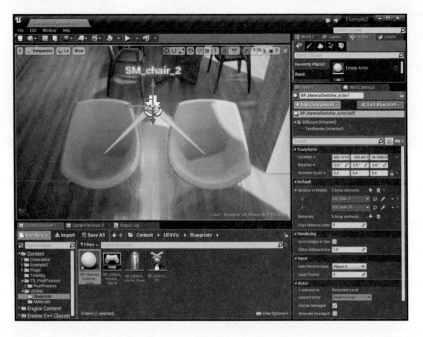

Figure 19.20 Meshes added to the Meshes to Modify array. The connect lines and Text label are also visible

Adding Materials

After you have your Mesh list populated, do a similar setup for the Materials. Instead of selecting the Meshes from the world using the eye dropper as before, select your Materials or Material Instances from the Content Browser because the Materials array is an Asset reference rather than an Actor reference (see Figure 19.21).

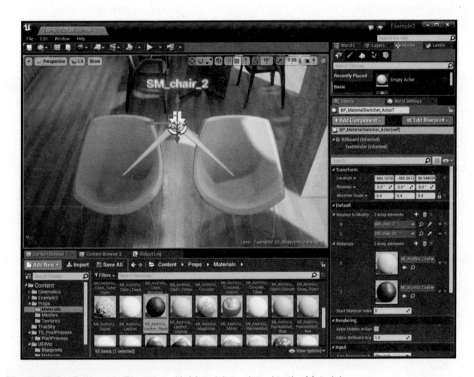

Figure 19.21 Fully setup Blueprint with Materials assigned to the Materials array

Setting Defaults

Not many options are available in this Blueprint other than the arrays. However, you can set the Start Material Index variable. This is an easy way of setting up the default look of your area and a way to preview the Materials before clicking Play.

Copying and Pasting

A great shortcut for setting up these Actors is the ability to copy and paste them like Variables. For instance, you can select the entire Materials array in the Details Panel and select Copy before pasting into the same property field on another Actor.

This trick isn't limited to Blueprints, either. You would be surprised at how many things you can copy and paste in UE4.

Playing the Application

All that's left to do is to test by clicking the Play button. You should be able move about the space, click on the various Actors in the Level, and change their Materials, creating a personalized interior space (see Figure 19.22).

Figure 19.22 Using Play In Editor to test the system—success!

After enough Meshes and Materials are set up, you can dramatically change the look of the scene with just a few clicks (see Figures 19.23 and 19.24).

Figure 19.23 Before mad clicking

Figure 19.24 After mad clicking

Summary

You now have a complete application with a fully fleshed-out feature that you could send off to your client, happy that you have met all your obligations. You have seen how simple Blueprints can have powerful effects in the game world with just a few nodes.

You've seen two ways of creating interactivity: using UMG and by directly interfacing with the Actors in your Level.

You've also seen a couple ways of switching out data in UE4, both with their own advantages and workflows. I hope you are encouraged to begin exploring and creating your own methods that solve the specific needs of your industry, your workflows, and your datasets.

CHAPTER 20

FINAL THOUGHTS

This book just scratches the surface of UE4. With access to C++ source code, a massive array of plugins and integrations, and some of the best developers on Earth improving it every day, UE4 is a true powerhouse that is poised to change the entertainment and visual communications industry. From visualization to movies and special effects, the future is wide open.

UE4 Continually Changing

Unreal Engine 4 is evolving more rapidly than any other software package I have ever used. The evolution of the Editor and the tools from my first exposure as part of the UE4 Rocket Beta has been astounding.

Constant improvements, innovations, and workflows are added with such regularity that it's become a large portion of my work to just keep up with all the improvements being made.

It's exciting to work with such a vibrant community and to see all the incredible things being made with it every day by thousands of individuals and teams across the world.

I can't see the future, but I regularly access many of Epic Game's planning tools, watch their myriad videos, and talk directly to the developers and the community, getting good insight into where the community and Epic want to see it go.

Future of Visualization

Visualization has always had a few core struggles. Delivering quality products that effectively tell stories and communicate complex information visually can be enormously challenging. Visualizations are often developed in remarkably short-time frames for remarkably tight budgets with remarkably incomplete or changing (or both) datasets.

UE4 can help alleviate these struggles significantly. Interactivity allows the Player to visualize the data on her own terms in a personal and affecting manner. Like video games, a Player using an interactive visualization is creating her own, unique story and doing it from her own perspective.

Also, by eliminating render time, data changes or last-minute client requests can be more easily accommodated. This leads to a better, more accurate, and useable product, a happier client, and a more productive studio that spends less time rendering and waiting and more time creating and improving.

Virtual reality, interactivity, and customizability via Blueprints and C++ means that UE4 is the most capable visualization tool available today—and with a massive head start on the competition that has seemingly yet to start down this path in earnest.

Next Steps

We've only scratched the very surface of what UE4 can do and what you can do with it. The examples presented likewise only represent a small fraction of the types of visualizations being created today. Datasets and client requirements range widely from one industry to the next and even from one project to the next.

I hope to have laid the foundation for you to be able to take your data and your vision and bring it into UE4. You'll undoubtedly find challenges I haven't encountered, thought of, or wrote about in these pages. When you do, you should find a plethora of resources available. So many people are using and learning UE4 that you are never alone when facing those challenges. Both Epic Games and the UE4 community are passionate about making UE4 the best engine it can be for everybody.

As you use UE4 more and more, I recommend looking at your workflows and see how you might adopt the workflows from UE4 into your overall studio approach. Like Hollywood and games coming together, you can learn many lessons from developing for games and interactive visualizations that you can apply to your day-to-day work that not only can improve your work, but can also enable an easier integration of UE4 into your work.

Virtual Reality

The most prominent and promising near-future technology that's being pushed hard is virtual reality. Almost every industry on Earth is embracing VR. It's very early in VR's life, but like UE4 it's evolving very quickly.

UE4 is playing a major role in the development of VR because it has supported VR since very early on and Epic Games has continued to push forward with VR innovation.

UE4 now ships with a VR mode for the Editor that lets designers and artists build VR worlds directly in VR with nearly all the capabilities of the Desktop version—it's an amazing feat.

This feature hasn't just been introduced and forgotten either. It's been actively and rapidly developed from a neat tech demo to a truly viable way of working.

Even if you're not using the VR Editor, Epic has done a fantastic job of exposing all the input, tracking, and other features of the various VR APIs and platforms, making developing for VR a breeze.

The tools, visuals, and passion from Epic for VR combine to make UE4 the premiere VR development platform.

Film Making

Hollywood has taken note of UE4 in a big way. Film makers face many of the same challenges as visualization houses do, but on a much larger scale. Any efficiency makes an enormous difference, so the rendering speed and toolset of UE4 make it undeniably attractive.

Game developers and movie makers have been feeding off each other for years, both taking techniques and technology from one another to improve upon their own products.

UE4 represents the culmination of all those years of integration. UE4 feels familiar to game makers and film makers alike. This is leading to collaborations between game makers and film makers that completely blur the lines between the two disciplines.

In a few years, we won't know the difference between many games and movies and our expectations for each will change drastically.

Content Creation

As UE4 matures, more and more content creation tools are being developed. In the latest updates, Epic has added full polygon modelling with subdivision surfaces (and it even works in VR Editor mode), as well as painting and sculpting tools.

UE4 also now supports Render to Texture (RTT). Using the Material Editor, Particle Systems, and any other tool available in UE4, you can create flipbook animations, textures, and other effects much like you would in an application like Substance Designer or Photoshop.

It will take a long time for UE4 to replace all the tools you need, but I spend less and less time in my 3D applications and more time in UE4.

Thank You

Finally, thank you, kind reader. I am excited that this book even exists. I have been pushing to combine my passions for gaming technology and visualization for more than a decade, and it's incredibly exciting to see how the visualization industry has begun to embrace real-time rendering and specifically UE4.

I wish you the best in your endeavors, and look forward to seeing all of your amazing creations and innovations.

GLOSSARY

A

Actor   An Actor is any object that can be placed into a level. Actors are a generic Class that support 3D transformations, such as translation, rotation, and scale. Actors can be created (spawned) and destroyed through gameplay code (C++ or Blueprints). In C++, AActor is the base class of all Actors.

Answer Hub   A searchable database of reported bugs, suggestions and questions about working with UE4. You can also submit your own bug reports, and ask and answer questions.

B

Blueprint Editor   The Blueprint Editor is a node-based graph editor that acts as your primary tool for creating and editing the visual scripting node networks that make-up Blueprints.

Blueprint   Blueprints are special assets that provide an intuitive, node-based interface that can be used to create new types of Actors and script level events; giving designers and gameplay programmers the tools to quickly create and iterate gameplay from within Unreal Editor without ever needing to write a line of C++ code.

C

Character   A Character is a subclass of a Pawn Actor that is intended to be used as a player character. The Character subclass includes a collision setup, input bindings for bipedal movement, and additional code for movement controlled by the player.

Class   A Class defines the behaviors and properties of a particular Actor or Object used in the creation of an Unreal Engine game. Classes are hierarchical, meaning a Class inherits information from its parent Classes (the Classes it was derived or "sub-classed" from) and passes that information to its children. Classes can be created in C++ code or in Blueprints.

Component   A Component is a piece of functionality that can be added to an Actor. Components cannot exist by themselves, however when added to an Actor, the Actor will have access to functionality provided by the Component.

Content Browser   The Content Browser is the primary area of the Unreal Editor for creating, importing, organizing, viewing, and modifying content assets within Unreal Editor.

Content Cooking   Content Cooking is the process of converting content from the internal formats used by Unreal Editor, such as PNG for texture data or WAV for audio, to the formats used by each individual platform; either because the platform uses a proprietary format, does not support the format Unreal uses to store the asset, or a more memory/performance-effective format exists.

Controller   Controllers are non-physical Actor Classes that can possess a Pawn or Character to control its actions.

D

Details Panel   The Details panel contains information, utilities, and functions specific to the current selection in the viewport; such as transform edit boxes for moving, rotating, and scaling Actors, editable properties for the selected Actors, and quick access to additional editing functionality (depending on the types of Actors selected in the viewport).

E

Editor Preferences   The Editor Preferences window is used to modify settings that control the behavior of Unreal Editor with respect to controls, viewports, source control, auto-saving, and more.

Event   Events are the starting point for Blueprint execution and only have an ouput Exec node. You may create Custom Events that can be called through Blueprint code as well.

F

Function   Executable method defined either through code or through the Blueprint Editor that has at least one output parameter or return a value.

G

Game Mode   The GameMode Class is responsible for setting the rules of the game that is being played. The rules can include how players join the game, whether or not a game can be paused, level transitions, as well as any game-specific behavior (for example, win conditions).

Gameplay Framework   The basic gameplay classes include functionality for representing players, allies, and enemies; as well as for controlling these avatars with player input or AI logic. There are also classes for creating heads-up displays and cameras for players. Finally, gameplay classes such as GameMode, GameState, and PlayerState set the rules of the game. Gameplay classes also track how the game and the players are progressing.

Global Asset Picker   The Global Asset Picker (Ctrl-P) is a fast-access means of editing assets or bringing them into your levels. In some ways, it is similar to the Content Browser but without limiting itself to the current folder you have selected in the Asset Tree. Not only can you pull assets specific to your game, but also anything from Engine, like lights or sound emitters. Because it offers all available assets in a list format, it is not intended to be used as means for browsing. Instead, it's perfect for those moments when you know the asset (or asset type) you need and just want to quickly type part of its name into the Search Line.

H

HUD   A HUD is a "heads-up display", or the 2D on-screen display that is common in many games.

L

Launcher   A UE4 application that allows you to manage your Unreal Engine 4 installations, Marketplace content, and other plugins. The Launcher also hosts the Community tab, Learning tab, and the Modding tab allowing access to a wealth of information.

Level   A Level is a user defined area of gameplay. Levels are created, viewed, and modified by placing, transforming, and editing the properties of the Actors it contains. In the Unreal Editor, each Level is saved as a separate .umap file, which is also why you will sometimes see them referred to as Maps.

Level Editor   Tools for viewing and editing levels. Container for many Editor functions.

Level Sequence   The Level Sequence is an Actor that acts as a "container" for your cinematic scenes and must be created in order to begin working inside the Sequencer Editor.

Level Streaming   The Level Streaming feature makes it possible to load and unload map files into memory as well as toggle their visibility during play. This makes it possible to have worlds broken up into smaller chunks so that only the relevant parts of the world are taking up resources and being rendered at any point. If done properly, this allows for the creation of very large, seamless levels that can make the player feel as if they are playing within a world that dwarfs them in size.

Lightmass   Lightmass is the static global illumination system which creates lightmaps with complex light interactions, such as area shadowing and diffuse interreflection from stationary and static lights.

M

Map   Map is a synonym for Level (see Level)

Marketplace   The Marketplace is an online store built into the UE4 Launcher that allows the communnity to buy and sell UE4 content.

Material   A Material is an asset that can be applied to a mesh to control the visual look of the scene. At a high level, it is easiest to think of a Material as the "paint" that's applied to an object. But even that can be a bit misleading, since a Material literally defines the type of surface from which your object appears to be made. You can define its color, its shininess, its transparency, and much more.

Material Editor   The Material Editor provides the ability to create shaders for geometry, using a node-based graph interface.

Material Instance   Material Instances are child Materials that use parameters to change the appearance of a Material without incurring an expensive recompilation of the Material.

Middleware   Middleware is applications that provide out of the box funcitonality to extend applications either as a standalone application or a plugin.

Modes   Modes are tools that change the primary behavior of the Level Editor for a specialized task, such as placing new assets into the world, creating geometry brushes and volumes, painting on meshes, generating foliage, and sculpting landscapes.

Modes Panel   The Modes panel provides access to the Editor Modes's settings and tools.

O

Object   The base building blocks in the Unreal Engine are called Objects, containing a lot of the essential "under the hood" functionality for your game assets. Just about everything in Unreal Engine 4 inherits (or gets some functionality) from an Object. In C++, UObject is the base class of all objects; it implements features such as garbage collection, metadata (UProperty) support for exposing variables to the Unreal Editor, and serialization for loading and saving.

P

Packaging   The purpose of packaging is to test your full game instead of a single map, or to prepare your game for submission/distribution.

Pawn   A Pawn is an Actor that can be an "agent" within the world. Pawns can be possessed by a Controller, they are set up to easily accept input, and they can do a variety of player-like things. Note that a Pawn is not assumed to be humanoid.

Physically Based Rendering (PBR)   Physically based rendering (PBR) refers to the concept of using Roughness, Base Color and Metalness to accurately represent real-world materials.

Play in Editor (PIE)   Play In Editor allows you to play the current level directly from the editor, so that you can test gameplay functionality, including player controls and level events triggered by players' actions.

Player   The player is the actual human being that is interacting without your application.

PlayerController   A PlayerController is the interface between the Pawn and the human player controlling it. The PlayerController essentially represents the human player's will.

PlayerState   A PlayerState is the state of a participant in the game, such as a human player or a bot that is simulating a player.

Plugin   Plugins enable you to add entirely new features and to modify built-in functionality without modifying the engine code directly, such as adding new menu items and tool bar commands to the editor, or even adding entirely new features and editor sub-modes.

Post-Process Effect   Post-Process Effects enable artists and designers to tweak the overall look and feel of the scene by applying effects including bloom (HDR blooming effect on bright objects), ambient occlusion, and tone mapping to the rendered scene before displaying it in the viewport.

Project   A Project is a self-contained unit that holds all of the content and code that make-up an individual game and coincides with a set of directories on your disk.

Project Browser   The Project Browser provides an interface for creating new projects, opening your existing projects, or opening sample content like sample games and Showcases.

Project Launcher   The Project Launcher tab provides a graphical front-end interface to build, cook, deploy, and launch your game.

Project Settings   The Project Settings editor provides access to configuration options that specify information about your project, as well as defining how the engine behaves when running the project.

Property Matrix   The Property Matrix enables easy bulk editing and value comparison for large numbers of Objects or Actors by displaying a configurable set of properties for a collection of objects as columns in a table view that can be sorted on any column.

R

Rasterization   Rasterization is the process creating rendererd images from vector data. UE4 uses rasterization over Raytracing to achieve interactive frame rates.

Raytracing   A technique for generating rendered images by simulating the path of light through the scene. This produces very high quality, but is very computationally expensive.

Real-Time   Real-Time refers to applications that resppond to the user's input immediately. This typically requires a response time of less than 1/30 of a second.

Redirector   A Redirector provides a reference to the new location of an Asset when it is moved or renamed so that content not loaded at the time of the operation can find the asset.

S

Sequencer   Unreal Engine's cinematic toolset that provides director-level control over cut scenes, dynamic gameplay sequences, and movies.

Simulate In Editor   Simulate In Editor enables you to run game logic in the editor viewport so you can inspect, edit, and interact with Actors in the world as the game runs.

Skeletal Mesh   Skeletal Meshes are built up of two parts; a set of polygons composed to make up the surface of the Skeletal Mesh, and a hierarchical set of interconnected bones that can be used to animate the polygons.

Skeleton   A Skeleton is an asset that holds bone and hierarchy information for a specific type of character or Skeletal Mesh.

Slate UI Framework   Slate is a completely custom and platform agnostic user interface framework that is designed to make building the user interfaces for tools and applications, such as Unreal Editor, or in-game user interfaces fun and efficient. It is the core technology UMG is based on.

In UE4, Source Code refers to the C++ code files that makes up UE4. These files are then compiled to create the Editor, Launcher and other UE4 tools.

Spawn   Creating a new instance of an Actor, either programmatically at run-time, or manually in the Level Editor at design-time.

Static Mesh   A Static Mesh is a piece of geometry that consists of a static set of polygons and are the basic unit used to create world geometry for levels in Unreal Engine 4.

Static Mesh Actor   An Actor whose visual representation is a Static Mesh.

Static Mesh Components   A Component that adds a Static Mesh to an Actor.

Static Mesh Editor   The Static Mesh Editor provides tools for previewing the geometry, collision, and levels of detail of a Static Mesh asset, as well as editing properties, applying Materials, and setting up collision geometry.

T

Texture   Textures are images that are mapped to the surfaces that a Material is applied to.

U

Unreal Editor   Unreal Editor is the complete suite of tools provided with Unreal Engine that enables developers to build levels, import content, create effects, and much more.

Unreal Motion Graphics (UMG)   Unreal Motion Graphics UI Designer (UMG) is a visual UI authoring tool which can be used to create UI elements such as in-game HUDs, menus or other interface related graphics you wish to present to your users.

V

Variable   A Variable is an named memory location that can store data such as numbers and text.

Viewport   Viewports are your window into the worlds you create in Unreal. They can be navigated just as you would in a game, or can be used in a more schematic design sense as you would for an architectural blueprint.

Volume   Volumes are three-dimensional areas within your levels, each of which serve a specific purpose.

W

Widget Blueprint   A Widget Blueprint is a specialized Blueprint used by Unreal Motion Graphics (UMG) to provide visual layout and logic editing functionality for widgets.

World   A World contains a list of Levels that are loaded. It handles the streaming of Levels and the spawning (creation) of dynamic Actors.

World Outliner   The World Outliner panel displays all of the Actors within the scene in a hierarchical tree view that can be filtered and enables selection and modification of Actors directly in the tree.

INDEX